AUTHORS AND APPARATUS

AUTHORS AND APPARATUS

A MEDIA HISTORY OF COPYRIGHT

MONIKA DOMMANN

Translated from the German by Sarah Pybus

CORNELL UNIVERSITY PRESS

Ithaca and London

Originally published as: *Autoren und Apparate. Die Geschichte des Copyrights im Medienwandel.* © S. Fischer Verlag GmbH, Frankfurt am Main 2014.

The translation of this work was funded by Geisteswissenschaften International—Translation Funding for Humanities and Social Sciences from Germany, a joint initiative of the Fritz Thyssen Foundation, the German Federal Foreign Office, the collecting society VG WORT and the German Publishers & Booksellers Association.

English-language edition first published 2019 by Cornell University Press

Library of Congress Cataloging-in-Publication Data

Names: Dommann, Monika, author | Pybus, Sarah, translator.
Title: Authors and apparatus : a media history of copyright / Monika Dommann; translated from the German by Sarah Pybus.
Other titles: Autoren und Apparate. English
Description: Ithaca [New York] : Cornell University Press, 2019. | Translation of: Autoren und Apparate : die Geschichte des Copyrights im Medienwandel. | Includes bibliographical references and index.
Identifiers: LCCN 2018047444 (print) | LCCN 2018048278 (ebook) | ISBN 9781501734984 (pdf) | ISBN 9781501734991 (epub/mobi) | ISBN 9781501709920 (cloth)
Subjects: LCSH: Copyright—History. | Copyright—Germany—History. | Mass media—History.
Classification: LCC K1420.5 (ebook) | LCC K1420.5 .D6613 2019 (print) | DDC 346.04/82—dc23
LC record available at https://lccn.loc.gov/2018047444

Contents

ILLUSTRATIONS

ACKNOWLEDGMENTS

Authors have no rights, only duties.

—Jean-Luc Godard, *Tagesanzeiger*, November 30, 2010

This book was created during a long journey into a foreign world of chic mahogany and marble libraries, well-ordered yet confusing mountains of paper, and an unfamiliar language to which I remain unaccustomed. I first thank the many librarians and archivists who, through persistence and imagination, allowed me access to the treasures in their care. I cannot mention them all, and so I thank Stephen Gray of PRS for Music and Ray Brewer of the Xerox Historical Archives, who dug up images from the bygone material culture of office technology. I thank my colleagues at the Forschungsstelle für Sozial- und Wirtschaftsgeschichte (Research Center for Social and Economic History) and the Historisches Seminar (Department of History) at the University of Zurich; the Internationales Forschungszentrum Kulturwissenschaften (IFK; International Research Center for Cultural Studies) in Vienna; the German Historical Institute in Washington, DC; the Max-Planck-Institut für Wissenschaftsgeschichte (MPIWG; Max Planck Institute for the History of Science) in Berlin, the Department for Art History and Communication Studies at McGill University in Montreal; and the Department of History at the University of Basel for answering questions, for their friendship, patience, and grants—and for their impatience, too. I would not have been able to write this book without the financial support of the University of Zurich, the Swiss National Science Foundation, the International Research Center for Cultural Studies in Vienna, and the German Historical Institute in Washington, D.C. I thank Jörg Fisch, Philipp Sarasin, and Tristan Weddigen for their valuable comments on my habilitation dissertation, submitted to the University of Zurich in 2011. I also thank Jakob Tanner for his absolute trust, even in times of radio silence and when my work came to a standstill. I am also indebted to Caroline Arni, Darin Barney, Regula Bochsler, Lorraine Daston, Christoph Graber, Valentin Gröbner, Michael Guggenheim, Michael Hagner, Vinzenz Hediger, Anke Hees, Ute Holl, Michael Hutter, Angelika Linke, Peter Passett, Regula Rapp, Alexandra Schneider, Karin Schraner, and Andrea Westermann. My thanks go to Alexander Roesler, for reading the book with curiosity and consideration, and to Sarah Pybus, who has rendered my prose into English with clarity and straightforwardness. One final acknowledgement comes, sadly, too late: Rudolf Braun, who pushed me to complete the manuscript as he enjoyed his Gauloises and Gugelhupf cake in Basel. The same is true of Marie Theres Fögen and Cornelia Vismann, both of whom left us at far too young an age. I owe to them the greatest thing an author can hope to gain from other authors: Inspiration and a desire to read. I therefore dedicate this book to them.

Abbreviations

ABA:	American Bar Association
ACLS:	American Council of Learned Societies
AEG:	Allgemeine Elektricitäts-Gesellschaft (General Electricity Company)
AFMA:	Anstalt für musikalisches Aufführungsrecht (Institution for Musical Performing Rights)
AKM:	Gesellschaft der Autoren, Komponisten und Musikverleger (Society of Authors, Composers, and Music Publishers)
AMMRE:	Anstalt für mechanisch-musikalische Rechte, GmbH (Institute for Mechanical-Musical Rights)
ASCAP:	American Society of Composers, Authors, and Publishers
BBC:	British Broadcasting Company
BIEM:	Bureau International des Sociétés gérant les Droits d'Enregistrement et de Reproduction Mécanique (International Organization of Societies for Recording Rights and Mechanical Reproduction)
BIRPI:	Bureaux Internationaux Réunis pour la Protection de la Propriété Intellectuelle (International Office for the Protection of Intellectual Property)
BMI:	Broadcast Music Incorporated
CISAC:	International Confederation of Societies of Authors and Composers
CONTU:	National Commission on New Technological Uses of Copyrighted Works
COSATI:	Committee on Scientific and Technical Information
EBU:	European Broadcasting Union
EDUCOM:	Interuniversity Communications Council
FICS:	Fédération internationale des Chasseurs de Sons (International Federation of Sound Hunters)
FIM:	Fédération internationale des musiciens (International Federation of Musicians)

GDT: Genossenschaft Deutscher Tonsetzer (Cooperative of
        German Composers)
GEMA: Genossenschaft zur Verwertung musikalischer
        Aufführungsrechte GmbH (1915–1933) (Cooperative for the
        Exploitation of Musical Performing Rights)
GEMA: Gesellschaft für musikalische Aufführungs- und
        mechanische Vervielfältigungsrechte (Society for Musical
        Performing Rights and Mechanical Reproduction Rights,
        from 1947)
GRUR: *Gewerblicher Rechtsschutz und Urheberrecht* (Industrial
        legal protection and copyright). Journal of the Deutsche
        Vereinigung für gewerblichen Rechtsschutz und
        Urheberrecht (German Association for Commercial Legal
        Protection and Copyright)
IFPI: International Federation of the Phonographic Industry
IIB: Institut International de la Bibliographie (International
        Institute of Bibliography)
IID: Institut International de la Documentation (International
        Institute of Documentation)
ILO: International Labour Organization
MPA: Music Publishers Association
MCPS: Mechanical-Copyright Protection Society
NAB: National Association of Broadcasters
NASA: National Aeronautics and Space Administration
NLM: National Library of Medicine
NSF: National Science Foundation
OSRD: Office of Scientific Research and Development
OSS: Office of Strategic Services
PRS: Performing Right Society
RGZ: Entscheidungen des Reichsgerichts in Zivilsachen (Verdicts
        of the supreme court of the German Reich in civil cases)
RRG: Reichs-Rundfunk-Gesellschaft mbH (Reich Radio
        Company)
SACEM: Société des Auteurs, Compositeurs et Editeurs de Musique
        (Society of Authors, Composers, and Publishers of Music)
SIAE: Società Italiana degli Autori et Editori (Italian Society of
        Authors and Publishers)
SSRC: Social Science Research Council
STAGMA: Staatlich genehmigte Gesellschaft zur Verwertung
        musikalischer Aufführungsrechte (State-Approved Society

	for the Exploitation of Musical Performing Rights, 1933–1944)
TSF:	Télégraphie sans fils (Wireless Telegraphy)
UFITA:	Archiv für Urheber-, Film- und Theaterrecht (Archive for Copyright, Film, and Theater Rights, 1928–1944), Archiv für Urheber- und Medienrecht (Archive for Copyright and Media Rights, from 1954)
WIPO:	World Intellectual Property Organization

AUTHORS AND APPARATUS

Introduction

A Media History of Legal Norms

Prologue

Like Waves of Water?

When the German legal scholar Josef Kohler published a 350-page tome on authors' rights[1] in 1880, the German Reich had existed for almost a decade; it was the same age as the 1870 regulation on literary and musical copyright that had been standardized throughout the Reich.[2] The systematization of this legal field within jurisprudence had only just begun.[3]

Kohler was among the jurists who, in the nineteenth century, established the right of inventors (patent law) and authors (*copyright* in English, *droit d'auteur* in French, and *Urheberrecht* in German) as an academic discipline. He set these legal areas firmly apart from early modern privileges ("given out of graciousness")[4] and shaped the concept of "intangible goods."[5] For Kohler, these intangible goods were "economic assets"[6] because their creation was a form of "work": "The philosophical basis of ownership and rights for intangible goods lies in the work, or rather the creation; he who creates a new thing is naturally entitled to it."[7] He justified creation qua work by referencing John Locke, but even more so by referencing the moral philosophers and economists of the eighteenth and nineteenth centuries, such as Adam Smith, David Ricardo, Jean-Baptiste Say, and Frédéric Bastiat.

Kohler compared ownership rights to air, gaseous substances, and "waves of water."[8] Describing intangible goods, he used the analogy of "flowing water" for temporary rights: As rights to water would flow on to neighboring shores, so authors' rights are "momentary" rights passed on to third parties after use. The comparison with water as an "eminent cultural factor"[9] is revealing: In the eighteenth and nineteenth centuries, running water was the raw material for electricity and the driving force behind industrialization, areas that, in Kohler's mind, had as much potential for progress as intangible goods. However, Kohler's "momentary" period is not actually that momentary when we consider that the German *Urheberschutzgesetz* (Copyright Protection Act) of 1870 granted thirty years of protection. Furthermore, Kohler saw intangible goods solely as the legal rights of individuals. In the act of creation, the individual would bond with the thing they had created, granting them sole control: "He [the author] alone shall determine whether, how, and to what extent it shall be published and made available to the world."[10]

Kohler's writings on authors' rights are praised by jurists to this day, sometimes questioned, and often quoted because they analyzed the problems of the era more sharply than other legal commentaries and proposed solutions. From a historical perspective, they are interesting precisely because they studied the law of the time and, in interpreting it, shaped it. They are an opportunity to observe an observer, and thus to take the changes he perceives and records in his own language and open them up to historical analysis.[11]

A professor at Berlin's Humboldt University starting in 1888, Kohler grappled with the traditions of his field during a period of transition within legal studies. He was among the jurists who distanced themselves from the "historical school" embodied by Friedrich Carl von Savigny and viewed law as "conforming to culture and following its progress."[12] For Kohler, the right to "immaterial or intangible assets" and the "right to literary, artistic, and industrial ideas" were the expression of an "industrial age" and a "contemporary culture."[13] His extensive focus on legal history, legal philosophy, legal comparison, and cultural anthropology topics[14] should be seen as part of this search for new notions and concepts for an era of change. He reinforced the validity and universality of the legal categories he formulated, not (like many of his contemporaries) primarily with reference to Roman law but with a wide range of examples from French, Anglo-Saxon, Spanish, and non-European law.[15] He was particularly interested in authors' rights and patent law and the laws of the postal service, telegraphy, and rail transportation; they were new, and he associated them with the hope embodied in the principles of international law.[16] He last outlined his vision of the "socialization of nations" and a "sensibly controlled" global economy on the eve of World War I; in hindsight, this seems like an act of desperation. However, the limits of Kohler's legal universalism also become clear:[17] For Kohler, "global socialization" was a project of the "Christian peoples together with the newly emerged East Asians imbued with European erudition." By contrast, the "states of Islam"—with their "simplicity of dogma" and "intuitively attractive promise"—were excluded from Kohler's universalistic concepts.[18] For these states, he envisaged "indirect rule" by means of a "protectorate relationship" and "financial control."[19]

The journal *Gewerblicher Rechtsschutz und Urheberrecht* (Industrial legal protection and copyright, GRUR) first integrated copyright into the ongoing legal discussion in the German-speaking region in 1896, together with patent law, design protection, and rights to protect legal business names as well as the topic of unfair competition.[20] Josef Kohler was selected to write the first article for the first edition, indicating his renown.[21] Copyright was developed as commercial law took shape and was debated within an exclusive group of stakeholders. The editorial in the first edition of GRUR explains why the journal was established: "The German association for the protection of intellectual property has tasked itself, with the assistance of its members, with determining the experiences and opinions of interested German parties, digesting the collected materials, and offering up the findings obtained for public debate. If this approach should succeed in clarifying an issue by gauging different interests, such that one may assume to have found a viewpoint that fulfils all relevant interests, the association shall also be obliged to distribute the relevant proposals to all legislative bodies in the Reich expressing the requirements and desires of the German industrial and commercial worlds."[22]

The End of Copyright?

In 1966—almost a century after Kohler's book on authors' rights—Benjamin Kaplan, a jurist teaching at Harvard Law School, gave a series of lectures at Columbia University in New York entitled *An Unhurried View of Copyright*.[23] While Kohler's commentary on authors' rights appeared at the start of his legal career, Kaplan spoke with the authority of an established expert. Kohler composed his arguments shortly after Germany's first national copyright was established; Kaplan expressed his opinions during the protracted revision process for the American Copyright Act of 1909, which would come to a provisional conclusion with the Copyright Act of 1976. While letterpress printing, lithography, and photography shaped

Kohler's world of authors' rights, jurists and judges were now asking how copyright was to be regulated for radio waves, photocopiers, cable television, and computers. Where Kohler systematically justified the newly codified authors' rights, Kaplan criticized the development of copyright *tout court*. Kaplan's main criticism was of the envisaged extension to protection periods, questioning the timeframe in which the author held exclusive rights to their work, a notion that Kohler had compared so prosaically to a wave of water: "Shall I now say in candor that I have sometimes dared to think even the fifty-six years is too much?"[24] He also believed that the central copyright categories of "personality" and "individuality" would be shaken by the rise of photocopies and information systems: "With mutations of machines, already imaginable, that foreshadow symbiotic relationships with the human brain, ideas of individuality and personality in relation to intellectual accomplishment may themselves be shaken."[25] He had been greatly affected by *The Gutenberg Galaxy*, published in 1962 by the Canadian media theorist Marshall McLuhan:[26] "Professor McLuhan, a professional soothsayer, says broadly that as the imperium in communications passes from books to electronic manifestations, as the 'Gutenberg galaxy' decays, not only is the relationship between author and audience radically changed but the author's pretensions to individual ownership and achievement are at a discount: his dependence on the past is better appreciated; he is seen somewhat as a tradition-bearing 'singer of tales,' as a kind of teacher peculiarly indebted to his teachers before him."[27] After reading McLuhan, Kaplan was certain that jurists had paid too little attention to copyright's technical environments. He interpreted the fusion of old publishing houses and new electronics companies as a sign of fundamental upheaval. In the future, global "systems" would replace letterpress printing and render national copyright obsolete: "You must imagine, at the eventual heart of things to come, linked or integrated systems or networks of computers capable of storing faithful simulacra of the entire treasure of the accumulated knowledge and artistic production of past ages, and of taking into the store new intelligence of all sorts as produced."[28]

The sluggish revision of the Copyright Act of 1909 showed that the strategy chosen in 1896 by the Deutsche Verein zum Schutz des Gewerblichen Eigentums (German Association for the Protection of Commercial Property)—to drive the legislative process by pooling commercial and industrial interests—had been reversed in the U.S. It failed due to diverging interests.[29] However, the draft revisions did agree on one issue, namely correcting the course of the American copyright tradition, which had so far been liberal compared with that of Europe. Benjamin Kaplan was not the only renowned jurist to criticize this development. He was soon followed by his student, Stephen Breyer, who criticized plans to strengthen and expand American copyright in the *Harvard Law Review* in 1970 and made a case for reducing the protection periods of 1909.[30] Back in 1880, Josef Kohler had justified authors' rights using eighteenth-century philosophers and economists; in 1970, Stephen Breyer reassessed the moral and economic arguments for copyright. Breyer no longer shared Kohler's interest in justifying authors' rights; instead, he questioned the economic consequences of abolishing copyright altogether. His legal argument used facts from the twentieth-century empirical economy to criticize the eighteenth-century moral philosophy that had been used as a basis for copyright: "The case for copyright in books considered as a whole is weak."[31] As early as 1970, Breyer warned against copyright protection for computer programs for competition policy reasons: "One must wonder, for example, whether, without protection, smaller hardware or software firms would not find it easier to use parts of IBM programs in their efforts to compete with IBM."[32]

The arguments put forward by Josef Kohler, Benjamin Kaplan, and Stephen Breyer were discussed only in specialist circles. This suddenly changed around 1970 when Nicholas Henry, an American political scientist who was not a legal scholar, published several articles about copyright—and not in a legal journal but in *Science*, America's most famous scientific journal. Copyright was no longer just a question of law, but one of politics. Henry did not want the science, technology, and information policy of the future to be regulated by the old concepts of copyright.[33] Around the same time, French philosophers and legal theorists discovered the explosive power of author concepts: Roland Barthes wrote about the death of the author in 1967, and in 1969 Michel Foucault questioned the social functions of authorship.[34] Bernard Edelman used the example of photography to give a Marxist critique of literary and artistic proprietary rights.[35] However, the cultural science debate expanded in the early 1970s failed to resonate. Authors' rights continued to interest only specialized legal scholars. It was not until the mid-1990s—triggered by the question of whether and how the Internet should be regulated—that a series of legal bestsellers were published in the U.S., receiving a response never before seen for publications about copyright.[36] Copyright discourse had suddenly been altered by the World Wide Web—or so it seemed. Copyrights had become copywrongs.[37] Lawrence Lessig announced that, in the future, norms would be created using binary codes, not just traditional laws.[38] This change was seen as abrupt: Authors spoke of the "digital moment,"[39] of the end of copyright "as we know it,"[40] and of a "tectonic shift" caused by the "construction of the information society."[41]

Object of Study

From a historical perspective, this notion of computers as deus ex machina is unsatisfactory because it does not explain the origins of this media and legal break or how the digital transformation differs from earlier radical changes. This book categorizes the backgrounds, driving forces, and social debates surrounding copyright using slightly longer timeframes than are usual for professions working with copyright (legal scholars, attorneys, Internet experts). It is questionable (or at least calls for an explanation) to speak of a break without understanding which traditions (concepts, practices, and norms) have been broken. Do we now find ourselves in a new epoch? Is it even helpful to call it an epoch? Hans Blumenberg has suggested speaking not of epochs but of epochal thresholds that are not tied to events with specific dates.[42] The following chapters will therefore examine a long period of transition between 1850 and 1980, the period in which new reproduction technologies developed that challenged letterpress printing in various ways.

In 1962, McLuhan argued that we cannot comprehend and describe a past epoch until we are aware that a change has taken place and can perceive and interpret the epochal threshold. His statements came at almost exactly the same time that observers outside the close-knit circle of computer scientists first became aware of electronic media: "It is because we have moved into another phase from which we can contemplate the contours of the proceeding situation with ease and clarity. . . . As we experience the new electronic and organic age with ever stronger indications of its main outlines, the preceding mechanical age becomes quite intelligible."[43] The presence of networked computers in the early 1960s prompted McLuhan to look back at Gutenberg's renaissance. He interpreted "renaissance" as an epochal boundary, triggered by the printing presses that shaped the form, mobility, and message of the new medium of the book. Today, McLuhan is read as a classical writer of media history. But his work, and particularly its reception, also shed light on social history. At the start of the 1960s, McLuhan formulated terms like "Gutenberg galaxy" to encapsulate electronic media; these terms were picked up by contemporaries such as Benjamin Kaplan and became the core of new media discourse.

This book takes the global spread of computers, epitomized in the term *World Wide Web* in the 1990s, as an opportunity to consider the radical media changes that challenged the dominant position letterpress printing had held since the nineteenth century. The media theory *turn* that McLuhan helped to initiate and that first linked literary studies with the world outside of high literary culture is characterized by the formulation of strong theories.[44] Media scholars have linked the historic change with the emergence of new media, in some cases tending to attribute teleological origin stories to these new media. In using narratives with a single explanation, this young discipline has at times moved closer to the mythical historiography that positivist historical scholars left behind in the nineteenth century. In contrast, historical scholars have continued to try to explain how one can know the claims one will make, a subject taken up by Marc Bloch.[45] Historical scholars also have a long tradition of "repurposing" legal sources for historic questions or, to reference Walter Benjamin, "going against the grain."[46]

This history of copyright is a legal history of media as well as a media history of legal norms. I am interested in the ways that new reproduction technologies have affected legal norms since the nineteenth century and, in turn, the ways that the law has shaped the use of new media. To explore the correlations between reproduction and legislation practices, I will look at norms and media *in the making*. As microhistorians examine Inquisition records to understand the mentality of the time, this book reads copyrights from a media history perspective and studies the disruptive effect that technology and media have on the law. To understand media development in a historical context, technology (copying devices, audio recording devices, and computers), media (records, tapes, photocopies, and data systems), and the law (court proceedings, legal revisions, regulations, and jurisprudence) must be considered together.

Premises

This history of copyright does not need to serve the law itself; it does not need to search for roots, back up its arguments with historic evidence, or emphasize continuity. It can address ruptures, disruptions, and ambiguities in the law. It can examine the area in which everything has supposedly been clarified—legal norms. And it can trace the social, political, and economic conflicts that these clarifications entail. It does not need to stick to differences between countries but can also look at the ways in which they overlap. And it can allow itself the luxury of moving away from the legal environment where necessary to track down the practices that the law was late to address.

We historians always come to things late, and what was once regarded as new is always outdated when seen through the eyes of Clio. As a profession, we are therefore skeptical when social and media theories claim that new contemporary media are innovative. Before you continue reading, I would like to point out that I began this book project with a desire to improve my understanding of new media and that this historiography of old media always takes new media into account.[47]

This book has five premises.

First, it is a media history of the law that takes the "materiality of communication"[48] much more seriously than has previously been the case for historians beholden to text hermeneutics. When sounds are recorded on plastic and texts are photographed, their storage and transmission brings about culturally complex changes to content with wide-reaching effects. If we focus solely on laws, international agreements, and public debates, we cannot understand how the media transformation changed the meaning of legal categories and classifications or the implications this had for society, economics, and culture. The public never notices media transformation until a very late stage. Between 1880 and 2000, Josef Kohler, Benjamin Kaplan, Stephen Breyer, Michel Foucault, Bernard Edelman, Nicolas Henry, and Lawrence Lessig were involved in a discourse on authorship and copyright that they analyzed both from a distance and with a feel for social contexts. This double role provides an insight into the history of copyright: They are witnesses to a change caused by themselves and others. However, their reports are not sufficient for a historical understanding of how reproduction and copyrights interlink: These reports must be supplemented by analyzing multiple accounts from all the people from different milieus who made passing statements in their roles as jurists, record producers, librarians, programmers, science policy makers, composers, "sound hunters," technology experts, and manufacturers of home electronics.

Second, this book questions the belief, common within economics and law, that the global networking of computers since the 1980s brought a well-established legal tradition and legal continuity to an abrupt end. Instead, I will start with developments in reproduction and legislation practices since the mid-nineteenth century, which are closely interlinked and mutually dependent.[49] Together with the booming global trade of the first wave of globalization and the flourishing sciences of the nineteenth century, photographic and phonographic recording technologies set a world in motion that since the sixteenth century had been largely shaped by letterpress printing. In the eighteenth century, new copyright regulations were introduced for printed materials as an economic mindset developed around the concept of "work"; barely established, these regulations were permanently eroded by technology and yet continuously expanded.

Third, I put forward a theory that legal history must always be viewed as the history of legal knowledge. The law is saturated with historical knowledge; as Niklas Luhmann states, "law never has to begin" but can "link to identified traditions."[50] However, perspectives on history are never untainted—certainly not in law—and definitely not self-evident. On the contrary, history's epistemic[51] status in law requires explanation. History is always present in legal literature. Anyone who claims to be correct, who revises the law or comments on it, always looks to the past. To take account of this fusion of history and law with a critical view of sources, we need an approach that analyzes the law "in action"[52] and regards legal concepts not just as the history of dogma or ideas but also as scientific, economic, and social practices.

History is also institutionalized in law: Legal history was established in the nineteenth century as a branch of university jurisprudence and remains part of the legal curriculum to this day. Legal and historical scholarship certainly have epistemic similarities. Both disciplines use evolutionary arguments and place great value on analyzing developments and emphasizing contingency. Both work hermeneutically, centering on interpretation and explanation, and use a comprehensive annotation system to substantiate arguments. However, they also exhibit differences, which have been noted by Marie Theres Fögen and Dieter Grimm.[53] Fögen emphasized that law is about "applicability" (all law is applicable), while history is about "contingency" (everything that has happened could or could not happen).[54] Grimm argued that law's occupation with the past primarily serves the law itself. Jurisprudence uses historical knowledge merely as a "reservoir of dogmatically useful knowledge." Grimm views this special development in legal history—which uses ad hoc and selective arguments, ignores social conditions, and stands out due to its ahistorical use of concepts and isolated consideration of norms—as even more incomprehensible than the focal objects of the law that lie outside the law. German social history, which flourished in the 1970s and 1980s and had a strong focus on social science, may have laid claim to "synthesis,"[55] but despite this integrated perspective, the law remained a gap in social history and was regarded, if at all, as a product of political decisions and was therefore subsumed under politics (as Dieter Grimm noted in a commentary on Hans-Ulrich Wehler's social history project).[56] To explain this vagueness, Grimm stated that social science considers legal norms far more than the application of law.

In comparison, works of social and cultural history see the law as a negotiation process. The distinction between legal norms and legal application common within legal history was thrown open by the concept of legal negotiation.[57] The concept of social negotiation is helpful but falls short when considering the first two theses in particular. On the one hand, social negotiation concepts must be expanded to include media and technology; on the other hand, legal practices are shaped by cultural techniques,[58] which must be reflected in legal history.[59] In addition, legal practice is not limited to the legal enactment and administration of justice: Legal practices are incredibly diverse, something that legal history long refused to admit. During media transformation in particular, norms emerge that are developed and modified not by countries but by institutions, companies, associations, and individuals at the local, national, and international levels.[60] These technical norms, guidelines, and agreements are often established when used within media and not as an act of legislative negotiation. They form parallel regimes to the law that manifests itself at the legislative level. This is particularly significant when we consider that technology develops much more quickly than laws are negotiated.[61] Furthermore, norms are more culturally diverse and fragmented (and much less homogeneous and uniform) than long believed in traditional legal theory: After all, different norms are established in different contexts that may conflict with or influence each other. For a long time, the legal history of copyright became lost in the history of nationalistic, legally dogmatic definitions, and the transfer and transformation of legal norms across national borders were overlooked.

Fourth, this history of copyright is also an economic history of culture and science. For example, organizing a global music trade would be inconceivable without authors' rights. Until recently, authors' rights were not seen as relevant to economics:[62] In economic theory, intellectual property solves the problem of public goods not produced in socially optimal quantities without market intervention.[63] For the economy, subsuming these under public goods solves the theoretical problem. The uncompleted 1966 study by Robert Hurt, a student of Milton Friedman, was for a long time the only attempt to research empirically the economic rationale for copyright. The study concluded that, from the perspective of economic theory, the general assumption that copyright contributes to general welfare is questionable and requires analysis: "The subject certainly deserves more investigation and less self-righteous moral defense."[64] In contrast to copyrights, the patents that protect technical inventions have been seen as phenomena of industrialization as well as a part of economic history. To understand the interest in patents within economic history, we need to consider the resonance of new institutional economics in the tradition of Douglass North. New institutional economics emphasizes the great significance of formal and informal norms and opportunities to implement these norms to reduce uncertainty, ensure stability, and aid the process of generating bursts of economic activity.[65] However, institutional economic interests do not focus on how norms are created or how they develop the stability to achieve all these things. In Northian institutional economics, norms largely remain a black box. However, the history of science has addressed the impact of patents[66] and copyrights[67] on the production of knowledge, showing that the notion of liberal, comprehensive "propertization"[68] based on a monetary economy does not go far enough. In the production of knowledge, economic property regimes based on monetary economy are diametrically opposed to academic reputation economies using peer review (citations, awards, or professorships). When securing their priority claims, academics find themselves stuck between these two competing regulatory cultures.

Fifth, this book takes an integral approach. The methodical requirements set out in the first four premises suggest that the legal history of new media also has implications for media, economics, and the history of science. This approach—which pushes the boundaries of historic specialization, does not respect national borders, and is committed to the transnational history of relationships[69]—requires carefully selected fields of study to exemplify the object of study in great detail. The timeframe encompasses the years from 1850 to 1980 and concentrates on the transatlantic space of Europe and the U.S. The book begins with the emergence of new recording media around 1850 and their integration into legal norms based on letterpress printing; this corresponds with the expansion of national laws and the internationalization of legal norms. The book ends in around 1980 following the enactment of the revised U.S. Copyright Act in 1976 and the key report from the National Commission on New Technological Uses of Copyrighted Works (CONTU), published in 1979. Congress appointed this commission to study the new automatic systems and mechanical reproduction techniques with regard to copyright.[70] This book continually establishes the relations and mutual inter-action between the national legal traditions (Anglo-Saxon copyright in the U.S. and Great Britain, German *Urheberrecht*, and French *droit d'auteur* and *propriété littéraire et artistique*). Unless explicitly indicating a specific national tradition, I shall hereafter refer to all these legal concepts as "copyright"; as global law converges, this is increasingly used as a metaterm.

We therefore take the transatlantic space as our geographic framework to study the media history of copyright since 1850; the Old World of Europe (with a long tradition of cultural production) and the New World of the U.S. (which began to catch up in literature, music, science, and business in the closing years of the nineteenth century) developed different reproduction cultures and legal practices within different economic and cultural constellations. These practices are, however, connected—the U.S.'s approach to the production, reproduction, and regulation of texts, images, and sounds affected developments in Europe, and vice versa.

Fields of Study and Sources

In this book, I shall pursue two strands of development in chronological order and relate them to one another.

The first field of study is the history of the photocopy. Here I shall ask how access to knowledge and information is mechanized and standardized in societies that since the mid-nineteenth century have increasingly seen themselves as modern, i.e., an ephemeral, transitory, and progressive presence.[71] I shall look at the recording and reproduction of library stocks, a topic that has now come to a head with debates about Google Library.

The second field of study, the history of music recording, asks how reproduction technology is linked with a complex network of exploitation rights. Here I shall look at the legal, organizational, economic, and technical practices that facilitate a global market with music media, constantly restructure this market, and in the last few years have become a social battlefield thanks to file sharing, spectacular court proceedings, and the establishment of pirate parties in numerous European countries and the U.S.

My corpus of sources encompasses material on national laws and international agreements;[72] extra-legal regulations and guidelines; legal commentaries; legal and technical handbooks; periodicals on law, economics, and information science; industry journals; publications from collecting societies; official letters; files from court proceedings and legislative revisions; and records of academic and political debates from Europe (particularly Germany, France, and Great Britain) and the U.S. To select these sources, I traced reciprocal relationships in the two fields of study and linked a wide range of sources from the people involved. Despite this integral approach, which ensures that source materials are not limited by specific interests, I must point out some serious shortcomings and blind spots in my corpus: While legal practices provide familiar paths by which to trace and reproduce legislative processes and their stumbles and failures with almost no gaps, uncovering the development of technology and media and the practices of the institutions and companies involved requires us to take circuitous routes, give ourselves over to obsession, or look at sources from a different angle. Sometimes it is a matter of sheer luck. Many archives (such as those of the collecting societies and record manufacturers) never existed in the first place; have been lost, forgotten, destroyed; or are inaccessible. Ultimately, this book must always remember one specific aspect of copyright's self-referentiality: The negotiation of law and its subsequent interpretation and commentary within legal studies have largely been cultivated by a small group of stakeholders. With a lack of alternatives, even the historiography of this field has no choice but to refer to texts created in a very small, almost closed circle.

It was relatively late when politics and media as a whole began to view copyright as the stuff of social dispute. The viewpoints of Josef Kohler (1880), Benjamin Kaplan (1967), Stephen Breyer (1970/1972), Nicholas Henry (1974), and Lawrence Lessig (1999) discussed at the start of this chapter reflect increasing public perception of a phenomenon long treated as a technical legal detail. Copyright could no longer be ignored as an eminent political topic when, in 2006, political parties were first founded (in Sweden and later in other European countries and the U.S.) that made copyright the most important part of their platform. Pirate party activists were mobilized when the Pirate Bay, the online sharing platform, was temporarily closed in 2009; they demanded radical reforms for copyright, patent law, and data protection as well as disclosures from various countries on how much they know about their citizens' electronic activities.[73] When pirate parties entered parliament, the political implications of media transformation became socially acceptable. In the following chapters, I aim to historicize the development of social conflict regarding reproduction; while this may have played out below the threshold of public perception until the 1990s, it had already caused great conflict in various milieus.

The first section (*Writing and Recording*) looks at the period from 1850 until around 1915, focusing on the creation of reproduction norms for new media. The second section (*Collecting Agencies and Research Materials*) looks at the period between 1915 and 1945, studying the archeology of two fundamentally different forms of reproduction, that found in libraries and in the music industry. The third section (*Private Copies and Universal Standards*) focuses on the period from 1945 to 1980 as well as looking to the present. It examines the genesis of the conflict between authors' rights collectives, consumers, and evolving notions of authors' rights following decolonization and in postcolonial discourse. We can also see how the latent social conflict regarding the regulation of reproduction accelerated and intensified in the 1960s.

PART I

Writing and Recording

CHAPTER 1

Sheet Music

Not every author is a capitalist; not everyone, in fact
only the minority, is capable of earning a living outside of the literary or artistic discipline to which his
special nature is often irresistibly drawn.

—Johann Vesque von Püttlingen, *Das musicalische
Autorrecht* (1864)

Between Nationalism and Free Trade

From Reprinting to Authorship

It was Michel Foucault who made the suggestion—which forms the foundation of this book—to examine the manifold epistemological dimensions of
the law.[1] Foucault's seminal shake-up of legal and criminal history cannot be
valued highly enough; this also goes for the history and theory of copyright.
Foucault grasped the explosive social power of the concept of authorship
at a very early stage when, in 1969, he asked the fundamental question of
what defined an author.[2] He identified authorship as the "pivotal point for
individualization in the history of the mind, ideas, and literature, and in the
history of philosophy and science."[3]

In a sense, the focus of the historical approach to copyright on the emergence of legal and aesthetic author concepts in the eighteenth century

followed on from the origin myth—maintained in law to this day—of the civilized author in the eighteenth century.[4] Up to this point, publishers secured the right to publication by means of privileges granted to them by rulers.[5] However, isolated instances can be found as early as the fifteenth century in which artists used authorship to control reprinting: In the 1490s, Albrecht Dürer used his monogram to gain control of the production process for his prints, and as far back as the sixteenth century writers brought actions against plagiarism and demanded exclusive publication rights. Reprinting privileges were granted by the sovereign. It is clear that the granting of privileges often depended on the approval of the censorship authorities. In law, the British Statute of Anne of 1710 is commonly referred to as the start of authors' rights. At its core, this was a copyright that restricted the old tradition of monopoly and was initially conferred for fourteen years (with the option to extend it for a further fourteen years). The idea of the author as the person upon whom the copyright was based was therefore placed at the center, but also incorporated due to publishers' interests. As Martha Woodmansee demonstrated for Germany, the birth of the author in the eighteenth century bore the hallmark of writers attempting to secure their social, economic, and symbolic position in the face of radical socioeconomic and sociocultural changes.[6] Eighteenth-century aesthetic and legal discourses influenced one another; legal knowledge played a significant role in aesthetic notions in eighteenth-century literature, art, and music.[7] Legal concepts were not simply an expression of the Romantic culture but genuinely helped to shape it through legal practice.[8] These legal concepts were themselves shaped by the change in printing techniques, as emphasized by Heinrich Bosse's study, written in the context of Freiburg during the incubation period of new German media studies, on the "development of copyright from the spirit of the Goethe era": "Work authority" (*Werkherrschaft*), the specific relationship between a creator and work that was institutionalized in Germany in copyright reforms at the start of the nineteenth century, is also to be viewed against the introduction of the rotary press, which mechanized and hugely accelerated printing technology in the mid-nineteenth century.[9]

Compositions in the Competition of Nations

Early modern printing privileges also included music, but only because, as printed matter, sheet music was protected against reprinting. The French law of 1793 was the first to explicitly mention compositions; elsewhere, composers were not declared to be authors until the 1830s and 1840s: in the U.S. in the Copyright Act of 1831,[10] in Prussia in 1837 in the *Gesetz zum Schutz des Eigenthums an Werken der Wissenschaft und Kunst gegen Nachdruck und Nachbildung*[11] (Act for the Protection of Ownership of Works of Science and Art against Reprinting and Replication), in Great Britain in the Copyright Act of 1842,[12] and in Austria in 1846 in the *Patent zum Schutze des literarisch-artistischen Eigenthums gegen unbefugte Veröffentlichung, Nachdruck und Nachbildung*[13] (Patent for the Protection of Literary and Artistic Property against Unauthorized Publication, Reprinting, and Replication). The concept of reprinting linked with early modern privileges was subsequently reinterpreted as a concept of reproduction that assigned the protection of the integral work to the composer.

This book shall analyze the contexts in which this new, legally influenced concept of reproduction emerged and their underlying cultural codes. Law may describe these changes as a continuum and jurists may emphasize analogies, but from a historical perspective they must be characterized as a caesura or epistemic break: First, what had previously been a discourse of aesthetics and law was increasingly displaced by economics and law. Second, with mechanical music, music media developed beyond familiar communication in the language of musical notation and outside the attention and control of the publishing system.

The new legal concepts for music are to be viewed in the context of debates about national legislative processes and the internationalization of copyrights. In France, for example, vaudeville artists were criticized because they incorporated passages from the repertoire of *opéra comique* and other vaudevillians into their shows and choral singing and because they were supported by a ministerial decree of 1807.[14] In the mid-nineteenth century, the French state also began to take systematic action against "counterfeiting" abroad and insisted on reciprocal recognition of authors' rights. The Prussian law of 1837 on the ownership of works of science and art could also be used by authors in all countries that granted protection to Prussian publications. The author ("during his lifetime") and his heirs (for thirty years) held the right to "reprinting" *and* "reproduction," a right that could be transferred:[15] "Each new reproduction, if performed without the approval of those holding exclusive authorization . . . is considered reprinting and is prohibited."[16] This right also applied to musical compositions. Compositions were protected more stringently than texts: While the "verbatim quoting of individual passages of a work already printed" was not classified as reproduction for texts, "extracts, arrangements for individual instruments, and other adaptations that cannot be considered individual compositions" were prohibited for compositions.[17]

The Austrian law awarded right of ownership to the "creator" of a "work," meaning "the person who originally wrote or made it." This protection applied in Prussia and the German Confederation.[18] The right "to use his products as desired, to reproduce and publish them in any form" and "to transfer these to others, in whole or in part" was also granted to customers, publishers, and businesspeople as well as to heirs and legal successors.[19] The Austrian law permitted more liberal use of music by other composers than the Prussian law: In Austria, it was permitted to use "themata of musical compositions" as well as "variations, fantasias, etudes, pot-pourris," and "arrangements."[20]

The 1853 discussions about the revision of the Austrian law of 1846 showed that the protection of authors' interests was not the only thing at stake and that copyrights also served as national instruments and cultural combative measures. These discussions took place in chambers of commerce and trade, among writers, publishers, and book and music dealers.[21] However, France's demand for mutual recognition of authors' rights was rejected in Austria as a threat to the interests of Austrian composers and music dealers due to France's stricter protection of literary and artistic property and the strong position of the French music trade.[22] The discussion of authors' rights was influenced by antagonism toward France: Authors' rights served as a means of fighting France's cultural allure, the dominance of French music (which "can be marketed outside France due to the prevalence of the French language"),[23] and the market strength of French publishers ("it is already a fact that artists of note turn to Paris to publish their works in that very place").[24] The protection of successful Austrian exports ("the compositions of Beethoven, Schubert, Proch, Strauss, and others") was weighed against free rein for the small fishes in the "domestic industry."[25] The commission therefore recommended that decisions on the mutual international recognition of rights be made on a case-by-case basis through diplomatic channels.

The Value of Works

Music rights were outlined only briefly in the legislation. In the 1860s, legal and economic commentaries began to discuss them in more detail, and the tone changed, the aesthetic/legal perspective displaced by economic/legal approaches. In 1864, Viennese jurist and composer Johann Vesque von Püttlingen wrote the first monograph about "musical authors' right(s)."[26] A state official of noble birth who also composed operas, masses, and songs, he formulated a concept for musical works that aimed to secure a middle-class professional existence for composers. He viewed compositions within the parameters of potential exploitation: While literary fragments were not suited to "speculation" (for example through separate printing),[27] economic value could be found in even "the smallest piece(s) of music."[28] It was not orchestra scores that were "sought out by a large audience" but piano scores and opera motifs, and this work was "exploited": "While just a few copies of the orchestra score are sold for the purpose of public performance and such scores are therefore not printed at all, but used only in manuscripts, copies of the piano score circulate in their thousands, at great advantage to the composer."[29] Because "individual, blessedly invented melodies often enjoy popular appeal," it was in the interest of the public and the composer "to publish these as independent works of art."[30] The composer and jurist wanted to see musical authors' rights formulated as commercial rights with the comprehensive power of disposal that also encompassed fragments of musical works (arrangements or short extracts).[31] His focus was on the value of works (their "pecuniary exploitation")[32] or, to put it another way, legal protection for capitalist composers.

One year earlier, in 1863, German economist Karl Richter formulated an economic justification for authors' rights.[33] Richter legitimized the "right to exploitation"[34] for works of science and art based on their contribution to progress and development. He explained that science and art are "important factors in civilization"[35] and that "intellectual work [is] a condition for economic development."[36] He stated that music requires particular protection under international law because, in contrast to literature, it can be understood by all, it is (therefore) generally available, and there are no cultural restrictions to its exploitation.[37] Richter advocated a sort of pricing theory for intellectual work: The greater the "education" and the higher the "general level of sophistication," the lower the "value actually placed on intellectual work."[38] By suggesting that prices would decrease for intellectual work, he implied that it required legal protection.

Karl Richter accomplished what had previously been implied in Prussian law—adopting the concept of reprinting: "Today, this term has only a historical context, because the first legal infringement to be recognized as such was, in fact, simply the exploitative reprinting of a printed book or written work."[39] He declared "the unauthorized and therefore criminal encroachment on the exclusive right to exploit works of art and science" to be the core of the crime. In this argument, reproduction and exploitation were directly connected.

Josef Kohler, who in the nineteenth century played a significant role in formulating the principles of twentieth-century authors' rights, drew a firm line between the new authors' rights and old privileges (reprinting rights for publishers). He too justified this distinction with an economic argument, that of value creation: He stated that privileges were commercial rights that the state had withdrawn from the general public and transferred to individuals; meanwhile, the author of a work enriches the national wealth with the economic value of this commodity. The author's rights are exclusive rights relating to this "newly created commodity."[40]

The economized discourse on authors' rights that became apparent in the nineteenth century must be viewed against two opposing tendencies: On the one hand, the easing and acceleration of global trade through the removal of customs barriers, the softening of protectionism, and technical innovations such as steam ships, the railroad, and telegraphy,[41] and, on the other hand, through the expansion, national standardization, and international harmonization of norms to protect literary and artistic property. The institutional entrenchment of international law endeavors was initiated in the 1850s by a Belgian committee of literary representatives and ultimately led to the foundation of the Berne Convention in 1886.[42] However, the economic grounding, conceptual expansion, and internationalization of authors' rights were accompanied by efforts to dissociate and exclude musical practices from this booming legal area; the expansion of copyright in the mid-nineteenth century also broke with oral traditions of cultural creation.

Authors against Traditions

Starting in the eighteenth century, the terms *creator/author* and *tradition* had a charged relationship. In the discourse on authors' rights, the basic assumption of modernity grew stronger that something new does not come from God or one's forebears and is not generated in communities but is created by an individual. The etymology of the German term *Urheber* (creator/originator), which is central to authors' rights, initially points to God, the primary creator, maker of the world, the one "who first creates a thing, and from whom it certainly originates, either wholly or to a large extent."[43] An ex negativo distinction has been formulated between the conceptual figure of the "creator" and "tradition." In the mid-eighteenth century, Johann Heinrich Zedler's *Universal-Lexicon* described *tradition* as follows: "Tradition, *lat. Traditio*, is as much a narrative that one can recite only from listening, but is not to be found written down anywhere."[44] Jacob and Wilhelm Grimm's German dictionary refers to the French origins of the term ("traditionnel = borrowed"), which was then viewed with increasing negativity: What has been "handed down" is "conventional," "normal," and therefore "traditional," a topos reflected in statements such as "a new shared atmosphere of learning developed . . . in contrast to the traditional ideas and insights."[45] On the other hand, as Hans-Ulrich Gumbrecht has pointed out, in the mid-nineteenth century the concept of "modernity" was redefined as a contrast to the "unalterable" and "eternal."[46] In 1859, the poet Charles Baudelaire formulated an aesthetic theory of modernity in *Le peintre de la vie moderne* (The painter of modern life) that he associated with a new sense of time: "Modernity is the transient, the fleeting, the contingent."[47]

Such perceptions of the new were also a constituent part of musical authors' rights. Vesque von Püttlingen justified claims to authors' rights with, as he put it, the "melodies" that contained the "individual core of a piece of music" and "attest to" the composer's inventive creativity.[48] Melodies—"happy inspirations of the creative spirit"—were "individual," "singular," and would distinguish themselves through "the imprint of newness distinguishable from all other melodies."[49]

In the nineteenth century, authors' rights were mentioned in the same breath as civilizing development, and the efforts to internationalize literary and intellectual property that resulted in the Berne Convention in 1886 directly cited notions of progress. Invitations to the preparatory conference for the Berne Convention sent by the organizing committee in 1858 spoke of "the competition of genteel peoples of all nations, who share their knowledge and love of progress,"[50] and this progress-related pathos consistently resonated in the discourse on intellectual property. Authors' rights were praised as the achievement of the "European cultural group of civilized states,"[51] which was always aimed against "American banditry, tolerated in the field of intellectual activity"[52] because, until the U.S. joined the Berne Convention in 1988, American copyright applied only to works produced in the U.S.

Lydia Goehr has argued that compositions up to around 1800 were produced for performance, reflected in the fact that the occasion of the composition and the performance date were listed on the sheet music.[53] After 1800, a paradigm shift took place in musical performance practices, as composers such as Ludwig van Beethoven and Hector Berlioz added more precise instructions to their notation and specified the exact tempo, rhythm, and instrumentation. According to the new ideal, the performance had to remain "faithful to the original." Written notes were authoritative, and the composer's notation for the instrument took priority over improvisation.

A cultural code that equated progressiveness with the rejection of tradition and that favored written notes over oral transmission is constitutive of music law in the nineteenth century. In the first legal commentary on musical authors' rights, Vesque von Püttlingen reflected this code by explicitly mentioning publishers of anonymous works as authors:[54] The "publication of folk songs, which are recorded as sung by the people" is an "artistic product of the publisher": "He [the publisher] first recognized the aesthetic, historic, or ethnographic value of the musical piece in its artistic significance and has published it with this in mind; through his own intellectual activity, he has rescued it from hiddenness or forgottenness and truly recreated it for the musical audience."[55] Elevating publishers to the status of actual creators resulted in their integration into authors' rights: "The intellectual activity employed to make accessible such hidden cultural treasures or interesting observations from popular life is certainly also entitled to the pertinent recompense and can find this only in authors' rights."[56] In contrast, Vesque von Püttlingen firmly excluded communally created music from authors' rights: "But a collective creation would go against the innermost essence of artistic production; in music, creative conception is typically tied to the inner life of the individual."[57]

This granting of author entitlements to the publishers of "observations from popular life" is based on the implicit presupposition that a work must take the written form to be created, an idea also manifested in the depiction of sample melodies in notation. Linking authors' rights to the written form created a paradigm of writing that was fundamental to the justification of musical authors' rights—and was also momentous. However, the line drawn in law between compositions created by individuals and folk songs created by communities was more porous than the categories purported. One episode involving none other than Richard Strauss, one of the spiritual fathers of the music royalty movement and a campaigner for composer copyright, reflects the complex breaches of legal codes in music production. Strauss returned from a Grand Tour through Italy (Mantua, Bologna, Florence, Rome, Naples, Sorrento, and Capri) in 1886 with the outlines of a composition. *Aus Italien* (From Italy) was first performed in Munich in 1887. In the finale, *Italienisches Volksleben* (Italian folk life), he used a melody that he described as an "old Neapolitan folk song." However, what he had taken to be a folk song actually turned out to be *Funiculì Funiculà*, a tarantella composed by Luigi Denza in 1880 for the inauguration of the funicular railway on Mount Vesuvius.[58]

Richard Strauss, the German father figure of copyright, had been listening out for music in southern Italy. In his natural assumption that this was authorless folk music, he neglected the man who had committed this folk music to paper and subsequently brought a successful action against Strauss. This demonstrates the inadequate boundaries drawn in musical authors' rights to reduce the number of potential composers to a marketable level.

Between the "people" and "composers," plenty of intermediaries were also at work who wanted to secure rights for themselves in the music business.

Mechanical Reproduction and Controlling Exploitation

While the legal framework for the sheet music trade was redrawn, a global mass market for music boxes was booming. The invention of music box technology by a Geneva watchmaker around 1800 had turned Switzerland into the global mecca of the music box industry: St. Croix, a village of 2,400 people in the Waadtländer Jura, was the center and symbol of music box manufacturing.[59] Swiss music boxes were presented at world fairs and became an export resource for the young Swiss state. In the mid-1860s, music boxes worth around two million Swiss francs were produced each year in Geneva and St. Croix alone.[60]

However, music boxes were seen not as art but as ornaments. In his report about the 1867 World's Fair in Paris, Pompejus Alexander Bolley, a chemistry professor at the Swiss Polytechnic founded in Zurich in 1855, described their sound as steely but pleasant: "Sound is produced primarily by the steel tongue, thus the high scales and the somewhat sharp, steely tone, which is to be expected from rather stiff, short, quickly oscillating pins. With pure tuning, that is careful work, the whispering sound of these instruments, which is clear but does not travel far, is pleasant to the ear, and has made them so popular."[61] In his opinion, the mass-produced metal boxes that found their "way to the world's remotest markets" were popular not just for their "musical value in and of itself"[62] but also for their "role as decorative objects or furnishings or objects of consumption."[63] Integrated into work boxes, cigar cases, photo albums, furniture, and carvings, these devices were seen as ornaments for the home and not as musical instruments.

In the 1860s, France sought to prevent free trade with music through authors' rights, and music boxes became another bargaining chip in international trade diplomacy when the first trade agreement was concluded between Switzerland and France in 1864. Switzerland, which since 1856 had only loosely regulated literary and artistic property through a network of half the cantons and, in contrast to France, had no national authors' rights until 1884, acquired a reputation for "counterfeiting" in France. In the discourse on intellectual property rights, forgery and imitation were stylized as the antithesis of invention, although in practice they often depended on and stimulated one another. Back in the eighteenth century, Adam Smith noted the importance of imitation in the development of innovations with regard to the emergence of modes: "Eminent artists" can bring about a change in modes by introducing new "fashions," who, in doing so, would be both admired and imitated. Through imitation, "his manner becomes the fashionable style in the art which he practices."[64] The juxtaposition of innovation and imitation has also been criticized from an economic history perspective: Maxine Berg has shown that in eighteenth-century mercantilist Great Britain, copies of foreign luxury goods centered around product imitation and not process innovation and that the actual innovation was therefore to be found in the imitation. Imitation was not simply about creating copies using cheaper materials but about creating new objects in new forms, occasionally in a more inventive, valuable, or unique form than the original.[65]

In the 1860s, however, the French courts began to view the transfer of musical works to music boxes as unauthorized reproduction.[66] Under pressure from France, a stipulation was added to the French/Swiss trade agreement (which opened up the French market to the Swiss export industry by reducing customs duties) about the mutual "protection of literary and artistic property." While Switzerland accepted authors' rights in exchange for trade facilitation, it remained tough on the conflict between authors' rights and music boxes. France and Switzerland reached a diplomatic compromise specifying that both countries would exclude music boxes from the rules on literary and artistic property.[67] This special rule for music boxes was finally enshrined in the trade agreement between France and Switzerland in 1882 and, thanks to Switzerland's efforts, was even integrated into the Berne Convention of 1886.[68] Composers and publishers now had a monopoly over the international exploitation of compositions, arrangements, and extracts ("now extended to pieces and so-called arrangements");[69] however, exploitation remained restricted to the sheet music trade, and notation remained the condition for protecting musical works. The idea of placing all music exploitation under the control of authors' rights did not yet prevail in the diplomatic world. Music boxes and sheet music continued to reside in parlors in reasonable harmony—one as ornament, the other as art.

From the 1870s, music boxes were followed by the Herophon, the Orphon, the Symphonion, the Ariston, and barrel organs mass-produced in Germany (particularly in Leipzig). Punched discs, cards, and volumes of *Lohengrin* and *Tannhäuser* could be bought for one mark per meter and first concerned the German courts in the 1880s.[70] In 1888, the Reichsgericht (Supreme Court of the German Reich) rejected an appeal by a producer of mechanical musical works who argued that his disks did not constitute unauthorized reproduction. The court's decision first established a new concept of reproduction in Germany that was no longer oriented toward reprinting. This was accompanied by the formulation of a concept of economic damage caused by reproduction through a change of media: According to the new doctrine, exploitation could also be "seriously impaired through reproduction in another form."[71] This paradigm shift can be seen in the arguments with which the Reichsgericht established breaches of a composer's authors' rights: Thirty years after Vesque von Püttlingen emphasized the value of musical works (particularly extracts) as potential value for composers, the Reichsgericht was already talking of the potential loss of value from a work through the repeated playing of small excerpts: Despite the "indeed minor form of reproduction—from the position of aesthetic artistic taste—limited by the means of reproduction," it is the "rapid deterioration of the composition of which the elite audience quickly grows weary." Sales of sheet music, "which are destined for human artistic activity," are therefore impaired.[72]

Ludolf Waldmann, the victorious composer and publisher, disseminated the court decision in a pamphlet.[73] He worked on a socially robust method of integrating mechanical musical instruments into the logic of the old copyright. A successful composer, he presented his legal pursuits as fighting for a threatened copyright and publishers' property. But Waldmann's musical repertoire was itself a manifestation of various transfer processes that led to the creation of new works: That his pieces were extremely popular, some even attaining the status of folk songs[74] and ultimately being reworked by Arnold Schönberg into new compositions,[75] clearly shows how those processes described by Waldmann as corrupting the original[76] could actually prove fundamental to creation.

With his plea for copyrights to be applied to mechanical musical instruments, Waldmann drew on two central social conflicts in the outgoing nineteenth century: The "social question," that is the antagonism between workers and manufacturers, and mechanization, or the replacement of human work with mechanized processes. According to Waldmann, changeable notated disks and their playback devices were destroying work. "The various musical professions will gradually become superfluous too and will be replaced by machines," he wrote.[77] "As a consequence of this new invention, there would be fewer piano schools within the next decade, many of their teachers would become destitute and, if industrialists were permitted to treat music publishers' right of publication as 'fair game' and the protection of intellectual property did not extend to the production of punched disks, the livelihoods of composers and publishers would also be at risk."[78] His polemic drew on arguments of aesthetics (distortion and fragmentation of the original by mechanical instruments), entrepreneurship (lost exploitation of new clientele through export to foreign countries), and class conflict (property of manufacturers). And he secured a decision from the Reichsge-

richt that he was owed part of the profits generated by the mechanical musical instrument factory he had sued.

Waldmann proved a shrewd entrepreneur who saw in mechanical musical
instruments a medium for dissemination and exploitation and a new field of
business for publishers: "Hopefully, some beautiful compositions will remain
that cannot be rendered abhorrent to the musical audience through continuous droning, and automated pianos will no longer prove too dangerous a
rival for pianists. However, publishers may later choose to cultivate the field
opened up to them, should the yield appear worthwhile."[79]

In later judgments, the German Reichsgericht reinforced the case law of
1888. Mechanical reproduction was no longer seen as destroying composers'
interests but as a means "to secure and enable the exploitation" of intellectual property.[80] The interplay of reproduction and intellectual property
resulted in stronger intellectual property for the exploitation of new reproduction technologies. It was certainly acknowledged that the new mechanical forms of reproduction opened up a new and different audience to musical
composers "than the audience to which music is performed using printed
notation." However, the prohibition of "reprinting" was not rendered obsolete. Nevertheless, authors' rights remained committed to the paradigm of
writing established in book printing: Only written compositions had a claim
to authors' rights, meaning that a significant proportion of music production—music passed down orally through the generations—was excluded
from concepts of authorship.

The exploitation of reproduction was based on rules that provided for
a transfer of rights and therefore enabled practices later described by Max
Weber as "market sociation."[81] The structure of authors' rights formulated
by legal theorists such as Josef Kohler as commercial rights and laws of
property enabled the impersonal transfer of a right originally tied to the
author's person. In the mid-nineteenth century, the question of the free use
of extracts from a musical work was riddled with conflicts in France, Prussia,
and Austria and regulated in different ways. However, the doctrine prevailed
that only the composer, publisher, or their legal successors had the right to
split up, break up, and rework music in line with the market. This established
a practice that at its core amounted to control of all potential exploitation
opportunities on different media.

Chapter 2

Images of Books

Such systematic reproduction of unique manuscripts and rare printed works would materially benefit the civilization of the future.

—Charles Mills Gayley, "The Reproduction of Manuscripts from the American Point of View" (1905)

Conserving through Copying

From Pen to Picture

Since libraries have existed, books have been read—and copied by hand—in reading rooms. The photocopy, the medium of modern offices and twentieth-century bureaucracy, was invented in nineteenth-century libraries and editorial studies. Before conquering the worlds of banking, insurance, courts, and administration, the photocopy and microfilm were developed as alternatives to copying by hand, as means of conservation and as techniques of rationalization and internationalism. These new methods of reproducing printed materials altered the relationships between publishers, authors, readers, and librarians. At first, this process was slow and went largely unnoticed. Thomas Edison's phonograph followed the music box, Emile Berliner's gramophone followed Johannes Gutenberg's letterpress, and a new music industry evolved alongside the old trade in sheet music. The copyright of old was remodeled as a right of reproduction that served the new channels of exploitation.

This was rather different to the situation in libraries, where the inventions of Louis Daguerre and Henry Fox Talbot were further developed for conservation and distribution, joining the Gutenberg legacy and fostering a culture of reproduction structured differently to that of the music industry. What were the driving forces behind this institutional and media reconfiguration? How did the invention of the photocopy alter reading habits, the way in which libraries were run, and how the academic disciplines perceived themselves? And what was the effect of this upheaval on the law?

As these new copying techniques were emerging, a move was taking place toward the "original" and handwriting, reflecting the professionalization and institutionalization of the archival and historical disciplines. The facsimile (Latin *fac simile*)—the detailed reprinting of manuscripts and documents—had been around since the seventeenth century.[1] And yet, in the nineteenth century, facsimile publishers highlighted the distinctive nature of their projects, seeing the focus shift to manuscript reproduction and the minimization of accompanying text.[2] The move from handwritten copies to images lends this development a cultural significance. To duplicate texts, it was no longer necessary to read them in advance and then transcribe and extract them letter by letter or word by word. From the mid-nineteenth century, the "pencil of nature" allowed texts to be recorded and stored.[3] Reading was no longer tied to a specific time and place.

In the 1830s, the École des Chartes in Paris—France's training ground for archivists and historians, founded in 1821—launched facsimile projects based on blueprints and lithographs. It had been possible to reproduce documents via photographic techniques since the 1850s; as evidenced by debates about whether documents and sources were faithful to their originals, the technique was seen as the scientification of historic methods.[4] Photography devotees criticized lithographs, branding them a manual "blueprinting process": "They could not remain faithful to the mechanical processes."[5] For them, the mechanical process of photography was more objective.[6]

Librarians initially resisted the use of photography in libraries because its technical requirements (light, water, darkroom) clashed with their conservational aspirations. Very few European libraries and archives set up special photographic facilities. In 1877, the Bibliothèque Nationale (National Library) in Paris installed an exposure space with darkrooms and running water for the photography of manuscripts and printed materials.[7] A regulation declared that permits were required for all photographic recordings in state libraries, museums, and archives. Before permission could be obtained for photographic reproduction, a negative had to be submitted to the ministry and two copies deposited at the library in question. This rule upheld the tradition of the "legal deposit" (a mandatory copy of printed materials) first cited in France in the sixteenth century, which committed publishers to providing copies to libraries.[8] The early modern obligation to submit printed materials aided censorship and continued in Great Britain's Statute of Anne of 1710.[9] Copyright regulation and the tradition of mandatory copies for libraries are historically intertwined in France, Britain, and even the U.S. Mandatory copies became one of the foundations of national libraries. When copyright was revised in the nineteenth century, librarians and publishers haggled over the number of copies and the duration of copyright protection. In the U.S., however, the librarians at the Library of Congress gradually won this privilege as the nineteenth century progressed. The 1846 act "to establish the 'Smithsonian Institution'" pledged to the Library of Congress (in addition to the Smithsonian Institution) copies of registered copyright literature "for the use of said libraries," "for the increase and diffusion of knowledge under men."[10] But publishers were very lax in complying: "We are surprised at the apathy shown of our leading publishers in complying with the law in relation to copyrights."[11] Congress therefore decided to use the postal service to ensure that intellectual works were archived and distributed; every postal office throughout the U.S. was able to send all registered works to Washington free of charge. Starting in 1867, anyone who failed to send their works to Washington was fined twenty-five dollars. Ties between the Library of Congress and copyright were further strengthened in 1897, when the register of copyrights was established and the Copyright Office's subordinate position to the Library of Congress created a direct administrative link between the Library and copyright management.[12] Librarian Thorwald Solberg was appointed the first register of copyrights in 1897. He and his successors were to play a central role in expanding American copyright. In fact, the Library of Congress would come to be the U.S.'s guardian of copyright.

The Rules of the Library

In the final third of the nineteenth century, facsimile projects evolved into nationalistic and patriotically charged endeavors and became an object of business for publishers.[13] However, the diffusion of reproduced library materials was limited by low circulation numbers[14] and "exorbitant prices."[15]

Permission to conduct photographic procedures in libraries was regulated. In the Bibliothèque Nationale in Paris, photographic recordings were permitted only under the supervision of a library clerk. The turn of the century saw criticism of the reproduction guidelines for libraries and archives. At Saint Catherine's Monastery on the Sinai Peninsula, the bishop's decision to prohibit photographic recordings of manuscripts brought editorial scholars and religious representatives to loggerheads. In an article in *Revue des Bibliothèques* (The Library Review), classical scholar Émile Chatelain denounced the rules and practices for photographic reproduction in libraries, where abbots and librarians were responsible for granting licenses.[16] Criticizing the regulations as draconian ("The most shocking thing of all is to see them being applied"),[17] Chatelain vehemently condemned the obligation, enshrined in French law since 1877, to provide expensive negatives and extracts: "The deposit of photographs, a practice we have renounced in France, is a persecutory and prohibitive measure."[18] Fearing that academic progress would be impeded, he called for the regulation to be amended. He also disputed the need for the "legal deposit," criticizing one of the foundations of state libraries, which required a library copy to be submitted before a printing license could be granted. For the classical scholar, access to the negative was no longer necessary once a recording had been made via heliogravure or phototype. Photography's potential for distribution questioned the monopoly of libraries as the only place in which manuscripts and printed materials could be archived and administrated. Looking back, Byzantine expert Karl Krumbacher speculated that there was a fear that copies would devalue originals and thus the status of their custodians: "There was a sort of jealousy that the photograph, a faithful copy, might detract somewhat from the value of the original."[19]

New Money for Old Rarities

At the International Congress of Librarians in Chicago in 1893, Otto Hartwig, a librarian in Halle (Saale), became the first person to call for an international society for the photographic reproduction of "the world's first-rate" manuscripts and rare prints.[20] Tracing back to his initiative, the first international congress on the photographic reproduction of manuscripts, coins, and seals (which took place in Liège in 1905) is to be viewed as part of the internationalism that flourished around the turn of the century. The congress also reflects the concept of a "global cultural heritage," which emerged during the initial phase of globalization around 1900 and boosted the conservation and dissemination of old manuscripts and printed materials. In these modern times, which saw the fleeting and transient elevated to a cultural principle, libraries evolved into counter-projects of permanent storage and timelessness.[21] Libraries therefore faced some competition for their role as "book-cases," or "chests for books" (*librarium*), particularly since their reliance on a specific location to store books was now considered a conservation risk. The Liège congress was in a state of shock following the Turin library fire of 1904, which destroyed one-off manuscripts and highlighted the mortality of these historical repositories. As the president of the congress announced in his opening speech, from Alexandria to Turin, "all libraries end up being burned to the ground eventually."[22] The introduction of dry plates meant that photographs were no longer considered a threat but a means to conserve and disseminate library stocks.[23]

Liège was the setting for the first encounter between the Old World, with its abundant library treasures, and the New World's demands for access to European stocks. Mills Gayley, a professor of languages and literature at the University of California in Berkeley and the official U.S. representative at the congress, took Liège as an opportunity to call for the foundation of a central copy and distribution body ("central clearing-house of research")[24] to produce manuscript facsimiles: "They are jealously guarded in the libraries of the Old World, and cannot be removed from them for love or money."[25] Gayley envisaged an exchange between Europe and the U.S. via a center in the U.S. (whose many new universities would urgently require facsimiles) rather than in the Old World, which had a rich vein of manuscripts but lacked the money to conserve or reproduce them.[26] He called for unrestricted access to knowledge "on liberal and unselfish terms."[27] To make his vision a reality, he proposed trading new money for old documents. A "bureau" was to be founded in the U.S. befitting the internationalist visions that initiated many global rules by establishing a central "bureau." This could be launched with start-up capital of around half a million dollars donated by foundations.[28] Herbert Putnam, head of the Library of Congress, had promised to help locate sources of funding. Libraries that made documents available for reproduction were to receive a backup copy, with the remaining copies available for purchase by libraries, collectors, and universities on the basis of subscription contracts and individual requests. The aim was to establish a "corpus codicum universale," a parallel library of every manuscript in the world. In Gayley's vision, books and manuscripts would circulate freely between Europe and the U.S., the high investment costs borne by a global network of libraries and collectors. As the originals were dispersed, so the costs would be shared. Given that these cultural riches were concentrated in just a few locations worldwide and that copies would be distributed to compensate for the potential loss of originals, this helped to spread the risk. But Gayley's vision was not one of decentralism; instead, he had in mind a U.S.-based "Bureau central"[29] that would receive decentralized support. There can be no clearer expression of the new cultural self-confidence felt by U.S. academics at the start of the twentieth century. The former Wild West was going head to head—and claiming equal status—with the custodians of the western world.

The American system of an international organization for the reproduction of manuscripts and rare books in the U.S. received support from the famous French archaeologist and art historian Salomon Reinach, who encouraged the congress to commission Gayley to found an international "bureau" on American soil.[30] However, the centralistic and internationalist American model was rejected by European librarians. Maurice Prou, head of the École Nationale des Chartes in Paris, feared an American monopoly: "No government will be able to grant a monopoly to a national office, as Mr. Gayley seems to be asking."[31] The Old World favored a decentralized system controlled by libraries and nation states. The only thing Gayley managed to extract from the international community of archivists and librarians in 1905 was a promise to advocate state intervention for liberal rules on manuscript reproduction. Gayley's proposition received tentative support and a commission was appointed to discuss these questions further—certain death for any visionary idea in global organizations.[32] The situation remained one of local solutions in European libraries from Brussels to Rome and Uppsala, where photographers offered to reproduce old printed works and manuscripts for any academics who might be interested.[33]

Mechanizing the Humanities

Expeditions with a Light Prism

Around the turn of the century, the reverse prism and microfilm were developed within editorial studies and libraries, significantly reducing the cost of manuscript copies and printed materials. Abbé René Graffin, co-founder of the *Patrologia Orientalis* editorial project, presented the light prism process for the first time at the 1900 World's Fair in Paris.[34] This process enabled photography directly onto photosensitive (silver bromide–based) paper. A mirror prism made the writing appear as white on black, or "positive." A darkroom was no longer required. The cost of recordings was halved.[35] This process was developed within editorial studies and was also initially used in the humanities. Early trial reports testify to evolving practices and a change in the self-perception of editorial studies. Editorial practices accelerated, lost their manual nature, and necessitated new working techniques.

Byzantine scholar Karl Krumbacher commissioned Paul Marc to undertake the "first expedition in which black-and-white photography was used on a large scale."[36] During his journey to Mount Athos in 1906, he made 1,307 manuscript recordings on silver bromide paper and 102 recordings on sheet film in twenty-two days—up to 230 recordings per day. In comparison, around twenty photographs were produced each day in the Bibliothèque Nationale in Paris in the 1880s. This equates to a tenfold increase.[37] Krumbacher saw the light prism as a technique of "objective precision"[38] and a means of conserving cultural "heritage."[39] This was accompanied by a reappraisal of research time; copies also became a way of "accelerating work."[40] Preparing for editorial projects (searching, traveling, transcribing) was now seen as a waste of time that ate away at "the best years of one's life."[41] Faced with this new copying technique, transcription lost its status as a scholarly craft and was reduced to mere "mechanical writing."[42] A task previously carried out by humans could be performed by a machine that swiftly revealed human achievements to be inadequate and flawed.

Breaking up books, the potentially fragmented access this offered, and the decontextualization of documents required loose pieces of photo paper to be labeled. In every media shift, information may potentially be lost when metadata is produced: "We are deluding ourselves if we believe that people

FIGURE 1. The birth of the photocopy in editorial studies: Mirror prism and book, 1906. Karl Krumbacher, *Die Photographie im Dienste der Geisteswissenschaften, Tafel 8.* Leipzig: 1906.

will actually enter this necessary information on every copy at a later point or even be able to remember it. This may have been possible previously, when every photogram was seen as something special."[43]

Copies were initially treated like originals, so it made sense to incorporate them into libraries too. However, this technique cast doubt on the tradition of storing negatives: If negatives were no longer being produced, they could not be stored. Academics and photographers once again criticized the deposit copy rule, which required all recordings to be made multiple times, while other forms of use (manual transcription or loans) required no comparable submission to libraries.[44] But why should libraries have to collect copies at all? Had the old library organization system not become an inadequate means of storing and distributing the new medium? After all, organizing, cataloguing, and administrating copies took up extra time, money, and space.[45] A notion was already emerging that copies could replace libraries and take on the role of conservation and dissemination.

Microfilm: A New Form of Book

As prism recording developed, documentation studies (a discipline that had emerged after the turn of the century) discovered microphotography, something with which Great Britain had experimented back in the 1860s.[46] Every historical account of documentation studies records the use of microphotography in the Franco-Prussian War of 1871 to transmit dispatches and postal orders to a besieged Paris. This narrative is based on an 1871 publication that described the daring use of balloons to transport cameras and pigeons to carry microfilms.[47] According to this tale of derring-do, fifty thousand dispatches were condensed to a weight of one gram, rolled up, and concealed in the pigeons' feathers. This fits almost too well with Friedrich Kittler's statement about the "misuse of army equipment"[48] and his associated argument that since the American Civil War, new media have always been developed for use in military technology. Could documentation studies, an internationalist and pacifist discipline that offered hope for the future of media, actually have been based on military technology?

However, it would be 1906—another quarter of a century—before the Institut International de la Bibliographie (International Institute of Bibliography; IIB, later IID) first discovered microphotography and discussed it as a way of storing and disseminating books, using the term *bibliophotography* ("Bibliophote" or "livre a projection," [book screening]).[49] The suitability of this method of compressing documents—which had been given a trial during the war—for documentary purposes focused on weight-, space-, and cost-saving alternatives to book distribution, on the vision of "absolute reliability," on standardizing and normalizing sizes and formats, and on sheer reproducibility.[50] Engineer and inventor Robert Goldschmidt and Paul Otlet, doyen of international documentation studies, got to the heart of the matter[51] in 1907: "Nowadays, books tend to be of a photographic nature."[52] Robert Goldschmidt left the intellectual property rights to his invention to the Brussels-based IIB. Photographic reproduction of printed materials was the "new form"[53] and the "book of tomorrow"[54] because, in addition to conservation and dissemination, it could replace the book itself. Although books had been around since the fifteenth century, they were not perfect. They took up space, were expensive to produce, and thus impeded the dissemination of knowledge: 60 percent of the world's books could be found in just twelve libraries, and there was a general tendency for books to be concentrated in large libraries.

As an alternative, the IIB presented the idea of a microphotographic book: A recording device would reduce the size of documents and commit them to film; index cards measuring 12.5×7.5 cm would hold seventy-two images and be stored in cabinets like those in libraries. These cards would be read via cinematographic projection devices. The IIB hoped that this new medium would revolutionize the structure of libraries, which would no longer be restricted to conservation and lending, but also become involved in reproduction itself—moving closer to the role of publishing houses: "Freely providing copies is in fact a publishing of sorts."[55] Here, thoughts turned to small print runs for specialist circles and to parallel publications, in other words to "publishing a work in a new form, publication that will be possible alongside the main edition."[56] For the first time, reproduction was being discussed not just for old and rare printed works and manuscripts, but also for extracts from current books, newspapers, and magazines. As the division of work increased within the academic disciplines, the IIB looked at new, tailored reading techniques and the compilation of "books" by readers: "It is increasingly important, therefore, to allow each individual to freely compose a book on a matter that he or she is studying, by taking extracts from these collective works."[57]

So it was not the microfilm but the reverse prism that initially conquered libraries and documentation centers. Given the huge interest in reproduction techniques expressed by American academics and librarians, it was no surprise that American libraries became the driving force behind technological development. The "photostat" (the U.S. term for black-and-white copies, named for the eponymous Rochester firm) was used in U.S. libraries and administrative bodies from the 1910s onward.[58] American librarians realized that the copy was the ideal medium for their new and vast academic nation. They wanted to redress their disadvantage against European researchers, whose plethora of libraries gave them much easier access to many libraries with large stocks, while American researchers had to make do with libraries that were much further away and had smaller inventories. In the 1910s, American librarians developed the vision "to put a photostat in one or more favorably situated cities in Europe and then copy such books and papers as they are needed."[59] Photostat copies were to systematically close the gaps in their stocks, allowing American researchers "to take the place on the learned and scientific world to which their energy, originality and intelligence entitle them."[60]

Although there was criticism—the black background of copies made it impossible to write notes, not exactly ideal for normal academic practices—it was outweighed by the new medium's potential. For example, copies could be bound and then reworked into new "books" that could in turn be copied as required.[61] The *book on demand* was born. The option to reproduce documents through images, rather than writing, also presented new reproduction opportunities for printed material in "non-European alphabets."[62] Reproduction was no longer the preserve of polyglot researchers; it could be performed by a device.

The photostat device made its way into American libraries and administrative bodies at the exact same time that Taylorist rationalization methods were being publicized and spilling over into Europe.[63] The ability of the photostat to quickly reproduce documents made it popular not only in universities and libraries but also as a means of preparing and mobilizing military forces in World War I.[64] As bureaucratic techniques, the photostat and Taylorism complemented each other almost perfectly for "so called efficiency purposes."[65] The machines were used according to the precepts of the cost/ benefit principle; as many copies as possible had to be produced to maintain a low cost per copy: "We found that in order to keep the operating cost of the photostat low per unit of work it is necessary to keep the machine in continuous use during at least five or six working hours each day, thereby permitting an economic utilization of the operator's time and of the chemicals used for developing. In this way we have found that the total cost may be kept down as low as 4½ cents per photostats print 7½ × 11."[66]

And so, quietly and unnoticed by the general public, the turn of the century saw a media revolution looming in the seats of the humanities, in libraries, and in a documentary movement with global ambitions. The book, the letterpress, and the library were moved aside by two alternatives: the reverse prism and the microfilm. American librarians, inspired by the project to get the young academic nation up to speed, and European internationalists like Paul Otlet, who dreamed of "more Taylorism"[67] in academia, set out to leave traditional libraries and the limitations of the letterpress behind with new photographic reproduction techniques. It was clear that they would at some point find themselves in conflict with the authors' rights of letterpress printing. Nevertheless, the custodians of international authors' rights did not initially believe that these new reproduction devices from the academic world would threaten authors. When *Le Droit d'Auteur* (Copyright), the magazine from the office of the Berne Convention, first reported on the microfilm in 1911, the microfilm was lauded as a progressive medium that served authors' interests. It was said that the microfilm could serve as an "instrument for transmitting their thoughts" that would provide readers with easier access to printed materials.[68]

While the discourse on authors' rights took an increasingly economic perspective on the reproduction of music in the nineteenth century, until the end of the 1920s reproduction techniques in libraries were viewed solely as working and dissemination media oriented toward libraries and academia that did not affect the interests of authors or publishers. Even promoters of intellectual property saw authors and academics as bearers of progress with common interests. No one had considered that microfilm might endanger copyright.

Chapter 3

Voice Recorders

> This storage and accumulation of artistic recitals for use at any time and in any place is far more important to the economic significance of the circulation of audio works . . . than the piles of notebooks containing mere written recordings of the same technique.
>
> —Ernst Eisenmann, *Das Urheberrecht an Tonkunst-werken* (1907)

Originality of Voice Recordings

In the nineteenth century, the creating authors and bearers of copyright—who had been invented as recently as the eighteenth century—found themselves challenged by self-recording devices. Photography requires no creator but is created by "hand" or "the pencil of nature"—at least so ran the argument of Henry Fox Talbot in 1844.[1] While photography offered no opportunity to reflect on legal theory and aesthetics in Anglo-Saxon law and was quickly integrated into copyright (in Great Britain in 1862 and in the U.S. in 1864),[2] in Germany it first had to be declared an art; the randomness and lack of intention emphasized so strongly by Talbot had to be negated[3] before reduced copyright protection could be granted in 1876.[4] Even so, the law remained ambivalent toward device-made images: They were not protected against the flourishing picture postcard industry, which used them as a means of sending messages. Even after their integration into the *Kunstwerkrecht* (Artwork Law) around 1907, they were protected against reproduction for just ten years, rather than thirty.[5]

Recordings of light waves on glass and paper were followed by the engraving of acoustic vibrations on wax.[6] The instruments required for this had been developed in the U.S. as devices for transmitting and recording language in the tradition of the telephone and telegraph. Thomas Edison initially saw his phonograph, a cylinder-based "talking machine" patented in 1878, as a recording device for stenography. As John Durham Peters put it, he was concerned with conservation, not repetition; with a "non-human secretary, an acoustically automatic writing machine," not entertainment.[7] Emile Berliner described his disk-based gramophone, patented in 1887, as an apparatus for "etching the human voice."[8] He focused on engraving the ephemeral onto material through electrochemical processes. By around 1895, for example, these machines were no longer being discussed as office aids and were no longer the sole preserve of hotel lobbies, saloons, and carnivals but had been further developed by the music industry into coin-operated machines and home entertainment devices.

Clearly, there was money to be made with these recording and playback devices. Negotiations were required on who should take a share. This was a challenge for copyright: While these devices captured the ephemerality of the human voice and the vibrations of instruments, the legal corpus was based on the written form. Who should own the recorded voices? Who should be able to exploit them? Under which conditions? And who ultimately profited from the new voice recorders? This chapter looks at the legal norms developed in response to the new recording media, the extent to which these norms coded the use of the devices and the form and content of storage media, and how these developments are to be classified within social constellations.

Phonographs initiated wide-ranging movements for devices, people, and legal norms: Phonographs, cylinders, licenses, sound recordings, factories, and tenors circulated between New Jersey, Berlin, London, Paris, Rome, and St. Petersburg. The raw material for the records came from Bengal, where the required shellac was extracted from tree resin.[9] The devices invented in U.S. telephone laboratories also found their way into the parlors of Europe. Recordings of famous European tenors like Enrico Caruso (whose frequency, with overtones and vibrato, was better suited to recording than "female voices"[10] or violin recitals) were exported to the U.S. Yodeling by American singers, who were recorded in America in the German language, sold like hotcakes in Germany.[11] And in France, Charles Pathé entered the phonograph trade in 1894 after listening to a phonograph at a fair in Vincennes. In 1896, he began to produce recordings in his own studio near the Opéra-Comique and also became a movie producer.[12] The final years before the turn of the century were a great time for the new media (phonographs and cinematographs), which were also used extensively to import, recombine, and re-export foreign cultures.

Protection against the Apparatus

From the outset, legal commentaries on the phonograph identified the differences between this apparatus and mechanical musical instruments like the music box or the barrel organ: In 1897, a jurist argued that this was a medium of "virtuosos, concert givers, and dramatic artists"[13] that, due to its "faithful sound reproduction,"[14] could create new needs for protection against these devices. He spoke of "sentimental interests" that could come into play with an author's heirs.

What are we to understand by this? Around 1885, a legal debate in Germany and the U.S. asked whether an individual has a right to privacy against the media and photographic devices in particular, a right to be left in peace by these devices and a right to one's own image.[15] This was also a debate of the culturally embedded notion that one's personality is manifested in one's portrait.[16] The legal norms established in the outgoing nineteenth century in response to the media's creation of publicity expressed a new sentimental culture that cannot simply be regarded as the effect of the bourgeois construction of privacy in public; they also drew new boundaries between the public and the private. For example, "public" figures (such as politicians and athletes) were excluded from this right by their decision to enter the public eye. At the same time, talk of the sentimental interests of heirs also alluded to the device's ability to store a person's living voice—and therefore to preserve their spirit in media after their death—and the question of whether the law should stop it from prolonging people's existence beyond their physical lives.

In 1900, the Berlin regional court ruled in favor of an opera singer who filed a suit after a phonograph cylinder containing a recording of his voice was duplicated by a manufacturer without his knowledge or permission.[17] The judgment ventured into lawless territory (a legislative amendment was being prepared) and justified the decision by stating that the form of recital reproduced the singer's "originality." In law, the reproduction of the voice emphasized its "originality." The court went as far as to call for a "right to one's own voice" along the same lines as the much-discussed "right to one's own image."

At the same time, a legal treatise on the phonograph appeared in Germany that proposed a conceptual reframing of copyright, which had previously been tied to musical notation.[18] Jurist Leo Eger released the concept of work from its fixation on the written form: "The phonographic cylinder contains the work; whoever has it may enjoy the poetic and musical creation whenever they desire."[19] He recognized at a very early stage that, in the future, the protection of exploitation rights would need to apply primarily to voice recorders and not to sheet music. In reframing the idea of a work, he also reformulated the concept of reproduction: "As the word clearly states, to reproduce something means nothing more than to produce a number of copies that share certain characteristics with the archetype."[20] Eger believed that the creator's rights were at risk because the work was found not on paper but on the cylinder, increasing reproduction, as he put it, "immeasurably."[21] Previously, works had been transmitted in writing or by memory. Suddenly, the cylinder offered a template for much more direct dissemination.

The new legal concept of reproduction was shaped by the revaluation of oral recital and the voice. Eger described the entry of the singer into the creative spheres as follows: "The artist exercises his or her own creativity and, in marrying his or her individuality with the composer's work, begets a new work that is independent in more ways than one."[22] This was a very harmonious description of a contentious issue: The relationship between singers and composers.

Protecting National Industries

The 1901 Reichstag negotiations on amended copyright legislation included an extremely "lively" debate about mechanical musical instruments. Tempers became heated when the topic of protecting this national export industry was introduced. In political discussion, mechanical music was debated within the codes of social issues. Members of the legislature discussed pianolas, meaning the interests of workers, authors, and industry. They also engaged in national trade protectionism: The advisory commission had been shown mechanical pianos (pianolas) from the U.S. to prove that there was very little difference between the playing of this instrument and the playing of a pianist.[23] The pianolas came from the Aeolian Company in New York, which was competing for customers with the mechanical music factories in Leipzig and vying with German composers for exclusive licenses for compositions. Like the compositions of the mid-nineteenth century, mechanical musical instruments became national symbols in the political discourse of the early twentieth century: The music boxes for which Switzerland had secured a copyright exemption in international law in the mid-nineteenth century were the quintessence of Swiss goods, and the pianolas were American products. In contrast to the mechanical instruments from Leipzig, American pianos were subject to copyright, enabling protectionist economic policies.

The first reading of the copyright amendment in the Reichstag in January 1901 merely touched on phonographs as the music of the future.[24] Arthur

Esche, the national liberal representative, mentioned them in his vote "more out of curiosity" because they could be viewed neither as "reproduction nor as public dissemination nor as public performance."[25] However, the phonographic industry—which to this point had helped itself to compositions without regard for legal niceties—followed the Reichstag debates nervously and tried to influence them.[26] None other than Emile Berliner, inventor of the gramophone and director of the Deutsche Grammophon-Aktiengesellschaft company, lobbied against the inclusion of phonographs in the new law by "calling upon the particularly relevant Reichstag members."[27] These actions resonated in the second reading in April 1901, when industry representatives made sure that the minutes explicitly stated that phonographs were excluded from copyright. Otto Arendt, economist and member of the Reichspartei (Reich Party), even called on Arnold Nieberding, state secretary of the Reichsjustizamt (Department of Justice), to clarify matters: "However, given the unease in the industry, I should like to take this opportunity to request that the State Secretary be so good as to make a declaration to help reassure this not unimportant industry."[28] A skilled mediator between political and legal camps thanks to his work on the *Bürgerliches Gesetzbuch* (German Civil Code), Nieberding fulfilled this request: "In our opinion, they [phonographs] are not among those instruments whose musical and mechanical recital is modeled on personal performance; therefore, they remain . . . free from the claims of composers and their publishers in accordance with the law and the committee's conclusions, as I believe I may be permitted to add."[29]

Over the following years, this brief comment by the state secretary during a parliamentary debate (transcribed in shorthand and published in the Reichstag stenographer's reports) was the only standard on the copyright status of phonographs, which inevitably led to it being cited even more frequently. Law does not need to be set out in legislation to be valid; decisive agreements are sometimes made and debated in the periphery outside of legislation. However, the pianola demonstration in the Reichstag achieved the desired legislative effect: American pianolas were explicitly enshrined in law as a breach of copyright.

Gentrifying Phonograph Sound

While phonographs were successfully exempted from copyright in the Reichstag, the talking machine industry was busy gentrifying phonograph sound. Before music performers could be integrated into the law and exploitation chains, the phonographic industry had to increase its cultural standing. This was achieved through recordings of opera stars as well as "phonographic

FIGURE 2. Caruso or gramophone, no difference! Advertisement for Caruso recordings, 1908. *Phonographische Zeitschrift* 9, no. 48 (1908), 1500.

competitions"[30] and "phonograph concerts,"[31] which had been filling Berlin's concert halls since 1901. Comparative recitals with singers demonstrated the phonograph's "natural rendition" and proved its "social acceptability." The term *phonograph sound* was used to refer to mechanical music, which was seen as inferior. The industry wanted people to use live concerts as a benchmark for listening to music with the help of a machine. The phonograph had to pass the voice test that Emile Berliner declared had been passed in the image of "His Master's Voice."[32] Berliner had trademarked the image of the dog and the gramophone in 1900; as the symbol of all products from the Victor Talking Machine Company, it soon became the icon of the talking machine industry as a whole. The enhancement of tenor voices and gramophone sound was a thoroughly reciprocal process: The gramophone turned Caruso into a reproducible mass product, just as manufacturers and dealers advertised gramophones to customers using Caruso recordings ("no difference!").[33]

The talking machine industry urged salespeople to be disciplined and preserve the ideal of originality, warning them not to experiment with the devices by varying the playing speed, for example: "Even a slight increase in speed renders the recording unnatural, unpleasant—which is almost the same thing—and, much more, accelerates the motion and therefore greatly raises the pitch."[34] They appealed to dealers to control playback and ensure a "beautiful" sound when demonstrating the devices to customers. They also emphasized the damage to reputation and value caused by playing "worn-out" phonographs in public places and at exhibitions.[35] Focused on standardization, the talking machine industry could no longer imagine people using phonographs for composition and resisting the urge to compare their quality with that of a concert.

The Search for Security

The talking machine industry was itself a victim of reproduction. Phonograph factories warned against copies of "original recordings."[36] The multiplication industry now stressed the importance of "originals" and manually produced "original cylinders," denouncing low-quality, mechanically reproduced "duplicates."[37] Technical copy protection had been invented—and new strategies would constantly be created to circumvent it. Phonograph companies attempted to fight copied cylinders on the market by announcing their name before the actual recording as a mark of quality: "Therefore, if the announcement is to be omitted before copying, the piece itself can only be copied imperfectly, that is without the opening bars."[38] Copiers worked around this measure by omitting the announcement when copying; in response, manufacturers would have the singer perform during the title announcement or add an "acoustic trademark" during the recording.[39] The acoustic signals were then visually duplicated through visible "characteristic spirals," an "unrecorded circle in the middle of the disk grooves."[40]

FIGURE 3. The beginnings of technological copy protection: Characteristic lines to warn against imitation records, 1908. *Phonographische Zeitschrift* 9, no. 43 (1908), 1327.

The association of talking machine dealers made its members commit to using original cylinders; in 1908, it passed a resolution admonishing copying as "unauthorized interference in the property of others" and ostracized producers and suppliers of "forgeries": "The dealer's association condemns the unauthorized copying of cylinders and records as theft."[41] In the battle to control reproduction, music publishers also began to raise exclusive claims to the use of musical works for phonographs and gramophones. Before the musical notation, they added a statement reserving the right to "use for mechanical instruments, incl. phonographs, gramophones, etc."[42]

The year 1905 was a pivotal one for codifying phonographs and cinematographs in copyright. The new media from the U.S. left its wild adolescence behind. These developments originated in France: On the one hand, the Tribunal de la Seine in Paris ruled against two film pioneers (Clément Maurice and Ambroise-François Parnaland) who had sold films of medical operations by the surgeon Eugène-Louis Doyen at carnivals and in theater halls.[43] On the other hand, the Parisian court of appeal prohibited the free use of "poetry and lyrics with or without music"[44] by the phonographic industry,[45] explaining that manufacturers would have a veritable library of text material that would breach the exclusive rights of authors. The court also decided that retroactive compensation was to be paid for rights violations, ordering that records be confiscated. The record industry thereupon entered into a "strike," and Pathé laid off 1,500 workers.[46] However, it abandoned this threatening gesture (which again alluded to social issues) that same year in favor of future joint business with publishers. The talking machine industry, publishers, and composers agreed on a licensing system, and royalties were reflected in a price increase for cylinders of ten and fifteen cents.[47] For the first time, an alliance was formed between the phonographic industry and the united composers and publishers; this was secured by a licensing system, and record consumers would foot the bill.

Although the court's decision spoke only of protected literary works, the French judgment triggered comprehensive restructuring of the legal relationships between composers, publishers, and manufacturers, on the one hand, and the revision of international copyright, on the other. Up to this point, the talking machine industry had rejected all claims for authors' rights related to music recordings and helped itself to musical material without any legal obstacles; now, the international industry was developing an interest in legal security, reflected in lawsuits and settlement negotiations for copied records and cylinders.[48] This tactic was also fueled by the hope of a trade-off: The phonographic industry speculated that the reproduction protection demanded for its recordings could be successfully integrated into copyright if composers were in turn granted copyright for phonograph recordings.

After French composers, poets, publishers, and manufacturers closed ranks, the German phonographic industry also changed strategy: "The situation in France, where talking machine manufacturers have for some time been obliged to pay money to composers, shows that it is possible to grant certain rights to composers without serious damage to the industry."[49] The industry now sought an alliance with publishers and composers and hoped, through payments to composers, to end legal uncertainty and achieve international protection for music recordings in a future revision of the Berne Convention: "Unauthorized copying would then violate not only the rights of the manufacturer, but also those of the composer."[50]

From Musical Notation to the Indescribable Voice

In 1907, Ernst Eisenmann formulated the pertinent legal justification for phonograph law. In doing so, he established a copyright theory of the "practicing artist," its importance underlined by its introduction, which was written by Josef Kohler.[51] What was new about this legal approach to sound recording? Or, to put it more generally, what made this legal commentary stand out from the crowd of legal theses and debates on the phonograph?

It was significant because he simultaneously broke with several historic copyright concepts: First, he rejected the separation of the artistic from the mechanical and instead emphasized the artistic use of the apparatus, drawing on the trivialization of the apparatus (which had developed in connection with photography) and emphasizing the artistic factor: The phonograph may provide a "mechanical rendition" of a sound performance, but its creation requires a "composer" and "musician" because it is "thoroughly artistic" and may only be produced through "artistic means."[52] Second, he did not reconnect the concept of musical works with the written form, instead emphasizing the indescribability of the voice; a phonographic recording of a voice contains the thing that cannot be fully grasped by musicology or physical analysis. The "distinctive tone of the voice, the 'timbre,' audible and striking to even the most untrained ear," cannot be explained scientifically.[53] He also refuted the paradigm of writing, arguing that oral cultures have always performed without musical notation: "Even before individual members of the tribe refined their minds to the point of learning to read music, the highly musical and far-flung Gypsy people have always managed without these means [notation] and nevertheless propagated all striking melodies and compositions by playing them with precision as they move from place to place."[54] He placed performers, the "musicians," on an equal footing with composers: In artistically bringing a work of sound to life—"turning the dead notation into sensorily perceptible sounds"—they are the first to "reproduce" the work.[55] Third, Eisenmann drew on the topos of "fidelity of rendition," the aim of the talking machine industry (from Emile Berliner's *His Master's Voice* and the Caruso gramophone comparison, to the standardized discipline of playback, through to phonograph concerts). Fidelity was now used as a reason to treat phonographic recording differently in copyright than other mechanical musical instruments. In this respect, the commentary also deviated from Josef Kohler, doyen of German copyright, who wanted to see sound recordings regulated not in copyright but in moral rights.[56]

Eisenmann based his reinterpretation on the "progress of cultural development"[57] and changes in the music market: The "storage and accumulation of artistic recitals for use at any time and in any place" is becoming "far more important to the economic significance of the circulation of audio works . . . than the piles of notebooks containing mere written recordings of the same technique."[58] By justifying a copyright paradigm shift, Eisenmann also questioned one of the pillars of classical music in the nineteenth century: That it could be described using a notation system. To use Friedrich Kittler's expression, Eisenmann had used the "pan shot" from the written form to the phonograph to the substance of a legal argument.[59] Eisenmann's legal commentary is a good example of the tendency for jurists to become technology and media theorists as part of their professional practice; at a very early point in the technology's use, they focused on the instrumental, media, and economic characteristics of the devices they described. Eisenmann saw the phonograph as an apparatus that recorded "artistic expression," precisely the thing that composers cannot transcribe into musical notation. This contrasts with positions within music didactics in the outgoing nineteenth century, which described musical performance with academic meticulosity and sought a language to establish performance as an activity that could be taught, like writing, reading, and arithmetic.[60] Eisenmann interpreted the talking machine as a medium that, due to its fidelity, was superior to playing from notation and a storage medium for new forms of scientific exploitation.

Two years later, in 1909, Josef Kohler also changed sides, believing that the reproducing artist is entitled to authors' rights.[61] However, he left no doubt that these rights would definitely not be granted to ephemeral improvisations and that the nature of a work lies in technical reproduction. Under no circumstances was the integration of the reproducing artist into copyright to result in the integration of all oral cultural production. Musicians were enthroned on the shoulders of composers, and musicians helped composers to safety in the new era of the phonographic industry. Where there were no protected compositions, there could be no vocal artistry worthy of protection or any associated rights—at least not for singers: "If one were to record the songs of savages, to which no authors' rights apply, in such a way and exhibit them," thoughts would instead turn to whether even the manufacturers of the musical recording should not also be granted these rights. This changed nothing about authors' rights, which were granted only to composers and publishers in the mid-nineteenth century. "Savage" non-authors remained outside of the law. However, Kohler wanted the door to the creators' realm to be left open to manufacturers. He cited the legal construct, connected to photography, that declared photographic recording an art in order to grant copyright to photographers. Was the "collection and definition" of sounds not also audio art? Was musical recording not also an "evaluative, discretionary activity"[62] and therefore worthy of protection?

The decisive question had been raised as to how far the authors' rights of the eighteenth century, which regulated relationships between authors, publishers, and reprinters, should be extended to regulate the music industry based on machine recording, a collaborative industry with factories and high capital expenditure. In terms of photography, this came down to the artist who uses the camera. But while photographic recording remained a profession performed by individuals and was therefore compatible with aesthetic/legal concepts based on individuality and creation, musical recordings were from the outset the product of well-funded stakeholders. In 1907, Albert Osterrieth,[63] general secretary of the Deutsche Verein für gewerblichen Rechtsschutz und Urheberrecht (German Association for the Protection of Intellectual Property), picked up on the demand for copyright for the talking machine industry. He believed that while phonographic recording deserved protection, this protection should be within commercial law, not copyright: "Phonographic technology as such has nothing to do with copyright."[64] Osterrieth was not impartial in making this assessment; he had represented the interests of composers as a longtime legal adviser to the Genossenschaft Deutscher Tonsetzer (Cooperative of German Composers). It could not be in the interests of composers and publishers to have manufacturers as co-creators. It therefore stands to reason that the copying of sound storage media was neither regulated in the Berne Convention of 1908 nor enshrined in German law but determined in court through lawsuits brought by the talking machine industry.

In 1910, the Reichsgericht (Supreme Court of the German Reich) ruled in favor of Deutsche Grammophon-Aktiengesellschaft, which had filed suit against people manufacturing copies of its recordings under the name "Divaplatte."[65]

However, the court largely worked around copyright law and based its arguments on the *Bürgerliches Gesetzbuch* (German Civil Code), that is to say, the "violation of good morals." Implicitly, the court made it clear that it did not want to see reproduction protection regulated in copyright. A distinction was being made between "work performance"[66] and "work creation," the legal categories of copyright clearly defined. There were now two categories for reproducers, those who violated morals and those who breached copyright. Authors—invented for literature and art in the eighteenth century and extended to include music in the nineteenth century—continued to keep to themselves. This was in the interest of authors and publishers, who did not have to share the privileges of authors' rights with interlopers from music transmission.

The German legal text from 1910 mentions composers, arrangers, and performers as the creators of music.[67] The small print reasoned that music recordings are to be accepted as an "implicit transfer of copyright" if this takes place "due to a special arrangement, an order, an existing service relationship, or a service relationship entered into for this purpose."[68] By contrast, British law specifically named copy protection for musical recordings in the Copyright Act of 1911 ("copyright shall subsist in records").[69] While British law had no problem integrating the work of sound engineers into the legal structure as the right of copy (copyright), German law took the indirect route, via the author. Despite converging developments, these two legal concepts—copyright as the right to copy and authors' rights as work authority—are reflected in international copyright to this day.

The contentious regulation of copy protection clearly shows that sound recordings created new, overlapping constellations of interests. The underlying reasoning for copyright—that legal rights belong to the author alone—was no longer accepted by the talking machine industry, a new type of publisher. Publishers and authors were now confronted with the phonographic industry, which was not interested in regulating the *reproduction of a work*, but in protecting the *reproduction process itself*. In principle this situation was not actually new but resembled the printing trade that had been around since Gutenberg and wanted to sell its printed materials before reprinters got there first. The reprinting privileges established since the outgoing eighteenth century were simply superseded by authors' rights. Legal categories no longer concentrated on media but elevated the work inscribed in the medium—inextricably linked with the author—to the core of the legal structure. These were the long-lasting consequences of the developments in authors' rights around 1800 appropriately described as "work authority" by Heinrich Bosse. Copyright regulated the question of "yours and mine" with the aid of the author.[70] The relationships that resulted from recordings and reproductions of their works were regulated in contracts outside of copyright. This created minimal legal security and substantial freedom of contract and already suggested that the record industry—the music publishers of the twentieth century—would switch to alternative legal norms outside copyright's legal corpus in the medium term.

CHAPTER 4

Canned Music

> I foresee a marked deterioration in American music and musical taste, an interruption in the musical development of the country, and a host of other injuries to music in its artistic manifestations, by virtue—or rather by vice—of the multiplication of the various music reproduction machines.
>
> —John Philip Sousa, "The Menace of Mechanical Music" (1906)

Talking Machines: Between Trust and Royalties

American Legislation at the Conference Table

Since the nineteenth century, Europe had viewed American copyright from the perspective of "progressive" universalism, criticizing the U.S.'s particularism with a certain degree of condescension and maintaining that the U.S. was "regulating legal relations with the aim of momentary advantage."[1] The Copyright Act of 1790, last amended in 1891, had made copyright protection for foreign authors dependent on the printed matter being produced in the U.S. (manufacturing clause) and therefore connected to import restrictions. This was not well received within the sphere of the Berne Convention, which had been established in 1886. The internationalistic Europeans believed that, when it came to law and culture, the U.S. was still a developing nation.

When Thorwald Solberg, the register of copyrights, began preparing a legal amendment for the U.S. in 1900, he envisaged moving closer to the laws of the Old World.[2] After the turn of the century, the attorney general—as legal adviser to the American government—also emphasized that a legal amendment was vital due to increasing ambiguities presented by the law: "Under this kind of legislation it is impossible to arrive at any satisfactionary conclusion to what the Congress really did intend by it."[3] New media and the growth of global trade with cultural assets had prompted a reassessment of U.S. and European laws.

Since the mid-nineteenth century, the music industry had focused on economics when discussing copyright; meanwhile, discourse on the misuse of market-dominating positions of power now shaped amendments to national laws and the Berne Convention in conjunction with the regulation of the phonograph. The notion that multiplication machines were accumulating in the hands of monopoly capitalists, leading to the destruction of evolved economies and the decline of culture, was reflected in a series of simultaneous and mutually influential national legal revisions (U.S. 1909, Germany 1910, Great Britain 1911) and the amendment of the Berne Convention (1908). Compulsory license systems regulated in law were introduced for music recordings. These license systems were a novelty in copyright, and they raise the question of how this abrupt change fits into social constellations. This question is important because the legal codification processes also shaped the symbolic coding of the new media. For the first time, the New World regulated copyright ahead of the Old World; for the first time, innovations in North America influenced developments in Europe. While the U.S. may have remained outside of international conventions in 1909 and created its own law, the compulsory license—a copyright norm enshrined in the U.S.—was exported to Europe.

In 1905, the chairman of the American Senate Committee on Patents instructed the Library of Congress to organize an advisory conference for an extensive revision.[4] The idea was to prepare a law together with all those "supposed to have an interest in such legislation."[5] This was entirely in the spirit of expanding copyright. Twenty-six associations were invited to the three conferences, which took place in New York and Washington in 1905 and 1906. Most of these associations wanted to see copyright expanded: Emissaries of authors, playwrights, artists, and composers (in particular the American Copyright League founded in 1883),[6] of book, magazine, and newspaper publishers (such as the American Publishers Copyright League), of photographers and lithographers, of music publishers, typographers, and printers; representatives of educational institutions and libraries; and the American Bar Association (ABA).[7]

As in the 1901 legal amendment debates in the Reichstag, phonographs were practically ignored in the U.S. at the advisory conference for a new Copyright Act. For the representatives, "reproduction" implied reprinting. The talking machine industry was not explicitly invited to the conferences.[8] It was the representatives of music publishers who in the second session brought "mechanical instruments" into the discussion.[9] Music publishers wanted "mechanical means" to be explicitly mentioned in the law as a new form of reproduction and attacked the talking machine industry: "These machines are beginning to be quite a commercial industry in this country, and the firm Mr. Thomae represents last year did a business of $38,900,000. We consider these gentlemen as enemy against us, because they have taken our copyrights without any considerations at all. The people Mr. Thomae represents are willing to associate themselves with us, and the rest should come in. One large concern, however has threatened to spend $100,000 to try to beat the bill."[10] The aforementioned Mr. Thomae represented the Victor Talking Machine Company from Philadelphia. It is worth noting that, on the list of participants, he was entered with the music publishers, and it was probably in the interests of his company that he did not speak on the question of mechanical music.

Ultimately, a draft bill by the register of copyrights was reworked at the conference and discussed in public hearings in Congress between June 1906 and March 1908. In his message to Congress, President Theodore Roosevelt called for a new law to be passed, echoing the opinion of the preparatory conference and voicing a massive threat to copyright holders: "Our copyright laws urgently need revision. . . . They omit provision, for many articles which, under modern reproductive process, are entitled to protection; they impose hardships upon the copyright proprietor."[11] It is striking that the question of mechanical music, touched on only briefly in the three preparatory sessions, became the center of the debate in the first hearing of the Committee on Patents. The hearings, which were perfectly orchestrated by the spiritual fathers and supporters of the draft bill, also reflect the links between the representatives and the legislative process.

Librarian of Congress Herbert Putnam and Richard Bowker of the American Copyright League got the ball rolling. Following the ratification of the law, Richard Bowker wrote an important reference work on the U.S. Copyright Law that has stayed in print up to the present day.[12] The referential relationship between lobbying, legislation, and jurisprudence is no cause for scandal; typical of law, this characteristic is particularly pronounced in the specialized field of copyright; representatives become experts and therefore have a say in the legislation—and, in the end, are also responsible for the accompanying legal commentary.

After the lawmakers, the artists had their say, specifically painter Frank Millet and composers John Philip Sousa and Victor Herbert.[13] John Philip Sousa was a popular composer of marching music. As a conductor of military bands and director of the United States Marine Band, serving the U.S. president, he was closely connected to the military and political spheres. The supporters of the law brought him to Washington's political arena precisely because of his patriotic aura. However, he was not a passive symbolic figure used to give a face to the author (copyright was an abstract legal concept) but was actively involved in debates about phonograph regulation and became a key figure in early culture industry criticism in the U.S.

John Philip Sousa: The Integrated Apocalyptic

In June 1906, Sousa initially appeared humble before Congress; he introduced himself as a brass band leader without the words to explain himself in a parliamentary setting. However, he did not mince his words. With rhetorical brilliance, he urged support for the law and stressed the urgency of giving composers a financial share in music recordings, stating that the bill would provide protection such that "in any production of our music by any of these mechanical instruments they must make a contract with us or with our publishers; that they must pay us money for the use of our compositions."[14] His rhetoric played on the central conflicts raging at the turn of the century: Industrialization, mechanization, market forces, developing market power through monopolies, and the loss of cultural certainties. His remarks clearly set "them" (the factories) against "us" (the composers and publishers). He spoke of moral rights and emphasized the clear allocation of property—"our music," "my property," "my publisher," and "my copyright." He also distinguished between interests and affairs of the heart. Sousa stripped copyright of its economic context, presenting it as a question of "pure" art and culture: "These talking machines are going to ruin the artistic development of music in this country."[15] By "culture," he meant "people" and "folk songs," the precise area of culture that was excluded from copyright. He contrasted human singing with machine music, which demoted people to mere operators. Although folk songs would not actually benefit from extended copyright protection, Sousa painted copyright as a question of ensuring the survival of a folk culture endangered by technology and talking machine manufacturers: "Last summer . . . I was in one of the biggest yacht harbors and I did not hear a voice the whole summer. Every yacht had a gramophone, a phonograph, an aeolian, or something of the kind."[16] He then showed how deeply he and his brass band were linked with this industry: "They were playing Sousa marches . . . but they were not paying for them."[17] In the 1906 hearings, Sousa emphasized that he had never set foot in a recording studio, and yet the short running time of marching music made it ideal for records. Although Sousa himself stayed away from recording studios, his band had made the first Columbia recordings back in 1895, as well as 260 recordings for the Victor Talking Machine

Company between 1900 and 1903.[18] Ultimately, Sousa's band was the greatest contributor to the Victor repertoire.

In the Washington hearings, a phonographic industry representative (American Gramophone Company) played on the way that Sousa switched between a record composer and a composing artist, stressing that Sousa's exclusive contracts with the Victor Talking Machine Company created a risk of monopoly: "He today is under contract, and he plays into these 'infernal machines' with his band."[19] Aside from the American Gramophone Company, only one of its rivals (the Victor Talking Machine Company) was represented at the preliminary negotiations; the company seized the opportunity to imply that links between composers, publishers, and the Victor Talking Machine Company could lead to the formation of a trust, pointing to the Victor Talking Machine Company's close relationship with publishers' associations. In doing so, the representative of the American Gramophone Company stressed the danger of monopolization and trusts in the phonographic industry, an argument that would dominate Congress debates and have a crucial influence on the international legislative process.

In the same year as the Washington hearings, Sousa consolidated his criticism of phonographs in an article for *Appleton's Magazine*, warning that mechanical conservation would destroy music.[20] This text and some of its catchy neologisms and metaphors have haunted culture industry criticism and criticism of culture industry criticism ever since.[21] Sousa's pamphlet is regarded as the origin of the "canned music" metaphor,[22] a term not just coined by John Philip Sousa but also powerfully shaped by the illustrations of Frederick Strothmann.[23]

The illustration shows a man picnicking by a river filled with fish and opening a "phonograph can" with a knife. The caption, "Incongruous as canned salmon by a trout brook," links music conservation with the canned food industry, which since the 1880s had symbolized the industrialization and mechanization of everything natural or human in the U.S. The criticism of mechanized slaughter in Chicago had hit a peak of public scandal in 1906 thanks to Upton Sinclair's *The Jungle*, a novel that was set in a slaughter-house.[24] Sousa's criticism of music conservation harked back to the songs of the first New England settlers and elevated the "living, breathing," public art of singing.[25] The phonograph symbolized the monopolization and commercialization of musical life ("wholly monopolized by commercial pursuit")[26] and the disappearance of the amateur. The apocalyptic mood of the fin de siècle also gained currency in the U.S. copyright debates. John Philip Sousa's cultural criticism was not written haphazardly; it was directed toward the copyright amendment negotiations in Washington. He demanded "absolute power of controlling my composition"[27] and stressed the imminent demise of culture.

Umberto Eco's 1964 analysis of culture industry criticism (and its counterpart, culture industry celebration) introduced the distinction between "apocalyptic" and "integrated" intellectuals.[28] These concepts can be used to classify Sousa's ambivalent relationship with the phonograph a little more precisely. To use Eco's words, Sousa is an integrated apocalyptic: He espouses a theory of cultural breakdown in order to integrate his profession into newly emerging music markets. His neologism "canned music" gets to the heart of this attitude. Conserving and therefore industrializing music is just the first step; this is followed by preserving the ephemeral, allowing it to be enjoyed outside of a particular time and space.[29] In this sense, Sousa's "canned music" metaphor was not a "fetish concept" in the sense of Umberto Eco's criticism of culture industry criticism. Unlike the concept of the "culture industry"[30] coined by Theodor W. Adorno and Max Horkheimer in American exile in the middle of World War II—which combines two words to suggest incompatibility and thus stops any further discussion of the phenomenon—Sousa's metaphor allowed the new medium to be interpreted in many ways; these interpretations may not have been intended but were implied in his neologism. For example, these might include preserving the ephemeral, prolonging musical enjoyment, or exploiting the metallic materiality of the storage medium.

The recordings of Sousa's compositions outlived their creator and developed a life of their own: To date, there have been over a thousand different recordings of his hit *The Stars and Stripes Forever*. Since 2011, anyone with a computer and an internet connection can access the National Jukebox of the Library of Congress website[31] and listen to seventy-nine recordings of Sousa's compositions and 2,230 recordings of Sousa's band from the Victor Talking Machine Company. The sounds of the instruments are preserved, including the rustling of objects near the microphone, the crackling that varies with the pitch and volume, and the rhythmic movements of the cylinders. John Philip Sousa's somewhat forgotten oeuvre is now experiencing an online revival in the National Jukebox. Why? Because one hundred years ago the music was stored using talking machines and has been transferred to a new medium; furthermore, it is out of copyright and the property of the Library of Congress, which has made it available to the public. This emphasizes one of the properties of new media, that it constantly brings old content back into circulation.

Compulsory Licenses and the Right to Reproduction

At this point, we must remember that law is not only clarified through law-making but also enforced in case law, particularly in the Anglo-American tradition. As Congress hearings were taking place in Washington, a few hundred feet away justices were advising on a suit brought by a music publisher against a manufacturer of mechanical music. The mills of justice had arrived at the mechanical piano.[32] In 1908, the Supreme Court had also come to a decision on what constitutes a copy in legal terms. The court distinguished between a general understanding ("a reproduction or a duplication of a thing") and a legal understanding ("that which comes so near to the original as to give to every person seeing it the idea created by the original").[33] Despite the increase in copying techniques, the justices maintained that the written form was required: "It is not susceptible of being copied until it has been put in a form which others can see and read."[34] It was decided that mechanical pianos were not copies. Remaining obtuse and, even in times of media transformation, clinging to reprinting and the associated paradigms of writing, copyright struggled greatly with the expanding concept of media. There was, however, another voice in the courtroom: Judge Oliver Wendell Holmes may have supported the judgment, but he left no doubt that the law-making bodies now had to adjust the legal definition of copying in legislation to include the new music reproduction techniques: "Anything that mechanically reproduces that collocation of sounds ought to be held a copy or if the statute is too narrow ought to be made so by further act."[35]

His wish was granted: In March 1909, Congress passed HR 28192, which came into effect on July 1, 1909.[36] The Copyright Act of 1909 amended the legal status of the phonograph by expanding the protection of music for commercial purposes ("for profit") to include all recordings ("any record whatsoever thereof"), although only for new works and not with retrospective effect ("copyrighted after this Act goes into effect"). In connection with this—indeed, to some extent offsetting this measure—a compulsory license was introduced that granted the same recording rights to anyone who paid royalties: "Any other person may make similar use of the copyrighted work upon the payment of the copyright proprietor of a royalty of two cents on each such part manufactured."[37] The introduction of the controversial compulsory license limited composers' demands for absolute control of their works. Through publication, copyright lost its right to exclusivity. Musical composer John Raymond Hubbell later described the law as "the lousiest, stupidest, most un-American clause."[38] Ultimately, the law was entirely in keeping with American tradition, uniting economic liberalism and state intervention to break up monopolies. This change to the law was initiated by the phonographic industry and some publishers, who linked reproduction with the spread and misuse of market power—an argument that has continued to hound new media all the way through to Google Books. Authors would no longer decide how their works were used—instead, this would be determined by a monetary transaction.

U.S. legislation pertaining to the phonograph had an economic basis. First, copyright was linked with antitrust measures, which was unprecedented. With the Sherman Antitrust Act of 1890, the U.S. Congress enacted the first competition policy standard, which paved the way for the legal prohibition and dissolution of trusts. The argument of market power abuse emerged in the U.S. after 1905 in Congress copyright hearings connected to mechanical musical instruments and talking machines; the argument in Europe then grew heated. Second, the law's commercial focus was reflected in the fact that copyright protection remained restricted to commercial purposes and was not, as in France, enshrined as moral rights for the author with comprehensive "work authority."[39] Third, it manifested itself in the standardization of business contracts, by which defined fees were to replace negotiations and prevent conflict. This allowed the exploitation of sound recordings to become a routine commercial process.

License Systems in International Treaties

European promoters of authors' rights such as Ernst Röthlisberger, the Swiss secretary of the office of the Berne Convention, did not hold back in criticizing the development of the American legal amendments when it became clear that the U.S. would adhere to the manufacturing clause and the formal requirement for registration. In Bern, the U.S. was described as the land of "business policy," against which the "idealists and intellectuals," like the register of copyrights, were powerless.[40] While negotiations to amend the Berne Convention continued at full speed in Berlin in 1908, the Copyright Act negotiations in the U.S. were followed closely. With the prospect of an international norm for the new medium, the pitch, volume, and even terminology changed when debating the legal status of sound recordings in Europe. Polemics from publishers and manufacturers heated up the debates. This was no longer about legal reasons for norms but the moral legitimacy of economic demands. The German phonographic industry seized on the monopoly accusations that had already dominated U.S. hearings on the new Copyright Act between 1906 and 1908. However, unlike the U.S., Germany had no tradition of legal remedies to stop corporations dominating the market. In 1897, the Reichsgericht (Supreme Court of the German Reich) even acknowledged that these corporations were admissible.[41] Nevertheless, the argument from the U.S. also took hold in the German copyright debate: The talking machine industry warned of the danger of a trust and "control of the arts" through the "greed and obsession of an international group of publishers and speculators."[42] It played the populist card of criticizing capitalism, with publishers cast in the role of greedy capitalists who have huge funds at their disposal and monopolize music. The talking machine industry presented itself as the voice of "the public," "the people," and "general interest" and as the guardian of free competition. At the same time, the music industry tried to play for time, to postpone national regulation and to hold out for an international solution.[43] It fought the retrospective application of legal regulations for phonographic recordings and voted for an automatic recording right for all manufacturers, a license system, and the definition of fixed royalties. The conflict surrounding the compulsory license—which saw particularly vehement disputes between publishers, composers, and manufacturers—demonstrated the constellations of interests at play in the regulation of the music trade. Copyright had granted authors exclusive control of their rights since the outgoing eighteenth century; now, the industry fought the exclusive exploitation of sound recordings with antitrust arguments and called for legal intervention to prevent monopolies in the sound recording business.

The 1908 Berne Convention (revised in Berlin) integrated mechanical music and phonographic sound recording into the international treaty. At the end of the nineteenth century, Germany had supported Switzerland's demands to exclude mechanical music to protect its music industry; however, in the run-up to the Berlin revision, Switzerland was the only country to fight the expansion of copyright to include mechanical music.[44] The Swiss federal government then decided to attach greater weight to publishers' interests in ratification than those of the music box industry. It "permitted signing" in order to "maintain good international relations."[45] Pulling out of the treaty would have cast Swiss international policy in an unfavorable light and jeopardized its status as depository of the Berne Convention.

During the negotiations, Germany and Great Britain championed the compulsory license. The Association Littéraire et Artistique Internationale (International Literary and Artistic Association),[46] founded in 1878 and one of the driving forces behind the internationalization and fortification of literary and artistic property in the late nineteenth century, saw the introduction of the compulsory license as the end of "unrestricted copyright." It vehemently spoke out against compulsory licenses, in which effort it found support in France and Italy. Italy also insisted that no music recordings should be permitted without the consent of the author. In the revised Berne Convention of 1908, individual countries were therefore permitted to include caveats against the compulsory license in their national laws.[47] The international treaty did not uniformly regulate international licensing, opting instead to leave the matter to the various countries.

Protectionism and Antitrust

Back in 1907, German representatives of the phonographic industry, publishers, and composers had started to negotiate the distribution of future royalties without agreeing on a distribution formula or the percentage of the license fee. The German talking machine industry regretted the failure to include an international compulsory license in the revised Berne Convention of 1908; at the same time, it was satisfied with the introduction of the license system. "The worst danger" had been "prevented."[48] From the publishers' perspective, a quick solution was now required after the Berlin revision of 1908. The aim was to "divide up the chickens . . . even before they hatched,"[49] as music publisher Ludwig Volkmann put it. While the talking machine industry warned against publisher trusts, publishers presented themselves as endangered small businesses engraving and printing music and as entrepreneurs bearing great risks in order to cultivate music—unlike the phonographic industry, which simply sought out tried and tested masters. Volkmann recommended that publishers act as intermediaries between manufacturers and composers. He called for a speedy resolution to forestall the development of a major movement for license-free music, much like the nineteenth-century associations that pushed through special regulations for "performance-free music." Volkmann proposed that they agree on royalties of between 1 and 3 percent, to be shared equally between composers and publishers. When it became apparent in the legal negotiations that the legislature was not going to define any fixed fees, the talking machine industry protested vehemently and called for legal definition to prevent "endless disputes."[50]

While negotiations between publishers and the industry grew more intense, the Reichstag debate of April 1910 left most parliamentarians cold. Six speakers had to settle for an audience of twenty. So as not to jeopardize the quick ratification of the 1908 Berne Convention, the material was quickly passed on to a commission for the final touches and accepted en bloc in the third reading without discussion.[51]

The revised German copyright law of 1910 introduced a compulsory license for sound recordings in the "interests of the domestic industry" to prevent the "formation of monopolies in the hands of large enterprises."[52] This had been aided by the argument that trusts could be formed by well-funded factories, "namely foreign ones."[53] Inspired by the U.S., the compulsory license was now used to fend off the U.S., the greatest rival to the German phonographic industry. Up to this point, the American and German phonograph industries had divided up the market between them: Devices from the pioneering U.S. occupied the high-price segment, while those of late-blooming Germany took the low-cost segment. But by 1910, the market was slowly becoming saturated, and the two industries were now competing in a mid-level price range.[54]

Most of the legal works on German phonograph law have stated that "legal logic" had been suspended in introducing the compulsory license and that purely "commercial considerations" were at work.[55] These legal works had two implicit presuppositions: First, the notion that law and economics operate independently of one another and independent of social developments; and second, the idea that the law must be timeless and unalterable. As the legal negotiations showed, these presuppositions are extremely questionable. Instead, they reflect the historical interpretation that these jurists believed that the law should remain the same precisely because conditions had changed (society, media, economics, politics, aesthetics).

Unlike in the U.S., German legislators did not dictate royalties, leaving them to be negotiated by contractual partners. In addition to Germany (1910), Great Britain (1911, Imperial Copyright Act) also followed the example of the U.S. (1909) by specifying a compulsory license and fixed royalties of 6.5 percent of the sale price. Great Britain (the old industrial nation) and Germany and the U.S. (major participants of the Second Industrial Revolution) all introduced an industry-friendly reproduction license standard. The split system of the compulsory license also proved advantageous in German/American legal relations when, in December 1910, the U.S. signed an agreement to mutually recognize mechanical music rights.[56]

Things developed differently in France, Belgium, and Italy. In France, the tradition of the collecting society had boosted the negotiating power of publishers and composers since the mid-nineteenth century. This helped to create a situation in which composers and authors did not have to share their exclusive rights with the talking machine industry. Furthermore, the early agreement on a royalty system in the wake of a 1905 court decision between publishers and the talking machine industry helped to find a solution that would not be overturned.[57]

The compulsory license meant that, after 1910, composers had to decide whether to release a work for sound recording and thus surrender some control over how their work was used. Once copyright was restructured, record-ing and reproducing music became a matter of licensing contracts. Although authors and publishers in the U.S., Great Britain, and Germany now lost their exclusive rights to the act of music recording, they remained the central legal reference point in the new network of relationships, particularly in Germany, where the protection of sound recordings was regulated as an implied trans-fer from the author to the manufacturer, while Anglo-Saxon copyright did not remove this "indirect route" via the author.

PART II

Collecting Agencies and Research Materials

CHAPTER 5

Collecting Collectives

> Musical copyrights are exploited to protect all entitled persons effectively and in accordance with the same principles by awarding the administered rights and applying consistent tariffs.
>
> —Genossenschaft Deutscher Tonsetzer (Cooperative of German Composers), *Grundordnung der Anstalten für Musikalische Urheberrechte* (1931)

Author Agencies

The Gaps in Economic Explanations

In the mid-nineteenth century, authors' rights increasingly described musical works as having value; this did not refer to any artistic and musical value but rather to their economic value. Initially, a requirement was simply formulated in law to treat works as economic assets that could be exchanged for money. This requirement was underlined when, in the same period, authors, composers, and publishers first united to enforce authors' rights. Authors now had a public presence: Their representatives visited cafés, theaters, cabarets, and concert houses with receipt books, filed lawsuits, and lobbied in the anterooms of national parliaments. They had to do this because they wanted money for something that had previously been free.

In the German-speaking region, the term *Verwertungsgesellschaft* (collecting society) had gained currency as a name for collective bodies that represented the interests of composers and publishers. Such bureaucratic appraisal, administration, and distribution organizations emerged in the mid-nineteenth century and influenced the formation of copyrights in Europe and the U.S. in the twentieth century.

From an economic theory perspective, these organizations emerged because transaction costs increased due to a multitude of media and the resulting complexity of authors' rights.[1] The collectivist perception of authors' rights enabled authors to prevent their works from being exploited at no charge. By applying the principle of reciprocity, the national organizations—which had a tendency to monopoly—gained global control of their rights. Economists also describe collecting societies as principal/agent constellations because authors have only limited control over the societies they commission. The economic methodology used to analyze these organizations has only three economic explanatory models (reducing transaction costs, monopoly formation, principal/agent). It remains incomplete to this day. There is no answer as to the constellations in which they developed, how they prevailed, and which social, political, and cultural factors played a role.

Through admission rituals and the valuation process, collecting societies influenced the form, content, and prices of exploitation and were therefore central to determining which music would be included in or excluded from exploitation chains. The following chapter explores in more detail the institutions that exploit authors' rights and analyzes the interplay of legal, economic, media, and cultural factors and how this influenced "social uses"[2] of music.

Initially, we focus on the development and diffusion of the French model of music exploitation and its expansion into an international system. Very few sources are available from the early days of collecting societies; due to the lack of archives, these are largely flattering self-portraits in periodicals. By looking at their regulations, we will therefore analyze their social logic and the associated attribution of economic value. By looking at the admission rules and valuation procedures, we can infer the mechanisms used to include and exclude music and the bases on which premiums were distributed by these organizations, which were central to copyright practice, strongly criticized, and yet extremely tenacious.

Fabriqué en France

The Société des Auteurs, Compositeurs et Editeurs de Musique (Society of Authors, Composers, and Publishers of Music, SACEM), founded in France in 1851, pioneered the organizational form that would be applied to the collecting society. It described itself as an "agency" that gave concert organizers permission to perform its repertoire, claimed fees for musical performances, and distributed the money to its members.[3] SACEM's aim was to establish performance—alongside sheet music—as a source of income for composers and publishers. Inspectors observed the activities of concert organizers. In doing so, they strengthened the actions of the French state, which had begun to push for authors' rights to be recognized abroad and to integrate them into international trade agreements (e.g., with Great Britain in 1851, Switzerland in 1864, and Prussia in 1865). The long protection period of fifty years in French law provided SACEM with a large repertoire of music that was protected by authors' rights. Furthermore, the foundation of SACEM and the integration of authors' rights into international trade agreements coincided with a boom in French music abroad.[4] The French state supported the export of French music and the associated aspiration to spread French values by subsidizing the music system. Musical magazines in Europe and the U.S. helped to further popularize French culture. As French cultural exports flourished, SACEM began to set up an international agent system— first in Belgium in 1878 and then, for example, in Alsace-Lorraine, Switzerland, Italy, Britain, Austria, and the U.S.—to thwart the free trade of French culture. At the same time, the French agency model was to be made universal by signing up foreign authors and publishers.

Royalty Economy

From the 1890s, organizers, composers, and publishers outside France criticized the activities of SACEM's agents.[5] SACEM was considered "international," which was not meant as a compliment; the organization was pilloried as foreign interference in national affairs. It was deemed centralistic, nationalistic, arbitrary, untransparent, chauvinistic, monopolistic, and quite simply, French: "The money that one manipulates in Paris is our legacy; it belongs to us, the Belgian authors and composers."[6] As SACEM was attacked, a counterattack was initiated with the goal of importing the French model of enforcing authors' rights. The aim was to get rid of SACEM and set up national societies based on the SACEM model: "What the French authors have done, we must also do *in our country*." "French authors would never put up with a *Belgian, Swiss*, or *German* association that conducted itself as the Société des Auteurs et Compositeurs comports itself in Belgium or Switzerland."[7] In Italy, the Società Italiana degli Autori et Editori (Italian Society of Authors and Publishers, SIAE) entered SACEM's field of activity in 1882; this was followed by the Austrian Gesellschaft der Autoren, Komponisten und Musikverleger (Society of Authors, Composers, and Music Publishers, AKM), which was initiated by publishers in 1897.[8] In 1903, the Genossenschaft Deutscher Komponisten (Cooperative of German Composers, GDT; also known as the Genossenschaft Deutscher Tonsetzer)—founded in 1898 with composer Richard Strauss as its figurehead—launched the Anstalt für musikalisches Aufführungsrecht (Institution for Musical Performing Rights, AFMA).[9] AFMA had been created to preempt potential SACEM agents who would "possibly even exercise the rights of German authors on German soil."[10] It was also founded because SACEM refused to pay out royalties for German works in France so long as fees for performing French music in Germany were not returned to France. Precisely because of its nationalistic bent, the French royalty economy model promoted the international alignment and payment of music royalties. In his 1901 commentary on the GDT's proposals, jurist and music critic Heinrich Schuster warned against "rocking the legality of adaptation."[11] He criticized proposals that deemed adaptations of compositions by bandleaders and arrangers to be violations of the composer's authorial rights and wanted to control musical performances in this respect. But it was the collecting societies that now set the tone.

In Germany, authors' rights royalties were collected based on the French example and the state's bureaucratic bodies: "Officials" monitored the music scene, inspected programs and posters, and visited establishments with receipt books. The central office in Berlin kept records of works, composers, lyricists, and publishers and created extensive administrative journals and registers. Music recordings were licensed using office technology and a system (established in customs authorities and postal administration) to confirm payment by sticking labels onto records; here too, France's publishers and phonographic industry had led the way back in 1905 by introducing licensed brands.

In designing the system—which was criticized by opponents as a "royalty economy"[12]—the collecting societies deliberately looked to their cooperative role models to counter the accusation that they were undermining "music for its own ends" in favor of profit. The system's opponents in publishing and the phonographic industry also argued that royalty collection was to be run as a "purely economic, commercial enterprise";[13] in response, the GDT emphasized that it was *not* a commercial business, pointing to its cooperative status. It also demonstrated its social focus by establishing a support and pension fund and using 10 percent of royalties to aid members in need; as stated within the GDT, "the humanitarian side was to be highlighted in particular."[14] The royalty economy legitimized itself as an "ethical moment"[15] in a world of merciless battle for economic survival. "Light entertainment" and "entertaining music" would keep "serious music" afloat: "The fashionable composer must allow part of his income to be diverted to his colleagues less favored by luck."[16] In social debates, it had to be concealed that when people spoke of musical values, they were thinking of money and not just of beautiful melodies. However, in criticizing capitalism to boost their credentials, the collecting societies struggled to legitimize themselves with German singing and concert societies, which also believed in the ethics of cultivating music for noncommercial reasons and fought the expansion of authors' rights to include performance.

From 1907, German publishers and composers came together in an alliance of convenience under the umbrella of the GDT. However, the alliance did not include all publishers, always remained fragile, and was constantly subject to public attacks due to the suspicion of monopolies and the criticism of capitalism that influenced debates. But what happened to the traditional music that fell through the net of authors' rights in the nineteenth century? Did its exclusion from copyright mean that it was also excluded from exploitation chains and the royalty economy?

Voice Archives

Since the mid-nineteenth century, music performance in Europe had been increasingly influenced by authors' rights restrictions. Associations of composers, publishers, and librettists that based themselves on the French model played a key role in this development. Following the decision in Berlin in 1908 (during the revision of the Berne Convention) to extend copyright to music recordings, their organizational structures enabled them to organize royalties for records. Alongside these economically minded collecting societies, institutions emerged around the turn of the century (Vienna in 1899 and then Berlin in 1900) that concentrated on collecting voices, sounds, and noises. Collecting and scholarly activities were established alongside the economic exploitation of music. In a sense, the voice, sound, and phonogram archives stand in contrast to the collecting societies, with their focus on researching and archiving oral cultural traditions outside of copyright categories. In doing so, they followed the tradition of American cultural anthropologists like Jesse Walter Fewkes and Franz Boas, who were among the first researchers to use phonographs as ethnographic recording instruments. Just like Native American music recordings made during the presidency of Theodore Roosevelt, these recordings were collected in museums, the Smithsonian Institution, and the cultural anthropology institutes of the newly founded universities. That these collections were established alongside the music markets shows how strongly the separation of traditional and composed music established in the mid-nineteenth century influenced the treatment of sound recordings.[17] Phonographic recording archives emerged in those milieus familiar with the archive as a place and practice of collection, organization, and conservation: Musicology, linguistic sciences, cultural anthropology, and research into the human voice positioned between psychology and physiology.[18] Researchers were interested in the dying (dialects) and the undiscovered (languages and chords not fixed in writing). However, sound recording was primarily intended as a medium to be transferred to the written form.

Nevertheless, the boundaries between phonograph archives and the phonographic industry remained porous: The German phonographic industry expanded its repertoire with music recordings that strayed too far from typical concert hall fare. Their brochures advertised "music from around the world" and "the voices of all peoples." They were probably alarmed themselves by the importing of culture via sound recordings when, in 1906, they called for more "German dialect recordings of folk songs" to be included in the repertoire: "Why are special recordings not dedicated to the individual peoples of our glorious German nation that meet their language, more precisely their dialects, their emotions, their idiosyncrasies, and their tastes?"[19] Comments in the *Phonographische Zeitschrift* (Phonographic Magazine) suggest that there was far more demand for the exotic than for maintaining domestic traditions. Musical recordings did not just bring sound storage media into parlors; acoustic signals from foreign cultures also infiltrated the home.

Recordings of indigenous peoples, tenors, and statesmen from the repertoire of the phonographic industry also expanded the stocks of the Berlin phonogram archive. Shortly before World War I, the production of "ethnic records" led the American phonographic industry to first discover the cultural creativity of immigrants and then to tap into new markets in these milieus. In the late 1920s, they turned to African American traditions and the culture of the southern states.[20] These were largely hindered by the stringent entry barriers of the American Society of Composers, Authors and Publishers (ASCAP), founded in 1914, which required members to have published five compositions. Harry T. Burleigh and James Weldon Johnson—a black musician and a black songwriter—succeeded in joining ASCAP.[21]

From Paris to Berlin, London, New York, Etc.

After 1905, the phonograph opened up new exploitation channels for music, and authors' rights were expanded to include sound recordings through amendments to national legislation and to the Berne Convention in Berlin in 1908. The organizational form of the collecting society therefore gained in economic significance. Now, the aim was to control the distribution of license fees for music recordings.[22] Following the introduction of the new copyright act, Germany had two institutions for collecting royalties, which over the following years amounted to between 5 and 10 percent of the sales price:[23] The Anstalt für mechanische Rechte (Institute for Mechanical Rights, AMRE), founded by the GDT in 1913 alongside AFMA, and the Anstalt für mechanisch-musikalische Rechte (Institute for Mechanical-Musical Rights, AMMRE), set up by the Verein deutscher Musikalienhändler (Association of German Music Traders) and the Société générale et internationale de l'édition phonographique et cinématographique (General and International Society for Phonographic and Cinematographic Publication) in Paris in 1909.[24]

AMMRE was a profit-oriented GmbH (German company with limited liability). In 1910, its contracts provided for a royalty of 10 percent of the sales price: Out of an income of 117,797 marks, 43,333 marks were paid to composers and publishers, followed by 173,498 marks in 1911 and 35,000 marks in 1913.[25] In 1911, AMMRE made payments to 406 members, which broke down as 261 publishers and 145 authors. Once royalties for music recordings were enshrined in law, the collecting society environment was fiercely contested at first: To gain an advantage on the licensing market alongside the GDT, AMMRE began to present new compositions at "novelty evenings" in 1913.[26] The "Hofjäger in Berlin" concert hall resounded with American rhythms, much to the displeasure of the trade journal for the German phonographic industry, which sneered at the "nigger or Yankee effects" that occupied half the program.[27] In 1915, fifty-one members broke away from the GDT and founded the Genossenschaft zur Verwertung musikalischer Aufführungsrechte GmbH (Cooperative for the Exploitation of Musical Performing Rights, GEMA), whose repertoire mainly comprised entertainment music; it merged with the Austrian AKM in 1916.

While collecting societies emerged in continental Europe at the start of the twentieth century to collect royalties for sound recordings, Great Britain and the U.S. did not follow suit until 1914.[28]

The foundation of the Performing Right Society (PRS) in Great Britain in the late 1890s was in fact a battle between music publishers and reprinters to prevent sheet music "piracy."[29] Britain's first major copyright conflict of the twentieth century was, again, a dispute regarding the reprinting of music. The dispute was driven by the development of photolithography, a piano boom among the English middle class, and the energetic presence (with private security) of members of the Music Publishers Association (MPA). Music publisher William Boosey, a central figure within the MPA who was also involved in developing the Copyright Act of 1911, was among those to initiate the PRS in 1914. Prior to its foundation, music publishers had a rapid change of heart with regard to their business strategy: Having considered defending sheet music as their means of survival, after 1911 they turned their attention to securing performance royalties. As in Germany, the PRS was founded in Great Britain to counter SACEM and its French agents in London. The first official act of the PRS, shortly before World War I, was to negotiate contracts with the German, French, and Austrian collecting societies and to publish lists of the PRS repertoire.

ASCAP's early history has become the stuff of legend. The story begins with a conspiratorial meeting in October 1913 between nine publishers and composers in Lüchow's Restaurant on 14th Street in New York City, a beer restaurant run by German immigrants that was popular with musicians and composers. Among their number were two composers, John Raymond Hubbell, who recorded his memories in a typescript in the 1930s, and Victor Herbert, who became an illustrious figurehead for ASCAP. An active member of the ASCAP board, Herbert had testified at the 1906 Congress hearings on the Copyright Act of 1909 alongside John Philip Sousa. Also in attendance was Nathan Burkan, a trusted attorney to music publishers who, funded by the growing ASCAP "war chest,"[30] was soon focused not just on rights for light operas and musicals but would make a successful case in the Supreme Court against hotels and restaurants that refused to pay royalties to ASCAP.[31] As its founding fathers openly emphasized in the U.S., the initial goal was to collect royalties in order to lay before the court the legal foundations to increase royalties in the future: "Of course ASCAP had to finance the costs of legal actions throughout the country."[32] What began over schnitzel and sauerbraten culminated in an official organization in 1914.

Admission Rules and Collection Categories

Measuring Performance Time

SACEM exported French organizational culture to Europe and the U.S. and played an important role in the musical copyright of the twentieth century. What do the regulations and distribution rules of the collecting societies in France, Germany, Great Britain, and the U.S. tell us about how these institutions saw themselves and the cultural coding of the royalty economy? And how did the Parisian agency model shape the social use of music?

SACEM's admission requirements expressed the paradigm of writing, established in musical authors' rights, that discriminated against oral cultural production, which was considered "ephemeral." Composers were only admitted who had published at least six works appraised by the society ("all published in the usual graphic format"),[33] paid an admission fee, been recommended by two members of the society, and had also taken a "technical examination" where requested. The examination required composers to write an accompanying melody for a song, while chansonniers had to notate a song with three verses. All aspiring music authors had to pass through a four-stage process, from "adhérents" (adherents) to "stagiaires" (trainees) and "sociétaires adjoints" (associate members) before finally being appointed "sociétaires définitives" (full members) and gaining the right to quarterly royalties and a pension.[34] By joining the collective, they also agreed to transfer their entire repertoire to the society for exploitation and not to grant any rights to third parties.

In addition to this admission ritual, SACEM used its assessment procedures in particular to standardize the value of works in authors' rights.[35] As a rule, royalties were divided equally between composers, lyricists, and publishers. This established an alliance between these differing interests that survives to this day. Classification was based on the decentralized collection and central evaluation of music programs in concert halls, restaurants, cafés, and at dances, of music recordings, and later of sound films and radio programs. Organizers of musical events were contractually obliged to provide SACEM's agents with programs listing the music played. A SACEM assessment committee evaluated the titles using a classification system; in the French model, this was based on the length of the performance. Long pieces (between forty and sixty minutes) were awarded seventy-two points, while short pieces (under five minutes) received six points. In 1900, SACEM employed around seventy "officials" in its headquarters in Paris; by 1929, there were one hundred "officials" in the accounting department alone processing sixteen million titles each year. They answered to a general directorate of fifteen people who conducted business on behalf of the members.

Valuating Reputation

The GDT based its admission rules on those of SACEM. The need for support from two members and proof of "independent sound works" established a German system also based on the idea of the notating composer. The delegate committee, which monitored the classification and distribution of royalties, included representatives from all three groups of beneficiaries—six composers, six publishers, and three librettists. But while SACEM stuck to its original metric classification system, which used length (duration of performance in minutes) as the benchmark for determining value, this was modified in Germany, the U.S., and Great Britain. The revised assessment criteria reflected a change in the way that authors' rights agents viewed themselves in the music market.

After initially basing its assessments on submitted programs in line with the French model, GEMA moved to a new assessment system in 1927, stating that evaluating programs required "a tremendous number of people and materials that cost huge sums."[36] A new assessment committee classified members by reputation, from the "Allgemeine Klasse" (General Class) to the "Prämienklasse" (Premium Class). This was fueled by more than just GEMA's ostensible rationale: It was the manifestation of a business policy that was no longer just about distributing royalties but treated "commercial music users"[37] (as organizers of performances and concerts, the film industry, and radio stations had been described since the 1930s) as market-conscious musical intermediaries.

Performing rights for musical works were no longer settled based on arithmetically measurable performance times but according to their "material value"[38] for GEMA. This is based on the logic of collective action: Now the focus was on maintaining an economically valuable overall repertoire. The collecting societies saw themselves as suppliers of music; the more attractive they could make their repertoire, the greater their bargaining power with music users. The stronger their negotiating position, the sooner they would be able to enforce their copyright demands. The assessment took into account an individual's celebrity, length of career, length of membership, and entire repertoire. It was believed that classification had to reflect both a member's current works and their total output.[39] GEMA needed prominent members to present itself as an agent of music. The assessment model therefore favored older, successful members. GEMA was also faced with the dilemma of keeping the number of beneficiaries as small as possible through stringent admission criteria while also making sure that future celebrities would be included in its repertoire.

ASCAP also used a translation of the French SACEM regulations as its template, adopting the French practice of making membership dependent on at least five published works and support from two members.[40] The classification committee determined the status of each member and assigned them to one of the eight categories. When the organization was founded, it was clear that popularity, length of time in the catalog, and trendiness should be important criteria. The society rewarded the things it deemed valuable: "The status shall take into consideration the number, nature and character of works composed, written or published by such member, the popularity and vogue of such works, the length of the time in which the works of the member have been a part of the catalogue of the society and generally the prestige, reputation, qualification, standing and service which such member has rendered to the Society."[41] Going against its original principle of sharing royalties equally between composers, publishers, and lyricists, in 1920 the power imbalance within ASCAP shifted in favor of publishers, who were now awarded 50 percent of royalties and half the seats on the board.[42] This meant that publishers in the U.S. earned a greater proportion of authors' rights than publishers in Germany. However, the U.S.'s greater appreciation for "producers" than for "authors" was concealed by using prominent composers like Victor Herbert and John Philip Sousa as figureheads.

In the early 1930s, ASCAP became the first collecting society to draw on the methods of empirical social research, using a program analysis technique (based on a program survey) that created a random sample for a specific day each quarter.[43] This created a points list that projected each individual member's percentage of ASCAP's income. The list was made available only to the members of the assessment committee and was otherwise treated as strictly confidential. This secrecy could have served the collective group spirit. Other collecting societies also practiced confidentiality: For example, at its general assembly in 1928, GEMA decided not to make public its member assessment list and instead informed individual members of the results.[44] In an organization set up as an alliance of comrades, the class system remained socially precarious and had to be mitigated by practicing discretion.

Evaluating the Serious

In Great Britain, royalty fees were set by the Board of Trade, the government's advisory body for economic matters. In 1914, royalties were 5 percent of the purchase price of a sound recording.[45] Composers received 40 percent, and authors and publishers each received 30 percent. For most musical works, royalties worked out to "less than one penny per work."[46] Binding royalties to the purchase price proved problematic when cheaper records arrived on the market in the 1920s; the Board of Trade therefore recommended increasing the license fee to 6.25 percent. This was guided by the criterion of "fairness" and aimed to balance the interests of copyright holders and the phonographic industry. The British PRS also used assessments from the outset: In the early 1920s, authors, composers, and arrangers were divided into no less than ten categories based on publisher assessments of the popularity and sales of their works.[47] As the repertoire was slowly consolidated, the PRS tightened entry requirements in 1926 and made membership dependent on whether composers and authors had published at least six works with a publisher in the PRS.

THE BROADCASTING DEPARTMENT, WHERE ALL BROADCASTS BY THE B.B.C. AND
THE IRISH REPUBLIC BROADCASTING AUTHORITIES ARE REGISTERED AND ANALYSED

FIGURE 4. BBC as a factor in royalty payouts: Radio department at the Performing Right Society, 1940s. Performing Right Society.

Royalties were distributed based on program analyses; the number of performances of a musical work was multiplied by a "point award" figure that allocated extra value to longer symphonies and "serious" music. As in the national society headquarters in Berlin, New York, Paris, and Vienna, in London too legions of female assistants evaluated concert and radio programs and drew up lists of repertoires and composers. From 1931, the British PRS experimented with punch-card machines to manage the sheer volume of forms produced by the growing societies and their overflowing repertoires. These machines had been developed in the 1880s for American population statistics and converted into accounting machines in the 1930s. In the mid-1930s, smaller and cheaper punch-card machines, first used to calculate dividends for wholesalers, entered the market in Great Britain.[48] In 1936, the PRS used Hollerith machines for program analysis and asked its members to trust in the mechanical calculation process:[49] "Those members who find it difficult to follow are kindly invited to inspect the system personally, for it has been devised solely in their interests and will be found on closer acquaintance to be far less formidable than might appear a verbal description."[50] But whether royalties were calculated by hand or by machine, whether they were rationalized with office technology or punch-card machines, they took away the individual's control. The invitation to inspect the new machines was a symbolic gesture to build trust.

A FEW OF THE ELECTRICAL ACCOUNTING MACHINES THAT PERFORM THE INTRICATE TASKS OF CONVERTING PERFORMANCES INTO CASH, AND APPORTIONING THE EXACT AMOUNT DUE TO EACH MEMBER OF THE SOCIETY AND ITS AFFILIATES

FIGURE 5. Royalties rolling off the calculator: Electric calculating machines analyzing programs, Performing Right Society, 1930s. Performing Right Society.

From Collection Agency to Repertoire Management

The first collecting society in France was founded in the mid-nineteenth century based on formalism and formalistic impersonality, conforming to Max Weber's hallmarks of bureaucratic administration.[51] The collecting societies in Germany, Great Britain, and the U.S. redesigned the classification systems for royalty distribution during the upheaval in the music industry between 1910 and 1935.

The collecting societies served as administration, valuation, and distribution bodies that measured, calculated, assessed, and thus determined royalties. An amount was awarded to an individual music producer on the basis of subjective negotiation and "objective" statistical calculation. The collecting societies also used royalty management as a means to strengthen their negotiating position with music users (phonographic industry) and to drive the expansion of copyright as applied to music use (to include new adaptations, new performance venues, and new media). A fragile yet firm alliance was forged between authors, composers, and publishers that presented a united front when dealing with music users. The publishers were the driving force, and the authors and composers were put on display.

However, some questions remain regarding the great financial, organizational, and lobbying outlay experienced by the collecting societies as they ran the classification systems: Why did the collecting societies allow such a system to cost them so much? Why did they stick with it, even though it continuously brought them to the brink of internal rupture and was heavily criticized? A historical perspective raises some speculation: The collecting society system was established in France in the mid-nineteenth century using the moral rights of authors and with resistance from commercial concert organizers. In the early days, this moral argument was linked with the bureaucratic argument of formalistic impersonality and tied to a measurable unit (performance time). Germany, Great Britain, and the U.S. abandoned this system in the 1920s in favor of subjective assessment. Complaints about the high administrative outlay caused by a large number of members "with only small and practically worthless output"[52] reflect this change in self-perception. Despite being founded as cooperatives, they had long since become "class societies." Royalties were not divided among members arithmetically. This may be precisely why the collecting societies developed such elaborate assessment and calculation procedures: To distract from their inner paradox as bureaucratic agencies oriented toward market prices that also had to ensure a balance between successful members and those who had failed on the market. The pathos with which the latter were represented in public (particularly in the 1930s), the practice of keeping assessment lists confidential, and the ever more complex calculation procedures associated with the growth of the societies certainly suggest that the collecting societies had developed into somewhat autocratic calculation machines.

Corporatism and Concentration

The shift in the collecting societies temporarily stabilized around 1930. This was partly due to the decline in income from the sheet music business, while new sources of royalties opened up with the phonographic industry, sound films, and the radio. Second, it became apparent that royalty management would be universal; the European (united in the International Confederation of Societies of Authors and Composers, or CISAC, since 1926) and American (ASCAP) collecting societies regulated royalty management through five-year reciprocal agreements. Now the focus was on administrating the "global repertoire."[53] Third, in the U.S. and Great Britain the state (which had traditionally favored a liberal approach) increasingly intervened in the regulation of the royalty economy; in this instance, royalties were fixed by Congress and the Board of Trade. Fourth, national collecting societies were consolidated and concentrated around 1930. This particularly applies to Germany, where collecting societies would ultimately be merged into a state organization during the National Socialist era. Back in 1929, the former rivals GDT, AKM, and GEMA had begun to negotiate a collaboration, resulting in the foundation of the central, Berlin-based Verband zum Schutze musikalischer Aufführungsrechte (Association for the Protection of Musical Performing Rights) in 1930.[54] The alliance of bitter rivals shows an emerging resistance among music users against the collecting societies. In 1930, a tract against the royalty economy was published with the title *Das musikalische Tantiemenrecht in Deutschland* (Musical Royalty Rights in Germany) that antagonized the GDT and GEMA to such an extent that they successfully fought for it to be removed from circulation.[55] The Reichskartell der Musikveranstalter (Reich Trust of Music Organizers), in which an alliance formed among the film, tourism, and phonograph industries, called for a central collecting body with standardized tariffs and the introduction of a state-supervised arbitration court for conflicts between music users and music organizers. Music users looked to the state, calling for legally defined royalties and even for the "nationalization of royalties."[56] The campaign peaked in 1932 with the demand to reconfigure German copyright. The alliance of music users, who presented themselves as the Arbeitsgemeinschaft der Verbreiter von Geisteswerken (Working Group of Circulators of Intellectual Works) and thus as disseminators of culture, also brought on board choral societies, department stores and malls, theaters, music directors, and bandleaders.[57] The collecting societies now found themselves confronted with opponents who spoke of "public right of access," demanded licenses for users, and protested France's strong, "individualistic" moral rights for authors. They were opposed to the demand for an increase in statutory copyright periods from thirty to fifty years (as in France). They also called for a "German copyright," a demand also directed against France's extensive authors' rights.

Music users' calls for a strong state were answered in 1933, during the era of National Socialism, when the collecting societies were forced to merge into the Staatlich genehmigten Gesellschaft zur Verwertung musikalischer Aufführungsrechte (State-Approved Society for the Exploitation of Musical Performing Rights, STAGMA).[58] The exploitation of music had already been subject to corporatist organization, making incorporation into STAGMA simply the final act. Once the proposal to "dismiss management members not of German origin" was endorsed without resistance at the last extraordinary general meeting of GEMA in March 1933, there was nothing to stop STAGMA from being founded in September of the same year. The Reichsministerium für Volksaufklärung und Propaganda (Reich Ministry of Public Enlightenment and Propaganda) declared STAGMA the sole facilitator of authors' rights. As with the invention of reprinting privileges in the early modern period, the management and control of reproduction were once again combined with censorship. The National Socialist state's interest in order and the centralization of power had come together with the capitalist interests of music users from industry and commerce in a central body for managing exploitation rights. The state was to ensure clarity and eliminate the conflicts, disputes, and ambiguities caused by capitalism and new media. The organized "music users" of the 1930s profited from corporatist and dictatorial organizational structures.

Chapter 6

Celluloid Circulations

Modern aids with no financial burden are turning every scholar's study into a reading room. The mechanically transcribed book is coming to the people.

—*Der Lesesaal von morgen* . . . [Photo-Copie GmbH advertising brochure] (1931)

That which we have before us is a prospect which, on the intellectual level, corresponds to railway and steamships at the commodity level—an opportunity to start free trade in ideas on a scale hitherto unapproached.

—Letter from Robert Binkley to James Shotwell (January 15, 1936)

Library Books on Film

The Study as Reading Room

On December 5, 1930, Photo Copie GmbH opened a branch in the large reading room in Berlin's Staatsbibliothek (State Library).[1] The busy jurist and economist Robert Koch-Hesse (1883–1970) had established the company in 1927 after his involvement in the one-kitchen house movement, fighting in World War I, and working as secretary to a trade association. In 1926, he had also set up (and closed down) a magazine for the Deutscher Reichsverband für Patent- und Musterschutz (German National Association for Patent and Design Protection) entitled *Die Erfindung* (The Invention). He was therefore very familiar with intellectual property, but it was reproduction that would soon become his major business. Initially, he thought only of reproducing patent documents in the Reichspatentamt (State Patent Office). Large orders soon followed from Berliner Gaswerke to commit drawings to film. Photo Copie GmbH expanded and opened photocopy offices on the second floor of the district and regional court and in the reading room of the Staatsbibliothek.

In the Staatsbibliothek, copies of "book passages, book pages, magazines, and manuscripts" that were "true to the original" could be made for a "modest fee."[2] Unlike the Bibliothèque Nationale (National Library) in Paris, whose employees had been producing photocopies since 1926,[3] the Staatsbibliothek delegated reproduction to another company. The service took between seven and twenty-four hours. In urgent cases, Photo Copie GmbH offered a rapid service of thirty to sixty minutes and sent the copies to the customer's home by post. Based in the old reading room, the company was a huge success: In its first weeks alone, it received roughly three hundred orders per day. According to ads for Photo Copie GmbH in 1931, modern technology was turning the scholar's study into a reading room, and books were coming to the people. This blend of intellect and money in the temples of academia was to prove explosive.

At the same time, a bundle of 139 pages of photolithographies pressed between two covers was published in Ann Arbor in the middle of the Great Depression in a run of one hundred copies.[4] It was authored by librarian and historian Robert C. Binkley and published by Edwards Brothers Inc., a company that specialized in the reproduction of manuscripts via alternative processes such as mimeography, offset, and microfilm. Neither its technical title (*Methods of Reproducing Research Material*) nor the unassuming name of its contractor (Joint Committee on Materials for Research, JCMR) hinted that this publication would mark the start of a critical phase of debates in

FIGURE 6. The Photo Copie GmbH branch network in Berlin, around 1936. *Nachrichtenblatt der Photo Copie GmbH Berlin*, no. 3 (1936).

the U.S. on academic policy, media theory, technology, and law. This phase would see the social consequences of moving from letterpress printing to new copy procedures in libraries and academia analyzed for the first time; copyright would be fundamentally challenged as well.

Revolutions were looming in libraries and academia. Copies had become a challenge to letterpress printing, and copyright had become a potential obstacle to visions of libraries. With the new copy machines in the hands of librarians, scientists, and scholars, some foundations became unstable: Letterpress printing found itself under scrutiny as the primary medium for storing and spreading knowledge. Some of the established copyright categories were no longer particularly helpful, for example the distinction between commercial and private copies or that between manual and mechanical reproduction. In addition, a new group (librarians, scientists, and scholars) was now making itself heard that opposed the tendency, encouraged by music recording, to constrict reproduction a priori to its economic exploitation, alternative interpretations of the copy, and, therefore, different ideas on its regulation.

How are these changes to be classified in the history of media, law, science, and academia? To what extent did they influence cultural relations between Europe and the U.S.? And why have these developments largely been forgotten and are almost being repeated in a different media landscape? This chapter looks at academic/science policy, copyright activism, cultural internationalism, and information and media theory *avant la lettre*.[5] Diverse activities against the backdrop of internationalist philanthropy, American cosmopolitism, the professionalization of science and academia, and technological futurism changed the understanding of the copyright question. In the 1930s, copyright was no longer seen solely as a battle for distribution between legitimized and illegitimate publishers and authors but for the first time as a way to regulate knowledge and communication and the circulation of ideas.

Preserving Confidentiality and Transcending Physical Presence

Thanks to photographic technologies, the word *copy*—which was derived from the Latin *copia* (*copia* = hoard, abundance, power and *ops, opis* = power, resources, might) and came to refer to a "duplicate" in administrative language[6]—had ceased to refer to manual duplication back in the nineteenth century.

At the start of the 1930s, various American and European companies (such as Leitz in Wetzlar, Zeiss Ikon in Dresden, La Cinèscopic in Brussels, and the Eastman Company in Rochester) were involved in further developing "bibliophotography," which was invented in Brussels as part of the documentation movement to capture checks and customer policies for banks and insurance companies as well as newspapers, books, and manuscripts for libraries.[7] The reverse prism process originally developed in France had been mechanized by photographic companies in the U.S. and Germany.[8] Ameri-

FIGURE 7. Machines as office aids: Rectigraph brochure, U.S., 1930s. Library of Congress, mm 78028043 Joint Committee on Material for Research, Box 13.

can photostat devices had reached the mechanization and automation stage at the end of the 1920s: They worked faster, required few staff, and performed development "more or less independently."[9] That photocopies were produced almost automatically was now seen as a quality of reproduction technology: There was a notion that mechanization could overcome the risk to confidentiality always associated with reproduction. By delegating reproduction to a device, confidential files and documents could easily be copied in companies and administrative bodies too: "In such cases, you can insert the documents yourself, specify the number of copies and deliver them to trusted persons, or you can monitor this process. The machine can process the photographic prints itself after exposure, which means that the operating staff cannot see the documents during the production process. The lack of negatives in our process also guarantees that no unauthorized copies can be produced once the photograms have been delivered."[10] In the Reichspatentamt (State Patent Office), copies had been accepted as surrogate documents in the patent process since the start of the 1930s.[11] According to ministerial decree, copies of extracts from the civil register were deemed of equal value because "sufficient safeguards against forgeries" were promised.[12] In legal terms, photocopies were already seen as documents.

For libraries, the microfilm cameras and photostat devices that produced white-and-black copies were another form of distribution; the library at the League of Nations in Geneva now sent copies of "international material" (statistics and statute books) to ministries, academic/scientific institutes, banks, and libraries.[13]

Copies served two contradictory logics: The library's principle of presence tied to a specific location and the League of Nations' identity as an international organization intended to cross borders.

Scientific Offensive after the Great War

After World War I, various new institutions endeavored to nurture international scientific collaboration: Organizations like the Conseil International de Recherche (International Research Council),[14] founded in Brussels in 1919, and the Institut für Geistige Zusammenarbeit (Institute for Intellectual Cooperation),[15] launched by the League of Nations in 1926, dedicated themselves to intellectual exchange. International collaboration between libraries, documentation studies, and the application of the new photographic reproduction technologies were to help bring the world closer together, cultivate the exchange of knowledge, and incorporate the accumulated knowledge into a common system. The two decades after World War I were a period of scientific awakening and internationalism—even in the U.S., which since the Great War had held back from internationalist engagement at the political level. The foundation of the Joint Committee on Materials for Research (JCMR) in 1929 under the aegis of the American Council of Learned Societies (ACLS) and the Social Science Research Council (SSRC) is to be viewed in this context. The ACLS was established in 1919 as the American branch of the International Academic Union, a Brussels-based international umbrella organization for the social sciences and humanities. The SSRC was formed in 1923 as a new research policy meta-association that united various disciplines—including archaeology and psychology and economics—under the label of "social sciences" and had been heavily involved in the scientification of politics since its inception.[16] In August 1929, the ACLS and SSRC, supported by endowments from Carnegie and Rockefeller, commissioned Binkley to study the new alternatives to letterpress printing with regard to analyzing, disseminating, and storing research data in the social sciences and humanities.[17] For science policy associations, reproduction and distribution media using light prisms, offset, and microfilm processes held as yet untapped potential for progress in the social sciences and humanities.

This study was reproduced "by the photo-lithographic process from [sic] author's own manuscript . . . reduced one-half"[18] in a custom-made small run for distribution among libraries, scientific / academic associations, and foundations; the media format symbolized the results of the study. Increasing specialization in the sciences and the trend for printing small runs of scientific and academic publications meant that the old publishing system was no longer suited to distributing scientific results. Book production costs could be reduced only through large print runs; therefore, scholars and libraries had to take the distribution of data and results into their own hands and use the new reproduction technologies for their own ends.

After Gutenberg Is Before Gutenberg

In Europe, the new discipline of documentation studies had experimented with microphotography as a medium for storing and distributing books since the turn of the century.[19] With library stacks bursting at the seams, in 1934 Paul Otlet, the founder of the new documentation movement, described storing printed matter on film rolls as the space-saving medium for recording and efficient archiving: "The saving amounts to eighteen times the weight and sixteen times the volume."[20] In these circles, archiving was declared a matter for copying technology. An advertising brochure from the Recordak Corporation contrasted the film rolls neatly packed in small cardboard boxes with the masses of paper stacked almost to the ceiling in the background. The film camera, which in 1895 captured workers leaving the Lumière factory in Paris and provided the public with its first confrontation with moving pictures, would forty years later bring into circulation the dormant treasures of libraries—manuscripts, rare old prints, and fragile, disintegrating newspapers. In naming its microfilm camera "Recordak" and its associated subsidiary the "Recordak Corporation" in 1928, the Eastman Kodak Company headquartered in Rochester, New York, suggested that "records" (a word that originally referred to written documents) would in future also encompass copies produced via cinematographic processes: "Microfilm is the answer to record problems—on the count of accuracy, permanence, space saving, and general practicability."[21]

Binkley's 1931 study on the new reproduction methods appeared in 1936 as a revised and much more comprehensive manual.[22] In this manual, he developed notable media theory theses and controversial theories on science/academic policy: According to his first thesis, the microfilm had created conditions comparable with the time before letterpress printing was invented. In the era of manuscripts, a distinction had not yet been made between the published and unpublished: "If a monastery maintained a scriptorium, and if its policy was to accede to requests for copies of its books, its whole library was, in a sense, 'published' material."[23] The microfilm had now reinstated this situation. His second thesis was that the microfilm had once again canceled out the distinction between collecting and publishing, fundamentally changing the epistemological status of libraries: "The library may come to be, not only a depository of printed material, not only a collector of existing records, but even a maker of new records."[24] His third thesis was that while the invention of letterpress printing had made books more accessible, this had in the meantime been reversed through the growth and differentiation of scholarship: "When many if not all scholars wanted the same things, the printing press served them. In the twentieth century, when the number of those who want the same things has fallen in some cases below the practical publishing point, the printing press leaves them in the lurch."[25] Unlike the capital-intensive film industry in which (according to his fourth thesis) reproduction had led to a concentration of media corporations, the reasonably priced microfilm would enable publishing and the sciences to be devolved.[26] After all, as Binkley stated in his fifth thesis, the production of beautiful books could now be left to calligraphers, while scientific/academic communication would concentrate on reproduction methods like the photostat, offset, and microfilm.[27] This would fundamentally change humanities work: Pure editorial work to access treasures from distant archives and libraries would become obsolete and could be left to librarians. Instead of spending their valuable research time on collecting and editing documents, scholars would finally start to share work with librarians.[28] According to Binkley, the purely physical work of editing had been confused with intellectual findings for too long.

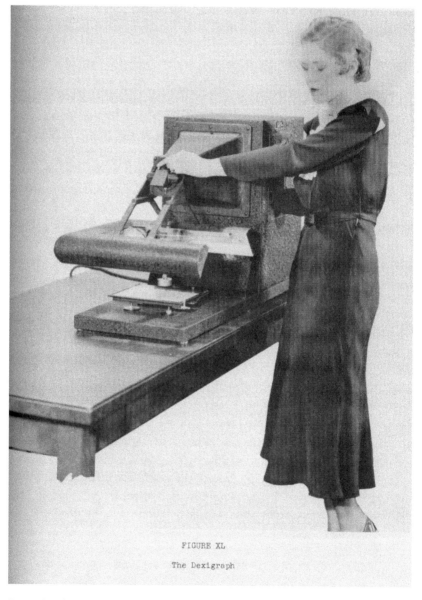

FIGURE XL

The Dexigraph

FIGURE 8.   Alternative to letterpress printing? Dexigraph, U.S., 1930s. Robert C. Binkley, *Manual on Methods of Reproducing Research Materials* (1936), 77.

The theses that Binkley developed in the 1930s on behalf of the JCMR were motivated by science / academic policy. In retrospect, they are also significant for media theory and the history of scholarship and should be seen as media theory *avant la lettre*; from microphotographic recording and the cinematographic projection of texts, Binkley concluded that the changes to

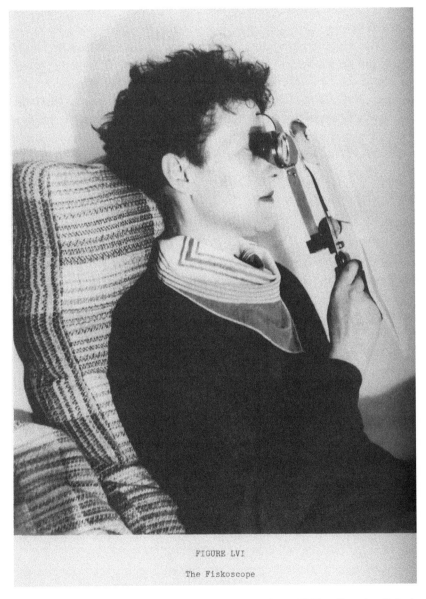

FIGURE LVI

The Fiskoscope

FIGURE 9.   Alternative to books? Fiskoscope, U.S., 1930s. Robert C. Binkley, *Manual on Methods of Reproducing Research Materials* (1936), 116.

recording and reading habits brought about by microfilm would also change production and the use of knowledge. He outlined ideas in the 1930s that Marshall McLuhan would then formulate much more thoroughly and radically as part of a media theory for the technological age.[29] In view of xerography, which in the early 1960s enabled the electromagnetic recording of texts, McLuhan spoke (as Binkley had three decades earlier) of the potential of the technologies that devolved book production, individualized book consumption, and brought with them a customized library service to replace mass-production via letterpress printing. With its progressive projects and plans to rebuild the knowledge and publishing landscape, the JCMR fit perfectly into the age of the New Deal under President Franklin Roosevelt: The JCMR's activities clearly showed that the age of the New Deal encompassed far more than anticyclical economic policy, social reforms, and infrastructure projects and also inspired new forms of knowledge organization and avant-garde media reflections. A young, aspiring academic nation was setting out its stall.

Old Prints for the New World

Binkley developed his thoughts in the context of extensive library microfilm projects. The New York Public Library, the Library of Congress, and the libraries at the University of Chicago and the U.S. Department of Agriculture, among others, began to film newspapers, manuscripts, and magazine articles in the mid-1930s.[30] Microfilm devices were also used in libraries in Berlin, Paris, and London.[31] Styled as symbols of intellectual collaboration, microfilms manifested the profound ambivalence in cultural relations between the U.S. and Europe in the interwar period: The Old World, with its library treasures, faced continued demands from the New World to access these cultural assets. It is therefore no coincidence that the American exhibition at the 1937 World's Fair in Paris, dedicated to the application of art and technology "in modern life,"[32] shrewdly loaded this new medium with multiple meanings. A year earlier, when the French government's invitation to the World's Fair landed on Robert Binkley's desk, he seized the opportunity to make microfilming the focus of the exhibition concept. The exhibition was to celebrate the microfilm as the original American "machine for intellectual collaboration" and a symbol of the international exchange of information: "In other words, I think that we can present Europe by 1937 with something that will be as striking on the intellectual level as the Taylor system of scientific management of the Ford assembly line work in industrial technology. Our objectives should be no less high than this. . . . That which we have before us is a prospect which, on the intellectual level, corresponds to railway and steamships at the commodity level—an opportunity to start free trade in ideas on a scale hitherto unapproached."[33] The concept of intellectual Fordism was to be represented by a rolling microfilm camera. The aim was to send Europe a message that it may have invented the microfilm process, but it was the U.S. that had developed it for automation and mass production. A plan was also made within the exhibition project to copy as many old documents as possible from Parisian libraries and make them available to American libraries.[34] With funding from the Rockefeller Foundation, the notion of "free trade in film at mass production prices"[35] was to be suggested to Europe, the "hunting ground for micro-copying."[36] American librarians like Llewellyn Raney of the University of Chicago criticized European libraries as paranoid custodians withholding treasures from the rest of the world in order to preserve their uniqueness.[37] With this negative image of the Old World defending old privileges, American libraries mobilized microfilming as a New World technology, a symbol of the free flow of ideas, a guarantee of world peace and understanding even as a world war loomed.[38] Cellulose acetate was the new material to protect civilization against the loss of printed materials in the face of future armed conflicts.[39] After the National Bureau of Standards verified the film material's very high stability in a 1935 material testing study financed by the Carnegie Foundation, cellulose acetate became the storage material of the moment, particularly as a replacement for fragile newsprint paper in libraries.[40] Thoughts had already turned to replacing paper originals with copies: "And it may be that the files printed on the most impermanent stock can be preserved only by film-copying them and letting the originals disappear."[41] Ultimately, the destruction of the "original" was no longer ruled out.[42]

When visitors to the 1937 World's Fair at the Trocadéro in Paris watched University of Chicago librarian Herman H. Fussler[43] and his wife filming copies of Le Temps and various French Revolution–era newspapers from France's Bibliothèque Nationale, they witnessed how the U.S. imagined machines would aid international intellectual collaboration in the future: The free flow of research materials throughout the world under the aegis of the U.S., facilitated by automated copy machines based on a medium that had granted the West Coast a new export industry. In the logic of the exhibit, described as an "expedition"[44] into European "hunting territory," the spoils would be shared among all participants: The negatives went to the American Library Association, with copies for the University of Chicago library and the Bibliothèque Nationale in Paris.

PLATE I

TWELVE YEARS OF THE *New York Times* IN ORIGINAL AND ON FILM

FIGURE 10. Twelve years of the *New York Times* in a few card index boxes: U.S., 1942. Herman H. Fussler, *Photographic Reproduction for Libraries* (1942), Plate I.

While the filming projects at the World's Fair were primarily a display of American vision, the administrative bodies and state research institutions around Washington, DC, had already begun to develop copying facilities. This was no longer an internationalist statement but one of science and academic policy. Even before American big science took off in World War II, libraries had begun to set up new research resources based largely on the use of microfilm. After 1934, notable institutes financed through endowments and the American federal state (including the U.S. Department of Agriculture, the National Institutes of Health, the U.S. Geological Survey, the U.S. Navy, and the Census Bureau) set up a "bibliofilm service" that provided researchers with copies from the latest academic journals ("in lieu of loan of publication or in place of manual transcription and solely for purposes of research").[45] In 1937, Atherton Seidell, librarian at the National Institute of Health in Washington, DC, proclaimed his vision of a film library of all journal literature and in 1939 championed the academic value of copies in a series of articles in *Science*, America's most renowned science journal. His first argument focused on its fidelity to the original, superior to transcription: "One of the principle advantages of microfilms is that they relieve the research worker of the task of making transcriptions of the original literature. The inconvenience arising from errors or incompleteness in such records is entirely avoided."[46] Second, he emphasized that microfilms are handier than bound journals and that reading would no longer be hindered by leafing through bulky and cumbersome books. Third, he saw an opportunity to use microfilm to create extensive documentation on specific academic topics. Fourth, he cited the reduction in costs compared with conventional lending and inter-library loans. He also addressed the criticism that exchanging copies would endanger academic journals, suggesting that journals with small print runs no longer needed to be printed at all but could be distributed on microfilm: "The microfilm has introduced a far simpler and more economical plan of distributing such reports to workers."[47] When World War II broke out, microfilm was definitely no longer just a technical topic of interest to technicians, librarians, and visionaries. These celluloid strips had now joined the ranks of the academic elite and would soon be used for military research.

New Media and Old Copyright

Photocopies and the Primacy of "Marketing Interests"

From the outset, American social sciences and humanities saw the copyright question as more than simply a minor issue within science policy activities to harness research resources. Binkley considered it to be directly linked to his investigations on reproduction techniques as alternatives to letterpress printing. In doing so, he set in motion a discussion in the U.S. about copyright problems for microfilms and photocopies that had been of little interest to publishers and authors.

At this point, Germany was already discussing the question of copyright for the new reproduction techniques. However, there were significant differences between the American debates in the context of the JCMR and those taking place among German librarians and publishers. In Germany, the question was *whether* copies should even be permitted as an exemption, while the U.S. was asking *how* copies could be permitted as exemptions.

Library representatives in Germany had raised the question of photocopying back in 1930; however, rather than asking whether library copies violated copyright, they asked whether libraries themselves would have a claim to copyright *for* the copies. This approach contrasted sharply with the legal debate that soon unfolded regarding copyright breaches *caused by* copies. In retrospect, however, this approach must be considered visionary; many libraries have since demanded license fees for their reproduction activities.

The photocopy conflict had been initiated in Germany by the new branch of Photo Copie GmbH in the Staatsbibliothek in Berlin.[48] The debate was opened by publishers in the *Börsenblatt für den Deutschen Buchhandel*, the German book trade magazine that had traditionally been amiable toward copyright. The German copyright law of 1910 included an exemption for reproduction for noncommercial "personal use." Now, publishers attacked this conceptual separation of noncommercial and commercial reproduction, arguing that copyright could potentially be undermined and that reproduction could jeopardize the existence of academic journals in particular. Bolstered by their attorneys, publishers and booksellers developed an argument that broke with the customs of scholarship and libraries: "But what is significant is that the photocopy takes the place of the original and is intended to take its place; the original can no longer occupy the place taken by the reproduction produced by means of photocopy."[49] Put plainly, this referred to the practice already established within the music industry of placing all reproduction under the control of authors and publishers and their "marketing interests."[50] The practices of libraries and academia—based on loans, exchange, and temporary use—stood in opposition to the practices of publishers, which were based on sales and property acquisition. Academic practices were now to take a subordinate role to the copyright rules developed for music markets. If books in libraries were often used and subject to wear and tear, the libraries would inevitably have to buy a second copy. Apparently, photocopies would endanger the purchase of multiple copies: "The copy is spared, the wishes of many borrowers can be satisfied simultaneously with a single copy. In addition, although he does not purchase the book, the borrower can add the section of the text that interests him to his permanent collection."[51]

The director of the Königsberg state and university library defied publishers' demands and pointed to the academic culture, which took a different approach to that desired by publishers: "The only thing he certainly will not do is purchase an expensive book to inspect a single section of text on one occasion. If he is interested in the entire book, and not just a single passage, then he must buy it; photocopies will be of no use here. Therefore, academic scholars are the sole and exclusive victims."[52]

In a 1932 legal dispute between an author and Photo Copie GmbH (regarding seventeen photocopied pages), the Leipzig district court ultimately ruled that Photo Copie GmbH had breached copyright.[53] Nevertheless, libraries did not stop their copying, instead declaring photocopies to be the legal form of use in libraries.[54] Reproduction companies attempted to protect themselves against lawsuits by concluding contracts with their customers to pass on the legal risk.[55]

In addition to tradition-conscious German libraries, the internationalist documentation movement also criticized the demands of publishers and authors. They countered the talk of authors' rights with the rights of the consumer and the "right of the reader": "This reader has the right to feed their soul at a fair price."[56] Ultimately, however, European documentalists also remained defensive and viewed photocopies as part of the fee-based license systems now established in the music industry. They proposed a tax that would be paid to the creator by the international documentation institute in The Hague via national documentation bodies.[57] European documentalists had already accepted that reproduction was linked to exploitation chains back in 1935 and had never considered alternative regulations. In addition, Fritz Ostertag (director of the International Bureau of Intellectual Property, the headquarters of the Berne Convention) had already made clear at the 1935 documentalist congress that the photocopy question was a "special question" that would not be included in any revision to the Berne Convention. He had made no secret of the fact that, for him, the "economic value of the creator's right of distribution" must not be impeded, no matter what the libraries and documentalists demanded.[58]

Incentive Systems and Distribution Channels

In the U.S., the JCMR took a much more offensive approach than that of Europe. For Binkley, letterpress printing and copyright were obstacles to his vision of the "free trade in ideas" and "free intercourse in the world community."[59] In these visions, microfilms not only brought dormant texts into circulation but also set nationalistic barriers in motion, established communities of global citizens, and hindered totalitarianism—properties that would all be attributed to the internet half a century later. In the formative years of a new medium, people always fantasize about creating new worlds. Binkley saw "in a sense a world of their own"[60] created by science using microfilm with its own global currency and universal laws: "Its credit is better than bank credit; its authority is more definitive and universal than the authority of any judgement of a court of law."[61] Microfilms went hand in hand with a belief that credit is inherent, indeed a belief in manifold validity, as reflected in the historical roots of the concept of credit.[62]

These euphoric visions were to be secured in law. In 1934, the JCMR therefore engaged a New York law firm to clarify how library filming projects could be protected against the risk of copyright lawsuits.[63] However, negotiations with publishers showed that they had no interest in integrating an exemption for libraries into a potential revision of the 1909 copyright law. The only concession that Binkley was able to wrest from the National Association of Book Publishers on behalf of the JCMR was a gentlemen's agreement sealed with an exchange of letters in 1935. In this exchange, the two associations consented that libraries would be permitted to create individual photocopies or microfilm copies for scholars if in place of a loan or manual copying. At the same time, however, this reinforced copyright as the exclusive right "to print, reprint, publish, copy and vend the copyrighted work"—even in light of new copying technologies.

In Germany, isolated figures voiced their wish to adopt the gentlemen's agreement model but received no response.[64] However, it became clear just how little sway U.S. scholars and librarians held with the gentlemen's agreement when, in 1938, the National Association of Book Publishers merged into a new organization and some publishers seized the chance to question the legal validity of the exchange of letters.[65] At conferences, various representatives (authors, publishers, radio stations, record companies, film producers, etc.) discussed whether the U.S. should pass a new copyright act and ratify the international law of the Berne Convention. Since the end of the nineteenth century, European supporters of international copyright—which was first institutionalized in the Berne Convention in 1886—saw the U.S. as a nation of oddballs because it had steered clear of the Berne Convention and granted copyright protection only to works produced and registered in the U.S.

American copyright laws may have been passed in Congress and brought into effect by the president, but they were drafted by various interest groups and law firms in New York and Washington, DC. The purpose of the Committee for the Study of Copyright, established in 1938, was to analyze the complex mosaic of interests within the copyright question and to help involve a broad range of representatives in the negotiations for a new copyright act. It was funded by endowments from Carnegie and Rockefeller.[66] The Department of State also drove the legislative activities forward. In contrast to Congress, the Department of State had declared U.S. entry into the Berne Convention as one of its goals since the early 1930s.[67] But at the negotiating tables, scholars and librarians—who poured blood, sweat, and tears into these conferences—were mere small fry; microfilms and photocopies were at best side issues.

While many librarians, who traditionally felt themselves duty bound to authors' interests, endorsed the ratification of the Berne Convention and therefore the extension of author protection, Binkley questioned the argument of "author interests" as early as January 1938. As he pointed out, conventional and academic authors do not share the same interests: "The author of a scientific or learned article has an equitable right to have that article become available to all his colleagues in the field."[68] According to him, these authors would gain more from reduced copyright than from increased copyright. And if the Berne Convention were ratified, the U.S. would be forced to agree to more copyright. Thus scholars should feel themselves obliged to oppose the ratification of the Berne Convention in the interest of a culture of academic internationalism.[69] He described the international copyright system as absolutely "out of line with the revolutionary technical developments in the graphic arts."[70] Binkley's position combined cosmopolitan engagement with an isolationist attitude, continuing an American tradition of openness toward the world while formulating its own idiosyncratic standards in the interest of the nation.

Binkley therefore became increasingly critical of the ratification of the Berne Convention. In light of the technical revolutions in reproduction media and their consequences, the new technology could not simply be integrated into the old law; a new ethics of copying had to be developed. In Binkley's eyes, the right to copy was not the same as the right to issue or publish.[71] Following his technological euphoria of the early 1930s when the new medium of microfilm allowed him to rewrite the old copyright, Binkley became increasingly disillusioned with the law firm's reports from the front line of negotiations. Toward the end of the 1930s, he realized that developments conflicted with the interests he represented. He now believed it absurd to regulate fiction books, films, music, and academic journals with the same law; these works were incomparable. Expanding copyright might stimulate the production of cultural assets in some cases but would be counterproductive in others. Binkley came to realize that media, academic, and economic circumstances must first be analyzed before writing new laws. In 1938, he offered an unrivaled synopsis of the fundamental copyright question: "What is the property system that will offer both an adequate stimulus to creators and the clearest channels to distributors?"[72]

The End of the Progressive Copyright Era

Behind closed doors, the negotiating tables in New York and Washington, DC, required strategy and tactics, not reflections on media and legal theory. Organizations that lobbied successfully (primarily ASCAP, which represented authors and publishers in the music industry) were the ones to set the tone. Academics and librarians were crushed between producers and commercial users. The attorney commissioned by the JCMR criticized Edith E. Ware, head of the Committee for the Study of Copyright: According to him, Ware did not hesitate to use academic interests as a pawn in her efforts to pass a draft law and submit it to Congress for consultation by any means necessary. In doing so, she apparently allowed publishers to make their mark as intermediaries between authors and consumers and to present the draft law as a sensible compromise, when in fact the interests of producers were the only ones being taken into account. The JCMR's attorney advised his client not to advocate the negotiated draft law. It may have contained an exemption for library copies of out-of-print publications, but overall, accepting the law would mean accepting changes that went against the interests of academia and libraries. He also complained that the law was "badly drafted and obscure."[73]

Ultimately, attempts to revise the Copyright Act and integrate the U.S. into the international copyright system ended in 1940 at the start of World War II. Opponents of an international solution seized the opportunity to let the bill peter out by warning against agreements with warmongering states and calling for the protection of American interests.[74] Interest groups strongly resisted the removal of the manufacturing clause and the elimination of the compulsory license for music recordings, which was not bindingly enshrined in the Berne Convention. Criticism from scholars and librarians of restrictions to their copying of foreign literature had little impact.[75] Ultimately, the chair of the U.S. Senate Committee on Patents announced in April 1940 that a decision had been made not to address the draft law in Congress.[76]

Thus ended a decade in which academic policymakers first became involved in the copyright question and formulated fundamental criticisms of copyright—with reference to new reproduction technologies and storage media—that questioned the network of authors, publishers, and librarians in place since letterpress printing was established. The new recording devices prompted Binkley to rethink copyright and the concept of authorship established within it. He no longer saw authors as individual creators, as they are described in copyright to this day, but as a link in a "chain of authors" in which the individual author aims to "[get] something from his predecessors and [pass] his contribution on to others."[77] As American internationalism boomed in culture, science, and academia, he developed a vision of an economy of flowing ideas, the free trade of information, and the protection of "world culture" under a liberal American protectorate. This was to defy the European traditions of authors' rights and the burgeoning totalitarianism in politics. In the fight against National Socialism, expensive medical and chemistry journals from Germany (which American libraries reproduced for their scientists) now gave libraries, which saw themselves as communication agencies, a welcome argument to vote against American integration into international copyright. Here they anticipated the U.S. science policy that would be officially initiated during World War II when the Office of Strategic Services (OSS) commissioned the filming of German scientific journals on a massive scale to aid U.S. military science.[78]

The Technical Limits of Celluloid Circulation

Despite the notion of distributing knowledge resources across great distances that was linked with the talk of the "flow of documents,"[79] microfilm technology was confronted with huge operational problems. The lack of suitable reading devices made it very difficult to read documents on paper or via projection. The familiar cultural techniques of reading manuscripts could only be applied to a limited extent: The eyes quickly grew fatigued and were no longer able to move as normal.[80] In addition, formats were not standardized, which thwarted the international exchange of celluloid strips. Although American foundations provided French libraries with equipment and technical expertise, the transfer of technology did not lead to a standardized procedure. Unlike in the U.S., for example, in France films were cut into strips (rather than rolled), packed in folders, and stored like books.

Ultimately, so much time was required in France to find individual articles in the endless rolls of film that the space saved became irrelevant.[81]

In July 1945, the American science policymaker Vannevar Bush encapsulated the limits of miniaturization and microfilm as a storage medium: "More compression, of course, is not enough; . . . one need not only to make and store a record but also be able to consult it."[82] He outlined a vision for a new way to store knowledge ("Memex") that, using microfilm, would surpass the existing methods of organizing and searching by creating a new type of index.

This can be seen in retrospect as the computer's primal scene, hinting that the future would bring further new reproduction technologies and that the solution to the copyright problem would be temporary at most.

CHAPTER 7

Performing Artists

> Reproduction is to be fundamentally separated from
> production, may reproduction be just as beautiful,
> clever, skillful, and successful.
>
> —Alexander Elster, "Die wettbewerbliche und die
> immanente Begrenzung des Urheberrechts" (1926)

Authors' Rights as Defense

Despite declining income from the sale of sheet music, the new medium of radio enabled the collecting societies to expand their royalty system in the 1930s. By the mid-1920s, radio receivers were no longer connected to headphones, acoustically disengaging listeners from their surroundings.[1] Now, electrical speakers filled rooms directly with sound. They transmitted a different sound to that familiar to phonograph listeners, louder and with stronger bass. It dawned on the collecting societies that radio would be the medium of the future. In 1926, the British Performing Right Society (PRS) declared: "Now Broadcasting is an accomplished fact. It cannot be disregarded, and it cannot be stopped. It must be accepted, and the musician who adopts a Canutelike attitude of prohibition is a fool."[2]

Microphones, radio receivers, and speakers boosted sound; that much was unmistakable. However, this chapter will explore the extent to which they would also shape the social, media, economic, and legal developments that began after 1900 with the phonograph. It will look at musical copyright during the period of radio expansion in the golden age of the 1920s, the Great Depression, and World War II. In doing so, it will develop the theory that the radio accentuated conflicts of interest (between authors and performers, authors/publishers, and the phonographic industry) and created new conflicts (between the phonographic industry and radio companies and between radio companies and collecting societies). It will also ask how these social tensions manifested themselves in copyright conflicts.

First, we will focus on European disputes regarding the integration of performers and music producers into copyright between 1925 and 1940. These developments will then be confronted with the conflicts between the musical collecting society ASCAP and the National Association of Broadcasters (NAB) in the U.S.

During these years, which are to be regarded as a key phase for the music economy, authors and publishers in Europe defended copyright against potential expansion. They resisted the integration of performers and record producers into authors' rights. Copyrights stagnated and formed only a limited framework for music broadcasting and conflicts of interest between authors, producers, consumers, and their numerous intermediaries.

In the U.S., however, once a commercial radio industry emerged, copyright conflicts were entirely shaped by the power struggle between ASCAP, the now-established collecting society, and the slowly forming interests of radio companies. ASCAP failed in its attempt to dominate the royalty system by establishing and controlling a repertoire—not least due to its rigid entry rules, which enabled the radio companies to sign up the repertoire that had been ignored or excluded and use this against ASCAP.

Performers and Their Legal Interpretations

The German term *Rundfunk* for the medium of radio referred to the technology's history in World War I.[3] During the Weimar Republic, radio was run privately by the state under the aegis of the Reichspost postal authority, following in the tradition developed for the telegraph in the nineteenth century of the state's sovereign right to broadcast news. In 1925, this organizational form became a state institution with the founding of the company Reichs-Rundfunk-Gesellschaft mbH (RRG).

In Great Britain too, radio was initially placed under the care of the postal service as a consortium of manufacturers.[4] The publicly financed British Broadcasting Company founded in 1922 (BBC, since 1927 the British Broadcasting Corporation) was then institutionalized as a corporation committed to public service without commercial intentions.

Hertzian waves moved freely through the ether, unhindered by national borders. Radio was therefore seen as an international medium, and standardized regulation in international law seemed all the more urgent. In 1925, the Union Internationale de Radiophonie (International Radiophony Union) was founded within the League of Nations for the international regulation of Hertzian waves.[5] In the same year, the first legal congress of the Comité International de Télégraphie sans fils (International Committee of Wireless Telegraphy, TSF) convened in Paris, where copyright was also discussed. The participants quickly agreed that the legal protection regulated via the Berne Convention should also be applied to "radioelectrical diffusion" in the future.[6]

With radio waves as a new means of transmission, old legal questions resurfaced. First and foremost was the issue of whether radio, which knew no bounds, was also to be subject to copyright restrictions. In this respect, the Reichsgericht (Supreme Court of the German Reich) had already clearly ruled in favor of creators' interests in two cases in 1925 and 1926: In the grounds for the judgment, the court determined that the radio companies in question had violated the copyright of writers Gerhart Hauptmann and Hugo von Hofmannsthal by broadcasting audio versions of dramas by both men without their express consent. According to the court, only the author had the right to "distribute his work on a commercial basis."[7] Once again, it was texts that paved the way for the enforcement of music copyright.

Far more protracted than copyright recognition was the old conflict regarding who should profit from this right as creator. The new medium set legal concepts in motion. Suddenly the future seemed open and everything seemed possible, even in law: "Legal development is in reality merely a part of human history, and if radio is called upon to speed up this development, it is because it has the ability to alter not just our milieu and our living conditions, but also the people themselves, to refine their ideas, their taste, and their spirit."[8] Great things were planned for the revision of the Berne Convention in Rome in 1928, and regulating radio was top of the agenda.

What had begun with the phonograph was now amplified by radio speakers: It was not composers but performing artists that everyone could hear—at home, in cafés, in theaters, and in cinemas, where talkies had gotten their foot in the door in 1926.[9] Now performers demanded copyright protection too. Should they be given equal recognition as creators? Their legal status had been upgraded thanks to the phonograph; however, this was due not least to composers' interests in exploiting their compositions on records. The rights of performers remained linked with those of composers.

The terms used to describe performers in legal debates indicated the implicit hierarchy that structured the discussion from the outset: There was talk of "recreating,"[10] "performing,"[11] and "reproducing"[12] artists, of creation "at second hand" and "in the shadow of the creator."[13] Fritz Smoschewer expressed what was at stake: "The performing artists . . . could attain a power over writers and composers previously unknown. Creating artists would be at risk of ominous commercial, moral, and even artistic dependency on reproducing artists."[14] Back in 1927, he predicted a development that could lead to polarization between broadcasting stations and collecting societies and "easily [escalate] into open battles through strike or boycott."[15] His prophesy would prove correct, although this would play out not in Germany but in the U.S. a good decade later.

The legal congress of the Comité International de TSF in 1925 included the first discussion of whether performers' rights should be handled in the old mode of authors' rights or created from scratch. Some felt that the question had been clarified within authors' rights and required no further action: "The question has been assessed, over-assessed perhaps a million times. The fact of reproduction is counterfeit if performed without the author's consent. That has nothing to do with the performing [artist]."[16] Others believed that performers were to be viewed independently of authors: "Let us not forget that this is no longer about authors' rights; we must concern ourselves with the rights of the performing artist."[17]

Representatives of authors, composers, and publishers—who up to this point had dominated the design of musical copyright—now introduced a momentous conceptual distinction between production and reproduction. Essentially, this distinction excluded practicing artists, recording, and broadcasting from authors' rights. In doing so, authors' associations laid the foundation for a legal area outside of copyright; this would be internationally constituted a good three decades later, at the 1961 Rome Convention, under the term "neighboring rights." Since then, neighboring rights have regulated the protection of practicing artists, producers of sound storage media, and broadcasting companies.[18] Nobody expressed this far-reaching separation more succinctly than German publisher and jurist Alexander Elster in 1926: "Reproduction is to be fundamentally separated from production, may reproduction be just as beautiful, clever, skillful, and successful."[19] Reproduction remained a mere derivative of production, based not least on a concept of work that prioritized authors over apparatus.

Disunity in Legal Unification

When the Institut international pour l'unification du droit privé (International Institute for the Unification of Private Law) was founded in Rome in 1926 by Benito Mussolini's fascist government, the movement for the international unification of private law gained an institutional framework.[20] In its charter, the institute under the auspices of the League of Nations stated the creation of standardized international private law as one of its objectives. The plans to revise the Berne Convention in Rome in 1928 were committed to this ideal. The Berne office (BIRPI) and the preparatory Italian commission had ambitious plans: In the spirit of international universalism, universal radio was to provide additional impetus for standardized international copyright. The focus was on a mandatory law for all members of the Berne Convention and the extension of the protection period to fifty years, in line with the French model.[21] In light of economic developments on the music market that would significantly affect performers, there was also a desire to anchor performers' copyright in the international contract: "New facts, new law. Legal theories must adapt to the requirements of the current economy so that we do not hesitate in recognizing an artist's artistic character, [even] if it is broadcast on the radio and has an economic value."[22] Performing artists were no longer to be mere co-contractual partners, but would themselves profit from radio broadcasts of their music through authors' rights. Furthermore, they were to be permitted to prohibit the broadcast of works against their will ("exclusive right to authorize broadcasting in this manner"). France vehemently resisted this proposal—successfully so.

In his 1938 history of international copyright, Stephen Ladas described the results of the conference, which took place in 1928 in Rome's venerable Palais Corsini, as fairly mediocre.[23] This is certainly true, given the huge ambitions of the Italian government and BIRPI. However, a historical perspective does not measure the significance of a result (unlike in law, for example) simply through the notion of "progress." In addition to securing radio broadcasts as the exclusive right of authors, the integration of the French concept of moral rights into the international convention was, from a media theory perspective, an illuminating expansion of authors' rights. Although it was left to the individual states to enforce these rights, authors now had the right to defend themselves against the deformation, modification, and falsification of their works. It is notable that the universalization of this French legal principle coincided with the spread of radio. The new medium had aroused fears that authors could lose their "work authority."[24] Now the law was to bring performance and sound recording under the control of authors too. This fostered a legal concept that regarded media solely as the carriers of a work. The law was to ensure that media did not interfere in or change a work. This inevitably brought the law into conflict with the media, which were not neutral channels.

According to Stephen Ladas, the Rome conference failed in its key objectives (such as scrapping copyright for performers and deciding not to extend the protection period to fifty years) because the Berne Convention had been expanded from sixteen to thirty-six member states. This is certainly a plausible explanation, confirmed by the minutes of the subcommittee debates (about radio and moral rights, for instance).[25] The discussions dragged on because more members wanted to have their say; the debates became protracted and participants lost sight of the formulated goals. International legal unification must follow these circuitous routes. All parties must be involved in the discussion to ensure they accept the later result. The focus is on the journey, not the destination. In addition to Ladas's argument of increased member states, the multiplication of interests also plays an important role. The radio had significantly expanded the circle of people who articulated their interests when copyright was formulated. When the subcommittee discussed the rights of performers in radiophony, France vehemently resisted rights for performers, citing authors' associations. When no agreement was reached, the protection of these rights was delegated back to the national legislators: "The governments that contributed to the Rome conference are taking steps to effectively protect the rights of the performing artist."[26] For the moment, performers' rights were off the table of international copyright diplomacy.

The International Labour Organization (ILO) and the Question of Performers

Various factors (media, economic, and sociopolitical) helped to stop performers' rights from being crushed in the mill of international legal diplomacy and increased social awareness of the issue. Following a decline in income from sheet music and a rise in income from records at the start of the century, demand for live music for silent films offset these changes to an extent. This temporary reprieve came to an end after 1926 with the introduction of the talkie.[27] The spread of radio may have given musicians new performing opportunities in the form of radio concerts, but orchestras could be replaced by records. The royalty economy became increasingly unclear; all interest groups were now discovering the license market. In Great Britain, the phonographic industry and the collecting societies vied for license fees for the playing of music in dance halls, theaters, and cafés.[28] In Germany, radio companies and the phonographic industry found themselves at loggerheads over the broadcasting of recorded music; the phonographic industry feared the loss of record sales and wanted to control or even ban the playing of records on the radio—or at least collect royalties.[29]

In the crisis discourse of the Great Depression, the radio was stylized as the singular cause of the economic crisis in the music publishing business and unemployment among musicians. This explains why, in the 1930s, the International Labour Organization (ILO) began to consider regulations to assist endangered performing artists outside of the Berne Convention.

The collecting societies, since 1926 merged into the International Confederation of Societies of Authors and Composers (CISAC), pursued a strategy to keep the topic of performers' rights away from the Berne Convention. In 1933, in the middle of the Great Depression, they passed this hot potato on to the International Labour Organization (ILO): "And desires that the officers of the Confederation keep in touch with the International Labour Office, to which the study of the problem of protecting performing artists has been allotted."[30] The ILO, founded in 1919 during the conclusion of the Treaty of Versailles, was brought into play because its focus on regulating working conditions had suddenly made it the point of contact for many social conflicts during the economic crisis of the 1930s. The ILO was duty bound to defuse the social question and fears of revolution through international labor law.[31] After authors spoke out against any mention of performers' rights in the Berne Convention, in 1938 the ILO convened an expert committee, including all interest groups, to seek a way of regulating the protection of performers outside of the Berne Convention.[32]

The ILO compiled a study, published in 1939, on the "rights of performers" as preparation for a 1940 conference that was then canceled due to the war. No recommendations were provided, and no international convention was devised. Nevertheless, the ILO study should not be underestimated. It was one of the foundations for formulating "neighboring rights" after World War II. The study is also interesting as a historical source because it addressed the conflicts in this question—previously discussed only among copyright specialists—from the "foreign" perspective of labor law. The ILO report is certainly comparable to publications by the American Joint Committee on Materials for Research (JCMR): In the mid-1930s, the ILO and JCMR sought new standards beyond the old author/publisher system. These discussions petered out around 1940 during World War II.[33] From a counterfactual history perspective, it would be interesting to ask how copyrights would have developed without World War II and whether the ideas for reform would have had a chance of being realized.

The ILO study began by observing that phonographs and the radio had altered the spatial and temporal coordinates of music consumption. If music could be consumed through the radio with a time delay and without spatial restrictions, then musicians need not be present. The ILO interpreted the high level of unemployment among musicians in the mid-1930s not as a temporary crisis phenomenon but as a social conflict caused by technological development and therefore a problem to be solved in the longer term. It proposed the same method that it recommended for all work conflicts: By formulating international legal standards, which would then drive the formulation of national laws.

The International Labour Organization compared the demands of performers—the right to authorization, the right to identification (i.e., the right to have the performers' names on all sound storage media and radio shows), the right to have their performance respected, the right to monitor technical recording, and the right to remuneration for every single broadcast of the performance—to the reprinting privileges that developed after letterpress printing was invented. Just as authors' rights had developed as a long-term consequence of letterpress printing, performers' rights would have to emerge from the new media of records and radio.[34]

The ILO report tied the major conflicts between authors/publishers, record producers, broadcasters, and performers to the logic of traditional conflicts between manufacturers and workers; it developed a theory of the value of the performing artist and grounded the legitimacy of performers' demands for protective rights not in the fact that an author's personality is reflected in their work but in the potential depreciation of the performance through uncontrolled media use.

The 1939 report explained that, unlike a worker, the value of the performer (that is, his or her reputation) is determined not by the manufacturer but by the audience: "The economic value of the interpretative artist's labour varies with his reputation and the favour he finds with the public. It is therefore most important to him that his name should be attached to the product of his labour and that this should not be distorted or altered in any way which may harm him in the public's eyes."[35] Sound recordings and their radio broadcast jeopardize the artist's reputation: "The reputation of a performer is at once liable to suffer if the *timbre* of his voice, his articulation, or the shades of expression are seriously distorted by a defect in broadcasting or recording technique."[36] Controlling the medium was therefore promoted as a measure to influence the value of the performer's work, advocating media regulation in order to regulate work. This demand by performers, taken up by the ILO, met with resistance from radio companies, who would not accept restrictions to their broadcasting activities.[37]

The ILO report was produced thanks to authors who did not want performers' rights to be regulated within the authors' rights framework after performers appropriated the old demands made by authors to control performance. Authors helped to transfer and transform authors' rights traditions and to justify new broadcast rights. Authors' rights had been buried in order to appear even stronger in a new guise. However, shifts could be seen compared with traditional authors' rights: It was recommended that arbitration bodies be convened in individual states to solve conflicts. Performers hoped that such courts, which would be appointed by representatives of all groups, would come to quicker and more competent verdicts than traditional courts with decisions based on analogies.[38] Ultimately, the call for arbitration bodies was a clear vote of no confidence in the old legal procedure of copyright, which no longer seemed suitable for the new framework of interests created by the medium of radio.

The Phonographic Industry Gets Organized

The interwar period was a time of international institutionalization and polarized interests for authors, performers, radio companies, and the phonographic industry. International copyrights were no longer written solely under the direction of authors and traditional publishers. Between 1925 and 1935, all key interest groups in the music industry organized themselves at an international level to strengthen their negotiating position when copyrights were designed;[39] first the International Confederation of Societies of Authors and Composers (CISAC) in 1926, then the Bureau International des Sociétés gérant les Droits d'Enregistrement et de Reproduction Mécanique (International Organization of Societies for Recording Rights and Mechanical Reproduction, BIEM) in 1929.[40] BIEM was originally a coalition of French and Italian music publishers and the Anstalt für mechanisch-musikalische Rechte (Institute for Mechanical-Musical Rights, AMMRE) in Berlin, who banded together with the phonographic industry to exploit royalties internationally. When the International Federation of the Phonographic Industry (IFPI) was founded in 1933, BIEM had a contractual partner with whom to regulate royalty payments in the future based on standard contracts.[41] The concept of standard contracts developed from the momentous formation of royalty trusts: When the compulsory license was introduced and a state-defined license fee implemented in the U.S., Great Britain, and Scandinavia, BIEM and the IFPI agreed on standardized license fees for all other countries. International royalty trusts had been brought into being that centrally controlled rates for authors' rights royalties. The contract between BIEM and the IFPI allowed the phonographic industry to produce music recordings from the huge BIEM repertoire unimpeded and without fear of legal intervention by individual composers.

The IFPI was founded in Rome in 1933. The publication to commemorate the IFPI's silver anniversary in 1959 explained that Rome had been chosen for its cultural history as the cradle of culture and the arts: "Nothing could be more natural or appropriate than that Rome should be chosen as the city which would give birth to the Federation and launch it upon the world. . . . The fair land of Italy, by tradition, by the artistic prowess of her songs through the ages, is surely entitled to be regarded, more than any other country, as the home of the arts."[42]

At the end of the 1950s, these florid musings on Rome's past may have been a way of obscuring the international organization's fascist roots. Domiciled in London, the IFPI had in the meantime become a respected organization that was present at the Berne Convention revisions as well as the negotiations for the Universal Copyright Convention (UCC)—founded in 1952 under the aegis of UNESCO and the U.S.—and the European Broadcasting Union (EBU), founded in 1950, and was also involved in drafting international contracts.

However, the IFPI was initiated in the early 1930s in fascist Italian industrial circles at the Confederatione Generale Fascista dell'Industrie Italiana (General Fascist Confederation of Italian Industry).[43] The IFPI founding congress was chaired by jurist Amedeo Giannini, who was active in Italy's fascist movement and coauthored Benito Mussolini's 1923 work *La nuova politica dell' Italia* (The New Politics of Italy).[44] Giannini had served under Mussolini as a diplomat, university professor, and (between 1937 and 1942) as general director in the Italian foreign ministry for economic affairs.

In 1934, in the journal *Archiv für Urheber, Film- und Theaterrecht* (Archive for copyright, film, and theater rights, UFITA), Giannini declared that an international association was required for the record industry because radio posed a great danger to the phonographic industry: "To bind industrialists together in one organization, they first had to be presented with a very serious threat, a threat that drove the industrialists to a common understanding of these problems, to enable them to withstand the pressure of the film industry and radio, something for which a common understanding seemed difficult, to some entirely impossible."[45]

The IFPI's origins recently caused an internet scandal when the IFPI removed references to its fascist past from its Wikipedia entry.[46] Articles circulating online developed conspiracy theories based on the fascist origins of the IFPI, now the most powerful lobbying organization against file sharing; from a historical perspective, these articles fall short and conceal more than they explain. There is no single one-way street from Italy's corporatist policies to the neighboring rights of the 1960s, which subordinated the rights of performers to those of producers. There were forks in the road: For example, authors' associations played no small part in this process, driving performers into a new legal structure with producers. It is safe to say that, from 1926 on, Italy's fascist government sought an international position as a supporter of legal standardization. In 1928, it also engaged in international copyright and organized the revision of the Berne Convention. Nevertheless, the fascist Italian regime was more open to the interests of the new media and industries (radio, film) than France or Germany, for example; this was particularly evident in the law titled "Protezione del diritto d'autore e di altri diritti connessi al suo esercizio" (Protection of authors' rights and related rights) of April 1941,[47] which granted record manufacturers exclusive rights to the reproduction and trade of their recordings for thirty years. In the post-war period, radio and television jurist Georges Straschnov praised this law as "modern law"; in his eyes, the legislator was ensuring justice for the new media ("that serve the distribution of intellectual works").[48]

The IFPI demanded that BIRPI provide internationally standardized pro-tection for records and license fees for the commercial use of records. At the founding meeting in 1933, jurist Alfred Baum was appointed legal advisor, a position he held until 1958. Baum had worked as an attorney for Deutsche Grammophon and Polydor starting in 1918 and entered the phonographic industry in the 1930s in test cases brought against radio companies by record companies.[49]

After the 1928 Rome conference, it became clear that the interests of per-formers and the phonographic industry should be regulated by a new legal area outside of copyright, an idea that was taken up by the ILO and the Institut international pour l'unification du droit privé (International Insti-tute for the Unification of Private Law).[50] In 1939, the institute invited a committee of experts to a conference in neutral Switzerland. After the war, authors spoke out against the integration of this legal area into international copyright during the 1948 revision of the Berne Convention in Brussels. The notion of regulating the rights of performers, manufacturers, and broadcast-ing companies within copyright was off the table for good. Alfred Baum, the IFPI's legal advisor, complained in Brussels in 1948 that "the opinion was clearly still prevalent" that only "creators and publishers [had] the right" to develop copyright further.[51] The phonographic industry and authors' asso-ciations began to fight for sovereignty over the interpretation of copyright.

From 1951, members of the Berne Convention, the ILO, IFPI, EBU, and the Fédération internationale des musiciens (International Federation of Musicians, FIM, founded in 1948) met in Rome to negotiate an initial outline of a new, separate legal area. Having failed in the 1930s, visions of legal unifi-cation were not revived until the 1950s. It was only after the Universal Copy-right Convention (UCC) was founded in 1952 on the initiative of the U.S. and under the aegis of UNESCO that representatives of the Old and New World met for the first time in 1955 to discuss a standardized global contract. Dashing the hopes of radio jurists in 1925, the universal medium of radio had not helped to make a breakthrough in international legal unification.

The Murder of Music and Radio Wars

ASCAP and NAB: The Start of a Relationship

Unlike in Europe, U.S. radio developed via private, commercially oriented companies that since the Great Depression had financed themselves through advertising with increasing success.[52] Music became the most important part of the program. A survey of the program content of the nine largest stations in New York, Chicago, and Kansas City estimated the proportion of music in radio programs at 71.5 percent in 1925 and 64.1 percent in 1932.

U.S. copyright conflicts were influenced by the polarization between the large commercial radio stations, organized in the National Association of Broadcasters (NAB) since 1923, and the American collecting society ASCAP. This conflict will be analyzed over the following pages,[53] revealing its media, social, and economic drivers and examining the extent to which the medium of radio shaped copyright discourse and practice.

Starting in 1922, ASCAP confronted selected radio stations and demanded license fees, provoking the as yet unorganized broadcasters to form the National Association of Broadcasters (NAB). This act was an early manifestation of the close relationships and mutual dependencies between the radio stations and collecting societies. In 1923, ASCAP began a series of test cases to add legal weight to its demands. The courts awarded ASCAP the right to license fees in three important cases between 1923 and 1926.[54]

The rivals then crossed swords before the legislature during various Congress hearings in Washington, DC.[55] The first hearing about copyright fees before the Committee on Patents took place in 1924. This was specifically due to bill S. 2600, initiated by Senator Clarence Dill in 1924, which aimed to free radios from ASCAP license fees. Eugene F. McDonald, president of the NAB, spoke first; the bill clearly bore the hallmark of radio stations. As in the hearings for the Copyright Act of 1909, ASCAP deployed composers Victor Herbert and John Philip Sousa ("I want their money")[56] to speak in Washington, DC. Again, ASCAP's strategy to celebrate representatives of "culture" versus the "commerce" of radio proved successful in Congress. Two years later, Dill presented a revised bill to help provide radio stations with license-free music. It failed, just like the other nine bills in the House of Representatives and all three draft bills in the Senate initiated in April 1926 alone.[57]

Propaganda for Percentages

The radio companies and ASCAP now found themselves negotiating license fees every few years. ASCAP offered the radio companies its repertoire at a flat rate, in the process influencing the music played on the radio. Blocking licensing rights allowed it to have a say in broadcasting frequency: ASCAP restricted the broadcast of certain hits from Broadway musicals by arguing that excessive play would shorten the life cycle of a hit or reduce the number of theater tickets sold.[58]

In 1932, ASCAP and the NAB concluded a new contract, although only at the last minute.[59] The three-year contract included an annual increase in royalties from 3 to 5 percent of the NAB's net income. A year later, ASCAP launched a press campaign to gain public support for the requested fee increases.[60] The campaign became even more significant in connection with the antitrust proceedings against ASCAP that were launched by the American authorities in 1934 and then dropped one year later.[61] The brilliant campaign depicted media transformation as a crisis at the pinnacle of the Great Depression and aimed to push through demands for fees.[62]

FIGURE 11. *The Murder of Music*: ASCAP pamphlet, U.S., 1933. American Society of Composers, Authors and Publishers, *The Murder of Music* ([1933]).

The cover of the 1933 pamphlet *The Murder of Music* (black background, white notes, white radio receiver, and red blood) dramatized media transformation as the relationship between an offender and a victim. The radio was cast as the weapon; the musical notes were the victim. To represent music, ASCAP drew on the original business of composers and publishers: the trade in sheet music. ASCAP employed the paradigm of the concept of musical works as developed in Europe in the mid-nineteenth century. This implied a threat not just to music but to the heart of musical copyright. The quotation from Shakespeare's *The Merchant of Venice* on the first page made it clear that this was also about the loss of cultural traditions.

Ten graphics expanded on the victim/culprit motif: Towering piles of coins for the cinema industry contrasted with a measly penny for authors, publishers, and composers. Radio receivers, whose numbers continued to soar, represented increasing advertising income for radio companies. These were contrasted with dwindling piles of sheet music symbolizing the declining income of publishers. Shrinking pianos indicated the collapse of domestic musical culture, and diminishing orchestras reminded readers of unemployment among musicians. With statistics depicted as images, invisible economic processes were made tangible.

How the Public Gets Its New Music, which contained text and was also published in 1933, was the counterpart to these graphics.[63] However, this text also presented the reader with figures of speech that conveyed the abstract argument (music is the raw material for the radio industry) through comparative examples from the industrial and agricultural worlds, offering evidence comprehensible to an industrialist from Chicago or a farmer from the Midwest. Just as cotton was the raw material for the textile industry and wheat the basis for the bakery trade, music was the raw material for the radio industry: "Farmers will not raise wheat unless they can sell or nor will composers write unless they can be sold to the great industry that depends upon an unending supply of them."[64]

The 1934 pamphlet *Who Uses Music and Why* expanded the raw material argument to include a message to the nation; music was now stylized as a national asset and America's new resource. The modern music industry, and with it ASCAP, became part of the folk song tradition and appeared to protect the history and customs of ancestors.[65] However, this traditional form of music creation was not represented within ASCAP. ASCAP linked this national and increasingly nationalistic argument with talk of the efficiency of the license system. Efficiency was not simply about reducing costs but also about creating order in the unclear and chaotic music industry. This argument—that ASCAP coordinated and created order—is expressed particularly clearly in an illustration from a 1937 issue of the ASCAP journal:[66] Without ASCAP, chaos would reign; with ASCAP, there would be order.

The rhetoric employed in the corporatist restructuring of Germany's royalty economy in 1933 under the state control of STAGMA was certainly comparable to the rhetoric of commercially organized, monopolistic licensing under the aegis of ASCAP in the U.S. or the Performing Right Society in Great Britain. Together, they emphasized the need for strong "central authorities"[67] and for bureaucratically organized "visible hands"[68] to master the market forces perceived as chaos.

Having targeted the public with pamphlets since 1933, ASCAP also began to promote academic copyright discourse in 1938 by founding and financing the Copyright Law Symposium.[69] This was a legal competition for law school students with a publication of the same name from Columbia University Press. The competition was launched in honor of Nathan Burkan, ASCAP's first in-house jurist. The foreword to the first issue reflects the journal's aim of helping legitimize copyright in academia and society: "The purpose of the competition is to encourage study of Copyright Law, analyses of the need and justification for, the social benefits derived from, and the wise public policy of enacting such law."[70] Until the 1950s, *Copyright Law Symposium* was the U.S.'s only specialized legal publication for copyright; ASCAP succeeded in controlling the intellectualization of copyright discourse. This historical study (and this chapter) were written using material from this ASCAP publication. In the 1930s, ASCAP and copyright became highly self-referential, a characteristic consistently found in historiography too.

World War II altered ASCAP's rhetoric without abandoning the arguments available to John Philip Sousa back in 1906.[71] For the first time, ASCAP not only acted as protector of American culture but also presented the American music industry as a new alternative to the old culture of Europe: "We must begin to give less and less attention to the culture of Europe. . . . We must develop and cultivate a culture that is typically Western Hemisphere, the culture of free man, living in an atmosphere of liberty."[72] But this was no ode to the capitalist American music industry—quite the opposite. Even after the war, ASCAP argued against the phonographic and radio industry by criticizing capitalism: "The great commercial enterprises that have grown up in the field of music are not enterprises which create music. They are enterprises which use, in the conduct of their business, the music created by others."[73] This rhetoric in no way reflected reality; since the end of 1920s, ASCAP had been intertwined with the film and music industry and counted large corporations among its members.

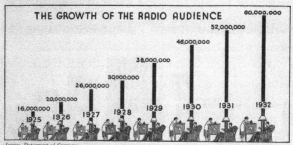

Source: Department of Commerce

The growth of the radio audience has been estimated by multiplying the number of radio sets in homes, as reported by the Department of Commerce, by four which is the average size of the American family, according to the last Census (4.1 is the exact figure). Proportionately as the radio audience has increased the sales of pianos, phonographs, records, and sheet music have decreased. At the outset of 1933 the radio audience in the United States was officially estimated at sixty-eight million persons.

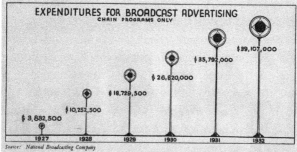

Source: National Broadcasting Company

During the depression money spent for radio advertising increased and still remains one of the bright spots of the critical period through which the country and the world have been passing. The figures in the chart represent advertising revenues of the National Broadcasting Company and Columbia Broadcasting System only. They do not represent the receipts of the hundreds of stations scattered all over the country. These figures are not available but they would further swell the impressive total annually expended for radio advertising. Music makes broadcasting interesting—this interest sells sets—the use of sets establishes the audience as a "circulation" which can be sold to advertisers. In eight years advertisers have paid more than *one hundred and thirty-four million dollars* to two networks only to reach this "circulation."

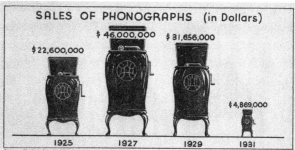

Source: Music Industries Chamber of Commerce

The phonograph industry was formerly one of our most prosperous. Sales reached a peak of $46,000,000 in 1927. Then, as radio became more popular, sales of phonographs slumped. In 1931, the last year for which the Chamber of Commerce has comparable figures, total sales of phonographs amounted to only $4,869,000. A decline of 90% was not caused by the depression. It was the result of a change in the musical habits of the nation.

FIGURES 12A–F. A graphic entrance into the radio war: ASCAP pamphlet, U.S., 1933. American Society of Composers, Authors and Publishers, *The Murder of Music* ([1933]).

TOTAL ROYALTIES FROM PHONOGRAPH RECORDS (in dollars) 1925-1932

OF THREE LEADING FIRMS

$780,568 $887,514 $877,723 $765,012 $598,150 $368,949 $169,248 $86,600

| 1925 | 1926 | 1927 | 1928 | 1929 | 1930 | 1931 | 1932 |

Source: Statistics of three leading music publishers

By Act of Congress, owners of musical copyrights receive a royalty of two cents for each phonograph record of their music. The royalty on a record with music on both sides is four cents. This was formerly one of the largest sources of income to the composer and writer of music. In 1926 three leading firms received $887,514 from phonograph record royalties. In 1932 their receipts had slumped to $86,000 (a decline of more than 90%), because fewer and fewer people are buying records. Music is more popular than ever, but people are listening to it over the radio.

EMPLOYMENT OF MUSICIANS IN MOTION PICTURE THEATRE ORCHESTRAS

19,000

3,000

| 1925 | 1927 | 1929 | 1931 | 1932 |

Source: American Federation of Musicians

A sad result of the mechanization of music is the effect upon employment of the professional musician. His employment in orchestras has declined to the vanishing point. One orchestra in a broadcasting station now renders a musical program to millions of listeners. Prior to the mechanical age in music, thousands of professionals would have been employed to render the same service. The sound film has deprived other thousands of their means of livelihood. What possible encouragement is there under such conditions for a youth to study music with a view to making it his profession?

THE AVERAGE LIFE OF AN OUTSTANDING HIT SONG

TOTAL SALE 1,156,134 COPIES

TOTAL SALE 229,866 COPIES

16 MONTHS

3 MONTHS

BEFORE RADIO — PRIOR TO 1925

AFTER RADIO SINCE 1931

Source: American Society of Composers, Authors and Publishers

FIGURE 13. ASCAP as visible hand: *ASCAP Journal* (November 1937), 5.

Music Popularity in the Testing Ground of the Music War

ASCAP became increasingly dependent on radio license fees; radio royalties made up 62 percent of ASCAP's income in 1936 and 67 percent in 1939.[74] In order to haggle with radio stations over royalty percentages, it was essential that ASCAP hold the majority of the repertoire. However, this monopolization was constantly endangered by powerful members within ASCAP who threatened to leave the association and conduct their own negotiations with radio stations and the film industry. Despite ASCAP's strategy of presenting itself to legislatures and to the public as an association with few well-known and many obscure composers, it needed the major music publishers among its members. In the mid-1930s, five of the largest publishers (united in the Music Publishers' Holding Company) were owned by Warner Brothers Pictures.[75] In 1936, this group left ASCAP for seven months until an agreement was reached regarding their royalty percentage (around 10 percent of an income of 3.2 million dollars). Naturally, only the most powerful ASCAP members could threaten such boycotts. These legal conflicts also influenced the musical offerings of radio stations; pieces by composers like George Gershwin and Victor Herbert disappeared from radio programs between January and August 1936.[76]

It was only a matter of time until the NAB became sufficiently powerful to withdraw from the deal with ASCAP.[77] This time came in 1939, as ASCAP

FIGURE 14A. Fighting ASCAP with cartoons: Pamphlet from the National Association of Broadcasters, U.S., 1941. National Association of Broadcasters, *Portrait of a "Protector"* ([1941]).

FIGURE 14B. Fighting ASCAP with cartoons: Pamphlet from the National Association of Broadcasters, U.S., 1941. National Association of Broadcasters, *Portrait of a "Protector"* ([1941]).

celebrated its twenty-fifth anniversary. The NAB now had the financial resources and the right degree of organization to take the fight to ASCAP. In August 1939, the NAB announced that it would look for music sources outside of ASCAP's repertoire in the future.[78] It countered ASCAP's campaign with its own pamphlets denouncing ASCAP as monopolists and publicly criticizing its organizational structure and regulations: "ASCAP is run by a self-perpetuating board."[79]

The battle to control royalties now reached its decisive phase. NBC had initially dropped the repertoire of ASCAP members in November 1940;[80] on December 31, 1940, the entire ASCAP repertoire disappeared from commercial American radio stations that were affiliated with the NAB. On New Year's Eve 1940, the *Herald Tribune* wrote of the bitter war: "It will be the

accustomed as I am to public speaking...

RADIO WAS FINALLY FORCED TO
PAY ASCAP FOR ALL PROGRAMS---
EVEN NEWS BROADCASTS, SPEECHES AND
OTHER PROGRAMS USING NO MUSIC.

FIGURE 14C. Fighting ASCAP with cartoons: Pamphlet from the National Association of Broadcasters, U.S., 1941. National Association of Broadcasters, *Portrait of a "Protector"* ([1941]).

first time in radio's history that ASCAP's tunes, which comprise most of the music written in the last fifty years, will be off the air."[81]

In place of compositions by John Philip Sousa, George Gershwin, Cole Porter, or Irving Berlin, arrangements of traditional folk music, Latin music, hillbilly music, and music by African Americans—at the time referred to as "race music"—were now being broadcast. Following the failure of ASCAP and the NAB to agree on a new contract regarding royalty levels in 1939, the NAB founded its own collecting society, named Broadcast Music Incorporated (BMI). BMI now signed up any music repertoire that was not maintained

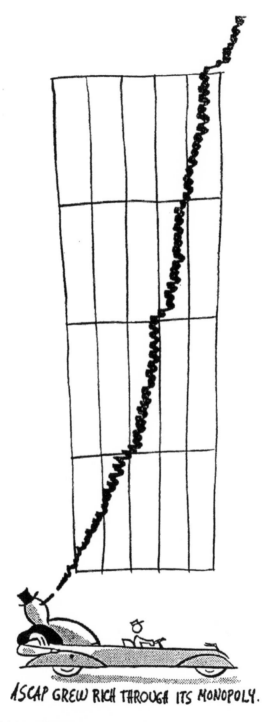

FIGURE 14D. Fighting ASCAP with cartoons: Pamphlet from the National Association of Broadcasters, U.S., 1941. National Association of Broadcasters, *Portrait of a "Protector"* ([1941]).

ASCAP MANAGEMENT
TAKES ONE-THIRD

PUBLISHING CORPORATIONS
TAKE A THIRD

FIGURE 14E. Fighting ASCAP with cartoons: Pamphlet from the National Association of Broadcasters, U.S., 1941. National Association of Broadcasters, *Portrait of a "Protector"* ([1941]).

by ASCAP or that had failed to meet ASCAP's admission requirements for exploiting authors' rights.[82] The Georgia Music Corporation, which specialized in race music, signed a contract with BMI, as did the Peer International Corporation, which specialized in country music. Thanks to BMI, blues, gospel, rhythm and blues, and jazz now had access to radio stations. BMI became the most important licensing agency for African American music. The music war was as positive for rural white music from the South as it was for race music. For ASCAP and BMI, the war ended with the division of the royalty market. This was due not least to the intervention of the Department of Justice, which investigated both institutions for monopolistic tendencies.

¼ OF THE ARTISTS TAKE 32% ?

¾ OF THE ARTISTS GET 1%

FIGURE 14F. Fighting ASCAP with cartoons: Pamphlet from the National Association of Broadcasters, U.S., 1941. National Association of Broadcasters, *Portrait of a "Protector"* ([1941]).

Without this intervention, it is possible that BMI and ASCAP might have found themselves in one large royalty trust.

In October 1940, *Harper's Magazine* concluded that the close relationships and increasing mutual dependencies between radio and ASCAP had made escalation inevitable: "Without radio ASCAP would lose two-thirds of its income; without ASCAP radio would be deprived of a tremendous percentage of its music supply."[83]

The Royalty Conflict as the Object of Empirical Social Research

For the social researchers under the aegis of Paul F. Lazarsfeld (who after emigrating from Germany to the U.S. offered their services to develop program analysis systems for American radio stations and the U.S. government's Office of War Information), the ASCAP/BMI controversy was the perfect topic for empirical social research.[84] In a 1944 survey about what makes music popular, radio analyst John Gray Peatman spoke of an almost ideal testing ground: "A more controlled, scientific experiment could not have been devised to test the selling power of radio. And as an experiment, such a test would have been financially prohibitive to any group of scientists. Costs ran into millions."[85] What experiment was this? And what was the underlying social science question?

This was the question, central to cultural industry criticism, of the extent to which a song's popularity is determined by frequent radio play, a practice known in the radio slang of the time as "plugging." To put it another way, it was a question of whether a song could only become a hit if (frequently) played on the radio. And, ultimately, it was a question of whether the social use of music was a consequence of advertising measures. After analyzing the BMI/ASCAP controversy of 1941, it was clear to Peatman that the medium of radio had a considerable influence on the sales of sheet music and records. In 1941, when the ASCAP repertoire was not played on the radio and BMI established its own repertoire, thirty million of the one hundred million records sold up to September 1941 came from the BMI repertoire. And of the fifteen songs listed in *Variety* in January 1942 as the bestsellers of 1941, only one came from ASCAP.

Once the dispute between BMI and ASCAP had been resolved, songs from the ASCAP repertoire once again "climbed to first and second positions, respectively, of the nation's best sheet music sellers."[86] The ASCAP/BMI war provided European cultural critics with empirically substantiated, sociological proof of their cultural industry theory that the radio industry had the power "to make or break the popularity of a tune through performance or non-performance."[87] Back in 1940, far from home and influenced by American exile, Theodor Adorno and Max Horkheimer had published a pamphlet with the New York Institute of Social Research (reproduced via mimeography and reflecting the new reproduction technologies pushed by the Joint Committee on Materials for Research) in which they lamented the loss of art as a scene of subversion.[88] For them, mass production had stopped art from being what it should be in the eyes of European aesthetic theorists: a sanctuary outside the logic of capitalism. Horkheimer's and Adorno's criticism of mass culture is to be seen as criticism of America; twentieth-century American production resulted in the expansion of mass production principles to all areas of society, something particularly evident in the commercially organized radio industry.

At the start of the 1940s, empirical social researchers were not the only ones to believe that the medium of radio could determine a song's popularity ("make or break the popularity of a tune through performance or non-performance");[89] ASCAP also agreed. Its strategy, founded at the start of World War I, to control the entire repertoire of "popular," valuable, renowned music was developed in the 1930s and transferred to the medium of radio. ASCAP then became dependent on radio stations; for its repertoire to be popular and economically exploitable, it had to be played on the radio. In turn, radio stations were dependent on the established repertoire of ASCAP's members to make their shows popular and attractive to paying advertisers. In battling to control the popularity and exploitation of music, the rivals were getting in each other's way.

Ultimately, ASCAP was doomed by the admission rules it had established at the start of World War I, taken from the European culture of the nineteenth century and giving preference to renowned music and music set down in writing. These restrictive rules enabled BMI to seek an alternative music repertoire, which it found in the white folk tradition, African American music, and jazz. This allowed it to capitalize on the exploitation logic ASCAP had imported from Europe by using American musical works not yet integrated into exploitation chains and to counter ASCAP's financial demands. BMI helped these genuinely American performing artists to achieve a media diffusion that did not stop at the East Coast, but in the postwar period also offered European listeners attractive alternatives, which were later denounced as "Americanization" by cultural critics.

PART III

Private Copies and Universal Standards

CHAPTER 8

Fees for Devices

It's Illegal—But is it Immoral?
—*Tape Recording and Reproduction Magazine* (1969)

Hunting is a passion.
—Paul Parin, *Die Leidenschaft des Jägers* (2003)

From the outset, radio listeners were not passive recipients. With their self-made receivers, hobbyists helped the radio to make its breakthrough. Even after the European states took the airwaves under their legislative wing and made people pay license fees to listen to the radio, some radio amateurs continued to be interested in more than just the messages they were receiving via their speakers. They were just as interested in how the medium was used and particularly what they could do with radio devices apart from listening, such as recording radio programs onto records.[1]

In principle, the Edison cylinder had been created as a medium for playback and recording. Given the complex pressing procedure for Berliner records, which was adopted by the record industry, the practice of amateur recording initially seemed to deviate from industrial production. However, as far back as 1925, descriptions appeared for devices that enabled users to record radio programs onto records, and the first devices produced for this purpose by the phonographic industry appeared on the German market in 1931.[2] These devices were intended for the technically adept, as were the detailed instructions that began to appear on the book market.

However, anyone purchasing such a device would find enclosed a note listing all the things they were *not* allowed to do with it, such as taping over records or using it in cinemas (with the exception of foyers, restaurants, and checkrooms).[3] The literature reassured hobbyists that they were permitted to record radio programs because they were for private, rather than commercial, use. The distinction between private and commercial formed the normative framework for these practices: "The procedure must never be used for commercial purposes. Selling the records is prohibited because radio programs may not be reproduced, and because recording using the amplifier tube is patent-protected. Nevertheless, nobody can stop users from recording the latest hits for personal use to play whenever they like."[4] The technology was still too primitive for classical music ("art") because it could not reproduce differences in volume.

For the next three decades, this paradigm—in which music recording was regulated by distinguishing between commercial and noncommercial use—continued to form the normative framework cited by amateurs and their suppliers from the electrical industry. Germany's legislative royalties for devices, devised in 1965, became the world's first technology licensing system that favored the creator. This chapter looks at the birth of fees for devices and argues that this was accompanied by a legal paradigm shift that altered copyright theory and practice. This shift was triggered by GEMA, the German collecting society that sued Grundig AG, Europe's largest producer of tape recorders. An analysis of the legal conflict between GEMA and Grundig should not simply examine its social and political context but also analyze the media and legal question of how use of a new medium interacts with legal norms in flux. The conflict between GEMA and Grundig is also particularly relevant because the expansion of copyright, in conjunction with device fees, was brought into question by a new type of consumer. Concepts of authorship legitimized in law were no longer self-evident, and they soon entered cultural and media theory debates.

Max Grundig: From Radio Amateur to Tape Producer

The name *Grundig* conjures images of the German economic miracle, reconstruction, and prosperity.[5] The 1978 portrait of company founder Max Grundig published in *ZEIT* magazine to mark his seventieth birthday is typical of the narrative that has surrounded the Grundig company since the 1950s.[6] The "patriarch of the German economic miracle" from the province of Fürth in Middle Franconia is described as a "self-made man" with a pioneering spirit who knew how to seize the moment.[7] The son of a warehouse manager and a passionate radio amateur in his youth, he began his first career in the radio trade before war broke out. During the war he supplied the German armed forces with transformers and control units for V1 and V2 missiles and electric detonators for antitank weapons, soon via

AEG and Siemens. His work supplying the arms industry earned Grundig a fortune, yet it did not pull him into the Nazi regime's gravitational centers. Politically unscathed, he could now reinvest the 17.5 million Reichsmarks (of which ten million were outstanding accounts with AEG and Siemens) he had acquired during the war. He remembered his youth as a radio amateur and, in the fall of 1946, began to produce and sell the Heinzelmann radio construction kit. Because the kits contained no tubes (supplied separately by radio dealers) and could be constructed by customers with no technical knowledge, the Grundig company was able to bypass the business regulations that were in place during the U.S. occupation. Grundig arranged the supply of tubes and other rationed raw materials through a network of former AEG and Siemens specialists who deftly negotiated the black and gray markets. Even before the 1948 currency reform, Grundig had conquered his segment of the radio market. He invested the profits in expanding the company and building production facilities in his hometown. This was Max Grundig's second career.

His third career, which is relevant to the history of copyright, began in 1951 when Grundig took over the Lumophon plants in Nuremberg and brought the first mass-produced German home tape recorder to market.[8] In his now-famous laconic about-face, Friedrich Kittler described the development of the magnetic tape by the German military technology companies BASF and AEG during World War II and their civil use in the postwar period as "misuse of army equipment."[9] However, tapes were a product of National Socialist research into substitute materials for a Nazi state set on expansion and conquest. After all, the sound recorder was made using synthetic material: initially cellulose acetate, until BASF developed a new tape material in 1944 from polyvinyl chloride (PVC), coated with a magnetic layer permeated with ferric oxide.[10] According to Kittler, the manipulation of recordings tested by the secret services became a specific media characteristic of tape: "Cutting and controlling listening allow the unmanipulable to be manipulated."[11]

This manipulability was what made tape so attractive to radio stations and the record industry. It aided censorship just as much as the production of accidental art, a function that would later make it the focus of domestic users passionate about hunting down sounds.

Grundig's business philosophy followed the Fordian principle of tapping into new consumer segments by developing ever cheaper devices: The first tape recorder from 1951, which cost less than 1000 Deutschmarks, was followed by the Grundig TK 5 (under 500 DM) in 1955 and the TK 20 (380 DM) in 1957, which became a "bestseller."[12]

FIGURE 15. Women, man, alcohol, and a magnetic tape recorder: Grundig advert for the TK 14, Germany, 1962. Rundfunkmuseum der Stadt Fürth.

Grundig's advertising brochures presented tape recorders as objects of desire and enjoyment, showing them being used by elegantly clothed women and men. The brochures celebrated West German postwar interiors, the background depicting small house parties where men and women drank cocktails and wine and smoked cigarettes. Tape recorders celebrated pleasure and prosperity. This increasing prosperity was even tangible at the radio and export trade fairs where new Grundig products were presented to consumers each year. Here, Max Grundig was photographed with Willy

Brandt, Berlin's mayor, and with Economics Minister Ludwig Erhard, the architect of the German economic miracle who also hailed from Fürth.[13] Before organizing the reconstruction, first as economics minister and later as chancellor, Erhard spent the first days and weeks after Germany's 1945 surrender traveling Fürth on behalf of the American occupation as head of the Ministry of Economics and predicted an upturn for the region's ailing economy. In 1956, the *Neue Zürcher Zeitung* was impressed by the meteoric rise of Grundig, Fürth's industrial company: "Ten years ago, this company did not exist—today, Grundig is Europe's largest producer of radios and tape recorders. . . . Exports have enjoyed a particularly steep upturn. In the last year, exports have increased by 80 percent to 73.3 million DM. This means that Grundig makes up around one third of all West German exports in this industry."[14]

As a company, Grundig represented success and a focus on exports. It produced products that epitomized "prosperity for all,"[15] and its founder appeared in public with well-known politicians. It was no coincidence that GEMA, the German collecting society, sought out this strong and prosperous opponent for its lawsuits on tape recorder royalties. Creators were to share in this success.

GEMA: Exploiting Music in the Federal Republic of Germany

In 1933 the collecting societies had been merged into STAGMA under National Socialist control; in August 1950, the occupying forces released its successor organization, the Gesellschaft für musikalische Aufführungs- und mechanische Vervielfältigungsrechte (Society for Musical Performing Rights and Mechanical Reproduction Rights, GEMA), from their control and confirmed Erich Schulze as the first director.[16] The new GEMA based its rules on the traditions established by the Genossenschaft Deutscher Komponisten (Cooperative of German Composers, GDT) in 1898 by positioning itself as a "non-profit" institution in the commercial music market. As before, membership was open only to those who had already made a mark on the music business: To join, composers had to have earned at least 1,200 Deutschmarks in three consecutive years or an average of at least 1,000 Deutschmarks in six consecutive years.

Unlike in the German Empire, however, the argument of the common good was no longer accepted so easily in the Federal Republic of Germany. At first, GEMA received a chilly reception in the German Bundestag in 1952,[17] and in March of that year the CDU/CSU questioned the German government on GEMA's practices of recording royalties and collecting fees. That

GEMA claimed to be a nonprofit organization and cultural mediator even as it accepted fees from the associations was strongly criticized. Once the criticism began, accusations followed that the organization was bureaucratic and monopolistic and was contributing to cultural decline, particularly because composers of popular music were profiting from royalties. Now cultural criticism came from the right, a decade after European aesthetics theorists Theodor Adorno and Max Horkheimer (from American exile and from the left) had criticized the loss of art as a place of subversion due to mass production. German choral societies also claimed to be a refuge outside the logic of capitalism. The strategy chosen during the Weimar Republic to unify the common good and to maintain a repertoire became a burden for the German collecting society. GEMA's directors were concerned about this new resistance so soon after the organization had left behind its National Socialist past: "What is important here is not the question of whether the allegations against GEMA are justified, but the fact that an attempt has been made to restrict copyright protection."[18]

GEMA responded to the allegations and its public image as an anonymous administrative body by lobbying in parliament with the aid of prominent cultural figures. First, it sent the Minister for Justice a telegram written by composers that was distributed to all members of the German parliament.[19] In this message, GEMA employed the notion of "theft of intellectual property" and drew on an original concept from the *Bürgerliches Gesetzbuch* (German Civil Code):[20] Everyone knows "that the theft of a movable object [is] not permitted," but few know "that the prohibited public performance of a work of sound is theft of intellectual property and [will be] prosecuted under both civil and criminal law."[21] Second, it called for the copyright law to be revised. Third, it began to demand royalties for tape recordings. And fourth, it pursued legal processes in an attempt to enforce these demands in law.

The question of whether magnetic tape recordings were to be subject to copyright dominated copyright debates in the Federal Republic of Germany between 1950 and 1965. After the war, the new director of GEMA gave top priority to magnetic tapes. In a letter from March 1950 composed with the phonographic industry, GEMA cautioned the people manufacturing and selling magnetic tape devices. They believed that recordings of radio programs and records violated the rights of creators, record manufacturers, and radio stations.[22]

The International Confederation of Societies of Authors and Composers (CISAC) first discussed magnetic tapes in 1950, and the German experts were quick to set the tone.[23] With the new medium of tape, the framework of interests between collecting societies, the phonographic industry, and broadcasting companies had shifted, and they now found themselves in a new alliance for tape royalties. This was also a rivalry between an old medium (records) and a new medium (tapes) and an attempt to expand the rights for old media so that they would include the new medium. This interpretation was highlighted when disputed by IFPI jurist Alfred Baum in a report on tapes: "Besides, the purpose of the warning letter was solely to preserve their own, justified interests based on copyright norms, with not even the slightest desire or even awareness that their own products would receive priority over those of the AEG."[24]

In 1950, Schulze presented GEMA's demand for a monthly flat fee for anyone who owned magnetic tapes.[25] To use an expression from researcher Michel Callon, he succeeded in "problematizing" the topic.[26] The new medium of tape became a legal problem and was prioritized over other topics. The arguments brought into play during this process are interesting from a media theory perspective. The first argument for device fees emphasized the loss of control for collecting societies: Unlike radio programs, for example, which could be controlled via program analysis, the "control device"[27] failed in the case of private users. The second argument focused on the potential for tape recordings to be deleted: "No other exploitation opportunity in the copyright field presents so many difficulties: Books, sheet music, and records can be defined as pieces of work; they cannot be deleted again and used to embody an unlimited number of other works. In contrast, the magnetophone tape allows popular music, eulogies, symphonies, speeches, and the like to be recorded and deleted in just a few hours."[28] The ephemeral character and manipulability of the medium were declared to be dangerous for creators: "'Overwriting' and 'recording' for personal use" had "overstepped the boundaries of the commercially irrelevant."[29] Commercial relevance was taken to mean potential loss of sales for the sound carrier industry. This was the same objection that publishers had used against photocopying in the 1930s—customers would make do with copies instead of buying books. Ultimately, the argument for device fees was based on the opinion that "all use of the device . . . [is] misuse" if permission has not been granted by the creator or if the owner of the tape has not acquired the right to use the medium by paying a fee.[30] It was now clear that, according to GEMA, all media usage should be linked to a license fee for the creator.

The demand for device fees did not go unchallenged. Talk of loss of control and the manipulability of the medium was countered by the argument for civil privacy. The liberal argument of "protecting citizens' private, noncommercial space against state intervention and spying"[31] was a novelty in German copyright discourse. The use of magnetic tapes was stylized as a symbol of private civil rights, a strong argument in the young Federal Republic, which was trying to leave behind more than a decade of dictatorship and censorship.

Neither the phonographic industry nor the collecting societies contemplated new commercial models for magnetic tapes in light of the media transformation. Siegfried Haeger, jurist at the Institut für Film und Bild (Institute for Film and Images, the successor organization to the Reichsstelle für den Unterrichtsfilm, the Reich Office for Educational Films), outlined such models, used media theory arguments, and brought the benefits of tape over records into the discussion. He referred to tapes' longer playing time and the possibility of "transferring records to tapes" to "create longer pieces of music" than were possible with records: "Then it is truly possible to record certain concert pieces, operas, etc. in their entirety on tape without breaks. If, in contrast, the piece of music is on two sides of a record, you must either have two records and two playing devices or interrupt the recording to flip the record. The inevitable pause can be cut out of the tape . . . (and reinserted)."[32] In 1954, he formulated a whole arsenal of alternatives to device fees, revealing the defensive attitude of the record industry, radio stations, and GEMA. In doing so, he anticipated many of the ideas of Digital Rights Management (DRM). Tape recordings could be prevented by technological design, rendered obsolete by radio programming, and developed into a business idea by the defensive phonographic industry. He advised the phonographic industry to provide consumers with whichever media they desired: "Why do you not fulfill the justified demands of tape fans by producing tapes with the desired music and selling them for personal use, just like records?"[33] License fees could then be collected from these tapes rather than taxing amateur recordings. Only those with the time, money, skill, and interest would record their own tapes. He suggested that radio stations pay more attention to their listeners and broadcast a second and third ultra-short wave program featuring the music they wanted. He proposed that the tape recorder industry produce cheaper magnetic tape devices for playback only.

The campaign for tape royalties must also be considered in light of the change from shorter record formats to long-playing records (with thirty-three revolutions per minute). Now that records cost less and contained more music, creators and producers locked horns over creator royalties, which were defined in the standard contract as a fixed percentage of the sales price.[34] It was now clear to the collecting societies that the conditions for exploiting music recordings could be questioned every time the medium evolved. Relations between the IFPI and BIEM were at an absolute low when the IFPI temporarily terminated the standard contract in 1956.

Hunting Sounds as a Revolutionary Act

The year 1949 represented a real turning point for the radical socio-technical changes discussed here; it was the year that France's first association of tape-recording amateurs was founded, which in 1958 became part of the Fédération internationale des Chasseurs de Sons (International Federation of Sound Hunters, FICS).[35] The aim of the association was to represent its interests in the field of tape recording toward radio stations, industry, and authors' rights societies, and starting in 1950 it organized an annual international competition for the best recordings. In 1960, FICS also concluded a contract with UNESCO to collaborate on the Sound Library.[36] An international "tape exchange" allowed people to socialize locally, nationally, and internationally.[37]

GEMA had been filing suits against Grundig since 1953, and one year later the director of GEMA began to attack the sound hunters.[38] The 1953 European sound hunter competition in Paris was the vehicle for Erich Schulze's criticism. He had nothing but scorn for the sound hunters: "Among them was an unusual recording of Chopin's Nocturne. The pianist had played the work from back to front. The tape of this recording was then played backward; the melody was unrecognizable."[39] The musical work—the basis of copyright and source of the royalty economy—was no longer safe from passionate sound hunters. Tapes established new forms of music consumption that were no longer connected to records and, therefore, to creator's royalties, and this could not be tolerated: "License fees from records form a significant part of their income. Every unregulated tape recording that replaces a record reduces the creator's income."[40]

It was at precisely this time that the first manuals and specialist magazines about taping technology began to appear, informing consumers about new products and offering music amateurs a forum to exchange opinions.[41] They discussed the merits and drawbacks of tape vis-à-vis records, emphasizing tape's flexibility in particular: "Tape is far more flexible than disc. You can cut it and splice it together again, eliminating sections you don't want. You can erase the magnetic impressions and use the tape again for some other piece of music. Moreover you can make your own recordings, whereas a phonograph pickup cannot be made to cut a disc. All sorts of advantages."[42] Anything that left the listener cold could be skipped or deleted: "If the result of any experiment is a continued coolness then the recording can be erased."[43] Always at risk of buying something they didn't like, consumers could now indulge their love of music unburdened: "One can then be glad that the impulse to 'acquire' the recording has nothing irrevocable about it."[44]

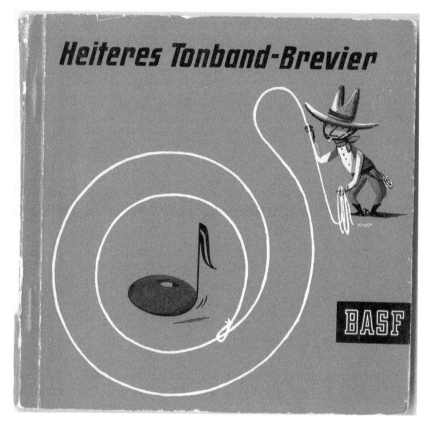

FIGURE 16. American cowboys and German synthetics: BASF brochure, Germany, 1960. BASF, *Heiteres Tonband-Brevier* ([1960]).

An American hi-fi manual emphasized the high cost of the devices and raw material, only to add that tape recording devices offered the "rich audiophile" "more fun" than any other device: "He can record an FM broadcast direct from his tuner. . . . The broadcast will be his to play, at almost its original quality whenever he feels like it. . . . When he's become a little tired of his record, he can erase the tape and use it again to lessen wear and tear on a later favorite."[45]

It was precisely this desire that economist Albert O. Hirschman denied to durable consumer goods (like refrigerators and automatic heating systems) because they provided mere "comfort" and no "pleasure"[46] and would therefore leave consumers disappointed. In comparison, magnetic tapes were consumer goods that provided constant enjoyment. The medium did not come ready to use, allowing the appetite for consumption to be constantly stimulated. Tape devices may have been a form of technology, but they were also a form of creativity: Anyone could cut and paste to create their own music from records, radio shows, and sounds they had recorded themselves.[47] They could even create malleable listening experiences by using different microphones to record on two parallel tape tracks (via double-track stereo) or using the four-track system of the Radio Corporation of America. The small red BASF brochure entitled *Heiteres Tonband-Brevier* (Jolly Tape Guide), its cover depicting an American cowboy ensnaring a music note with his lasso, compared music recording to magic: "Stereo tape devices enable 'spatially malleable,' stereophonic listening. . . . Because the sound travels at the same speed, two microphones positioned far apart record different instruments . . . with a phase difference that produces the spatially malleable impression when played back."[48] The mixer could then be used to layer sounds. Consumers were now doing something that was previously the reserve of studio-based music producers and radio stations: Producing their own music.

Tapes became a hobby and a pastime.[49] It was a "medium of creativity" in the technological age, as social historian Detlef Siegfried stated in his study of consumption and politics in West German music culture.[50] Not for the youth culture—until the mid-1960s, these devices were far too expensive for teenagers—but for technically adept (often male) hobbyists, who regarded tapes as an act of electronic revolution way back in 1959: "The tape recorder is part of the electronic revolution which is changing our lives from day to day; but unlike many other products of that revolution it does not contribute to the process of standardisation and regimentation. The tape recorder is on the side of individuality and imagination."[51] As well as entertainment, tapes presented an opportunity to escape from some of the frustrations of modern civilization: "It offers a medium of self-expression that is adaptable to a wide range of creative ability."[52] In the Cold War, tapes were stylized as a positive alternative to the atomic bomb that countered crippling passivity with active use of technology: "The tape recorder may not save us from the hydrogen bomb, but it can help to prevent civilisation . . . from being wiped out by standardisation."[53] Mass-produced home electronics devices, filled with standard components, were to fend off the standardization of everyday life and the horrors of mathematically calculated mass destruction; these were the ambivalent beginnings of the home electronics revolution. To paraphrase Robert Pfaller, tape devices were also interpassive media that enabled pleasure to be dispelled or deferred through replacement or delegation to a recording device.[54]

FIGURE 17. Tapes on the shelves of the economic miracle generation: Philips advertisement, UK, 1958. *Tape Recording and High Fidelity Reproduction Magazine* 2, no. 6 (1958).

This deferral of listening pleasure is also made manifest in advertising: While British specialist magazines emphasized the erase and rewind functions of tapes, Grundig's advertisements focused on the memory function of the new medium: "How much . . . is a memory worth?" asked one 1957 Grundig ad in the British periodical *Tape Recording and Reproduction Magazine*.[55] Like the camera, the tape was also to be integrated into family rituals as a medium of the culture of memory. Grundig promised its customers personal, acoustic memories saved on media; a child's first words or the sound of a house party. The tape industry provided customers with the necessary formats to integrate the acoustic storage media into the old order of living room books: "Tape Library. You should get Philips" said the Dutch tape manufacturer in 1959. Tapes were packaged in such a way that they could be stacked on shelves with books and relegated to the wall units of the economic miracle generation.

Royalties for Tapes? GEMA versus Grundig

Grundig courted consumers' attention for its wide range of home electronics devices and all possible uses of tapes (recording voices, dictating, self-monitoring for musicians, etc.), deliberately ignoring the application described in detail by the manuals and specialist magazines, recording from radio stations and records:[56] "You can make records of programs from your radio as easily as from your microphone; in fact many Grundig owners regard this facility as being more important than any other."[57]

GEMA had brought a series of lawsuits against Grundig in Germany since 1953 and was found to be in the right in almost all of its claims.[58] In its ruling of 1955, the Bundesgerichtshof (German Federal Court of Justice) summarized the question to be clarified: "The core question of this legal dispute is whether a work from the music repertoire managed by the plaintiff that has been transferred to magnetic tape encroaches on the rights of usage applicable to the plaintiff if the work has been recorded on tape for personal use only and with no intention of generating income from it."[59] This distinction, which made the breach of the creator's rights dependent on the commercial nature of reproduction, had been sacrosanct until this point. Now it had been lifted. This paradigm shift was justified in that "this new type of private reproduction of created works is by nature capable" of "placing the creator at significant commercial disadvantage if not [included] in his or her exclusive rights."[60] The court therefore accepted the argument put forward by GEMA since 1950 that the use of the new medium *could* cause the old legal structure to collapse entirely. As Margarethe Freiin von Erffa, legal advisor to GEMA, stated in 1955, they could not wait until "our German phonographic industry is on the verge of collapse and creators receive no more royalties for records."[61] The interests of GEMA and the phonographic industry were seen as identical here.

Although GEMA was deemed to be in the right, the law remained more controversial than in previous judgments. The sale of magnetic tape devices was allowed to continue, but Grundig was now obliged to mention in its advertising that GEMA's permission was required before recording protected works onto magnetic tapes. Later, GEMA was defeated in court when it requested retrospective information from Grundig about everyone who had purchased a tape recorder (customers were required to show personal identification) so that it could request a fee payable to GEMA.[62]

The big question—how magnetic tape recording was to be regulated in law—remained open. Ultimately, this was a question of whether the obligation to pay royalties was to be enshrined in law. The Ministry of Justice wavered: In 1954, a ministry representative declared that private recordings could not be prohibited "because the sense of justice for such a ban is not yet so widespread that such a legal provision could be justified."[63] The payment obligation was initially enshrined in the government draft bill, but the Bundesrat (German Federal Assembly) overturned it.[64] Together, the collecting societies and the sound carrier industry appealed to the Bundestag to maintain the payment obligation,[65] using the argument of the social constitutional state and referencing the exorbitant wealth of the Grundig company ("Grundig has recently begun the construction of a large tape recorder plant in Nuremberg. It will have halls and office buildings spanning 25,000 square meters with space for 2,500 employees").[66] They also quoted Ludwig Erhard's election campaign slogan: *Wir sind ein sozialer Rechtsstaat* (We are a social constitutional state).[67] With their recourse to law uncertain, they tried a political argument, citing a social state's duty to creators. GEMA (which formed an alliance with the record industry in this matter) appealed to the Bundestag to treat creators as members of society who needed the state to intervene and protect them against the dangers of new media. This strategy was to prove successful in the Federal Republic of Germany. The Bundestag accepted GEMA's position and enshrined the payment entitlement in law.[68] Manufacturers of tape recorders were now required by law to transfer 5 percent of sales revenue to the collecting societies.[69]

Germany entered new territory with the introduction of device fees for magnetic tape recorders. Creators' rights were significantly expanded in Germany in 1965, especially considering the extension of protection periods from fifty to seventy years. Foreign specialist magazines for home electronics also followed and commented on the legal dispute between GEMA and Grundig.[70] An American sound hobbyist living in Berlin and writing under a pseudonym mocked the legal case: In *Confessions of an Illicit Tape Recordist*, he warned his American colleagues that the situation in Germany could also take hold in the U.S.: "As the poet might have said, gather ye FM rosebuds while ye may, for as the other poet might have said, if GEMA comes, can ASCAP be far behind?"[71]

FIGURE 18. Keep Your Eye on Grundig: Tape recorders for the global market. Grundig advertisement, UK, 1962. *Tape Recording and Reproduction Magazine* 6, no. 11 (1962), 28.

While GEMA's demands were enshrined in law in Germany, sound hobbyists in Great Britain and the U.S. continued to practice fair use. The specialist hi-fi magazines held onto this argument.[72] The Mechanical-Copyright Protection Society (MCPS), a British collecting society for mechanical rights, first called for license fees in 1959.[73] The Federation of British Tape Recording Clubs resisted such a request and the demand for license contracts.

It emphasized that it could not and had no desire to monitor its members' activities.[74] Its members were interested in the medium of tape recording and not in (protected) works: "Now, the common interest, which leads individuals to form tape recording clubs, is in the common interest in the *art and science of recording*. . . . It lies not in the work itself nor yet in the manner of its performance; the interest lies in the recording as an example of recording technique, or as an indication of the quality of a particular piece of recording equipment."[75]

With magnetic tapes, a new type of confident consumer had emerged who no longer considered the rules of copyright, let alone was prepared to accept the expansion of these rules. This was a new development, one that could be traced back to the end of the 1950s. Tape hobbyists argued that they had a right to use the media and technology, rather than claiming that they had a right to works central to copyright. They felt themselves bound to an electronic revolution and fell back on irony as a stylistic device. Naturally, these weapons were insufficient in the face of the law. It was therefore no surprise when, in 1969, the *Tape Recording Magazine* in Great Britain asked the long overdue question: "It's illegal—but is it immoral?"[76]

By this point, some consumers had long since developed their own morality outside the law. For them, taped copies were not substitutes for records—at least that's what they claimed: "A taped copy is no substitute. Just a plain box. No pictures, no notes, no names of the artists, no repertoire. The program might have been copied, but nothing else has been. All visual attraction has been lost and very few people are prepared to accept such a loss."[77] The medium was the message and the message was sometimes secondary; this was the argument of a new generation of consumers entirely in line with Marshall McLuhan, who in a 1966 interview emphasized that it was not "the mass-produced package" that characterized electric technology but "the immediate personal service."[78] Mass-produced products held a great deal of potential for personal services. Now, consumers wanted not to buy sound carriers but to hunt sounds themselves. And they believed that buying the medium also gave them a moral right to make copies. By 1969, the electronic revolution had long since begun. It was just that very few people had noticed.

CHAPTER 9

Flow of Information

> I am suggesting that copyright or the larger part of its control will appear unneeded, merely obstructive, as applied to certain sectors of production and that here copyright law will lapse into disuse and may disappear.
>
> —Benjamin Kaplan, *An Unhurried View of Copyright* (1967)

> It is possible that information-system operators will make their own contracts with the authors and ask them to prepare their works especially for dissemination through the computer.
>
> —Julius J. Marke, *Copyright and Intellectual Property* (1967)

In the spring of 1945, the European theater of World War II came to an end. Vannevar Bush was already working intensively to explain to the American president the principles he envisaged for a postwar scientific offensive.[1] In July 1945, the head of the Office of Scientific Research and Development (OSRD), the agency that had been responsible for organizing military science, presented Harry S. Truman with his proposals for establishing what would become the National Science Foundation (NSF). The document, titled *Science—The Endless Frontier,* talked greatly of the "flow" of knowledge, technology, publications, and in particular information that was now to take place. The term *information* had dubious connotations; the military research of the 1940s had seen scientists from a wide range of disciplines join together under the auspices of a new information theory. Bush's outline of state-financed basic research even mentioned support for scientific and technical libraries, which were essential to the flow of information: "Adequate technical libraries are an indispensable tool for research workers."[2]

This chapter focuses on copyright between 1950 and 1980, when librarians had new tools at their disposal (Xerox copiers and computers) that enabled them to meet the great demand for information and helped to shift discussion from the flow of information to the "information explosion."[3] With the emergence of science and technology policy, a new type of regulation gained in social influence that challenged the traditional modalities of law and politics. The claim to the "American Century"[4] made in *Life Magazine* in 1941 was also reflected in copyright discourse: For the first time, the U.S. largely defined copyright discourse in science and technology policy. In 1967, the questions of whether copyrights should be reviewed for reasons of science and technology policy or whether technological development would trigger an expansion of these licensing schemes (as licensing schemes had been significantly expanded for music through the collecting societies and through the introduction of license fees for tape recordings in Germany in 1965) escalated into a real power struggle between two incompatible systems with regard to the legitimacy of library copies: *Williams & Wilkins Co. v. United States of America* became the landmark decision in the matter of how information societies should deal with copyrights. This Supreme Court case can be used as an example of the upheavals of a period in which "information society" evolved from a cipher into a description of the society itself. In this landmark case, a scientific publisher from Baltimore went head to head with the National Library of Medicine in Bethesda, Maryland, a reproduction agency that had pioneered services for scientific research since the 1930s. This supports the theory that the Supreme Court's ultimate failure to reach a decision in this landmark case and the American legislature's simultaneous decision to appoint an expert committee to regulate Xerox copiers and computers reflected a new vacuum in the copyright discourse. Scientific methods of establishing the truth had defied legal decision-making processes in the U.S., at least temporarily.[5]

Fair Use for a Reputation Economy

The U.S. scientific frontier movement influenced by Vannevar Bush in the postwar period had a consistently internationalist bent. As John Krige emphasized in his study of American/European scientific relations in the postwar years, the U.S. sought access to knowledge from abroad through cultural and scientific exchange. At the same time, the U.S. was convinced that, with the support of American foundations, promoting peaceful basic research in Europe (and the decolonialized states) would help to create a safer world.[6]

American librarians saw themselves as part of this international postwar awakening under the aegis of the U.S. During an American Library Association conference at Princeton University in November 1946, traditions from the 1930s promoting reproduction as a medium for international cooperation were revived that had developed within the American Joint Committee on

Materials for Research (JCMR) and the Europe-based Institut International de la Bibliographie (International Institute of Bibliography, IIB).[7] American librarians expected that the foundation of the United Nations Educational, Scientific and Cultural Organization (UNESCO) after the end of the war would bring them a new forum for the issue that was interrupted by Robert C. Binkley's sudden death in 1940.

The British scientific community, which was also involved in Allied military research during the war, had also evolved as a result.[8] In 1948, the Royal Society took up Binkley's efforts, initiated in the 1930s, to promote science policy and to enshrine reproduction technology in law. It organized a "Scientific Information" conference, and the "Fair Copying Declaration" developed at the conference coincided perfectly with the start of debates about revising the British Copyright Act. By launching this topic at an early stage, it could influence the course of the debates and the composition of the law. The Royal Society's declaration held firm that a "non-profit-making organization, such as a library, archives office, museum or information services" was authorized to make individual copies of journals published by the Royal Society[9]—and it urged other scientific societies to follow its example.

In its report, the Copyright Committee of the Board of Trade (the government's economic advisory body) proposed that exceptions for library copies also be enshrined in law as part of fair dealing.[10] This position was welcomed by the scientific journal *Nature* in 1952, but it was criticized in other quarters for not going far enough. Leslie Wilson, a contributor to the Copyright Committee, emphasized that authors and scientists had different interests: "The scientific man's financial return is often nil, or a merely nominal sum. His real profit is in the form of an increase in professional reputation. Indeed, his interest, like that of scientific progress, demands that his work should be circulated as widely and as freely as possible."[11] He called for the "relaxation" of the "anomalous and outmoded" law.

Things were very different in Germany, where since the early 1950s the question of library copies had always been discussed in connection with the conflict surrounding tape recorders. The passivity of librarians and scientists may have been partly to blame for the fact that legal discourse viewed photocopies merely as "trade." Photocopies were to be "subject to fees"[12] under the aegis of a collecting society. A Berlin reproduction company (Mikrophot) had committed itself to license payments by concluding a framework contract with publishers in 1948, defining the path that further developments would take.[13]

In Germany too, alternative models were suggested to regulate reproduction on the basis of the reputation economy: At the conference of the

Deutsche Gesellschaft für Dokumentation (German Society for Documentation), Arno Winter of the Welt-Wirtschafts-Archiv (Global Economic Archive) in Hamburg called for "all researchers" and "the entire population" to be included in the deliberations alongside creators and publishers.[14] Winter's suggestions were based on the Anglo-Saxon fair dealing model and pre-empted the now-commonplace common public licenses; when submitting their text, researchers were to explain how they wished reproduction to be approached: "Legitimate use, including reproduction of any kind, permitted and desired."[15] This suggestion was essentially a strategy to empower scientists who wanted to determine how texts were used, rather than leaving them (as publishers wanted) to the mercy of rules on expanded copyright with license fees for copies.

In 1955, the U.S. Library of Congress began to prepare a revision of the Copyright Law, commissioning thirty-four studies.[16] This broke with the procedure of 1905 / 1906, in which the old stakeholders drafted a law in closed conference. This time, the law was to be supported by a short history of American copyright and prepared on the basis of "objective studies" ("research and analysis").[17] Commentaries and expert reports were obtained for each study, and their arguments would be incorporated into the final version. In 1955, it was thought that "better understanding"[18] would improve laws and in particular that this process would enable the law to cover future developments (futurology was flourishing). Two of the thirty-four studies—on fair use[19] and library copies[20]—are particularly interesting for library copies. The studies honed in on the major conflicts: In the case of library copies, the demand that framework conditions for exceptions be enshrined in law was pitted against libraries and researchers, who valued the flexibility provided by the lack of legal provisions. In the case of fair use, the fundamental questions were whether an agreement would be reached at all, how the common law concept (which was open to interpretation and allowed flexibility) should be defined more precisely, and whether it would actually be desirable to abandon the U.S.'s previously liberal attitude to this matter. This was the state of legal research. But the status of technology had also changed, and it was optimistically assumed that the future would bring further technological revolutions.

Xerography and Information Systems

Copying in the Cold War

In 1937, Chester Carlson, a patent attorney from New York who had studied physics, patented a process that he called "electrophotography"; it was based on the interaction between electrostatic charge, a light-sensitive surface, and a toner powder.[21] The patent was not a success. It was not until 1947 that Haloid, a company that produced photographic paper, decided to invest in the technology. In 1951, the journal of American documentalists commented on Haloid's new procedure ("xerography") with cautious optimism; perhaps something revolutionary was brewing in Rochester that would improve the speed and efficiency of duplication methods.[22] American libraries first came into contact with a fully automatic, electrostatic Haloid copy machine in the mid-1950s in the form of "Copyflo," Haloid's microfilm printer.[23] Only libraries with a high demand for copying, such as the National Library of Medicine and the Library of Congress, could afford to rent the huge device. As the head of copying services at Columbia University warned in 1959: "Once you have it, you must keep it busy or else you find that you are working for the Haloid Xerox."[24] However, it was now possible for the first time to produce individual copies of a book for around thirty-five cents per page. In Europe, Rank Xerox Ltd. in London sold the Copyflo device, which had been presented in Germany at the 1959 Hanover trade fair: Catalog cards, microfilms, and even out-of-print books and lost pages could be produced more quickly and cheaply than with any previous reproduction device. Librarians criticized the Xerox aesthetic of these substitute duplicates: "With their too-narrow binding margins and sometimes almost complete lack of side edges, which moreover are defaced with ugly black-gray strips of powder, these volumes do not make a nice impression."[25] As records had been compared with voices, Xerox was compared with letterpress printing—in the early years of new media, copies always struggled to step out of the shadow of the original.

In 1959, Haloid presented the Xerox 914, the model that would soon become synonymous with copying.[26] The Xerox 914 could produce six copies per minute on conventional paper (rather than special, photochemically treated paper) without the use of liquids. In 1930, Photo Copie GmbH had set up a branch in Berlin's Staatsbibliothek (State Library). Now Xerox (and its European partner company Rank-Xerox, founded in 1956) rented the device to libraries for ninety-five dollars a month; this was expected to bring in more customers than selling the expensive machines. The company conducted its business wherever there was a high demand for copies: in offices, libraries, and heavily frequented places like train stations. Librarians raved about the copies, which they said sometimes exceeded the quality of the original because the typography was rendered in a more even black than in faint or uneven prints or typescripts.[27] However, copies of halftones and photographs did not meet expectations. Stapled pages and originals on thin paper (which created a see-through effect) required special treatment. There was a limit to automated copying. The device was also prone to faults. Paper jams interfered with the philosophy of information flow and disrupted library work; they heated up rooms, created noise, and emitted a specific electrostatic odor that is associated with the procedure to this day.

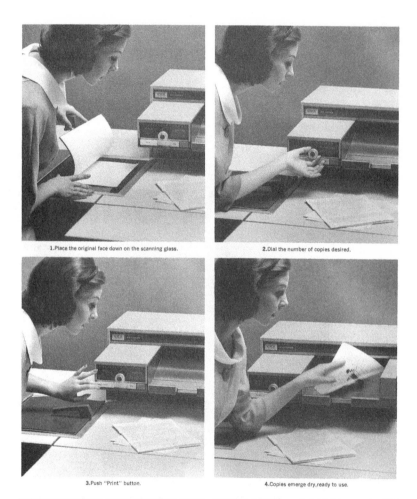

1.Place the original face down on the scanning glass.

2.Dial the number of copies desired.

3.Push "Print" button.

4.Copies emerge dry,ready to use.

DIMENSIONS: Length, 45"; width, 46"; height, 31" (42" to top of control panel); **Weight**: 648 lbs. **ELECTRICAL RATING**: 120 volts, 60 cycles, 20 amperes. **SIZE OF COPY**: 9" x 14" maximum. **COPY-PAPER SIZES AND WEIGHTS**: 7" x 7" to 10" x 15½". Standard paper stocks 20-lb. minimum, card stocks up to .006 thickness and selected offset paper masters. **SPEED**: Up to seven copies a minute. **CAPACITY**: Paper—one-third ream, or a ¾" stack of 20-lb. This is 200 sheets. Card stock— 100 sheets. Selected offset paper masters— 100 sheets.

XEROX   ROCHESTER 3, NEW YORK

CORPORATION

BRANCH OFFICES IN PRINCIPAL U.S. AND CANADIAN CITIES—OVERSEAS: RANK-XEROX, LTD., LONDON

PRINTED IN U

FIGURE 19.   Don't buy an office copying machine! Borrow ours! Brochure for the Xerox 914, U.S., around 1962. Xerox Corporate Library.

Haloid charged just under five cents per copy with a volume of at least two thousand copies per month. Looking back in 1964, the head of the reproduction department at the University of California in Los Angeles said that the Xerox 914 had awoken new desires for copying in libraries.[28] The number of copies skyrocketed. Libraries quickly extended the opening hours of their copy services to include evenings and weekends and acquired extra machines. In addition to changing the way they organized and managed their work to accommodate the large number of copy orders, librarians also began to sell their customers "Xerox Credit Cards": Worth ten dollars, the card would be punched every time a copy was made, saving the library an expensive accounting system.[29]

One thing was clear: The automation of the process, the trend for self-service, and the spread of machines in places such as train stations made it impossible to say who was copying what and how often. However, people ordering lots of copies had to expect questions from librarians, like the young female student who produced over one hundred copies of the same document.[30] She was earning a little extra on the side by copying an original signature from one of the Beatles. At a cost of twenty-five cents and a selling price of two dollars, she had a profit margin of 400 percent. Not even memorabilia, auratic objects, were safe from the Xerox machine. Was their aura really stunted by technical reproduction, as Walter Benjamin's 1936 statements suggested?[31] How were Xerox copies perceived by their users?

The social uses and media characteristics of photocopies can be analyzed using studies initiated by science policy commissions and associations in connection with the copyright conflict. An initial quantitative study from 1961 by the Joint Libraries Committee on Fair Use in Photocopying surveyed three American libraries in 1959 about the extent of copying and the collections affected.[32] A second qualitative study, commissioned in 1962 by the National Science Foundation (NSF) in connection with publisher demands for copy fees, interviewed scholars, publishers, and librarians about copying behavior.[33] The studies indicate how the new technology was used and perceived by scholars and how they viewed the question of copyright for academic publications.

Between 50 percent (Princeton) and 92 percent (New York Public Library) of all copied texts came from journals, almost exclusively from the twentieth century. Half of the articles had been published in the last ten years, over 40 percent in foreign countries. More than 90 percent of the scholars interviewed stated that they kept the copies after use. Just as many researchers reported that they passed copies on to other scholars. Academics clearly regarded photocopies as a medium of diffusion. They knew little about copyright and did not see it as important. They were far more concerned about "piracy" and the "misuse" of research results through lack of citation, misquoting, and the use of research results by commercial companies. They also complained that copying took away their readership overview: "You don't know who is interested in your work."[34] The ability to request copies from libraries meant that there was no need to order reprints from the author. The personal correspondence required to order and send reprints began to

FIGURES 20A–C.   Magazine copies for the free flow of information: The reproduction service at the National Library of Health, Bethesda, Maryland. U.S. National Library of Medicine.

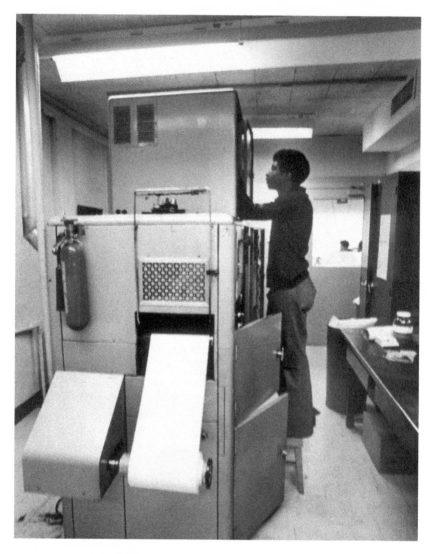

FIGURE 20D. Magazine copies for the free flow of information: The reproduction service at the National Library of Health, Bethesda, Maryland. U.S. National Library of Medicine.

dwindle. The study identified that copies had changed social relationships and communication practices. The German sociologist Niklas Luhmann described the lack of personal interaction between sender and receiver as a characteristic of mass media: "Interaction is excluded by the interposition of media."[35] This perfectly describes how photocopies transformed contact between researchers: Personal communication (for example when ordering a reprint) gave way to communication via a technological mass medium.

The practice of "swapping" copies with other scholars also meant that Xerox copies had great potential for circulation and a multiplier effect. A copy created a copy created a copy, and so on.

The international scientific offensive after World War II was soon displaced by the rhetoric of the Cold War. Once again, faced with the Communist threat, science was to serve as a weapon. In the West, the free flow of information was now a countermodel to the control of information and reproduction by the enemy in the East, for example in the GDR, where a 1959 regulation decreed that state permission (*Druckgenehmigung*) was required to produce printed and reproduced materials.[36] In 1957, UNESCO launched a meeting of government experts with the catchphrase "Free Flow of Information" to facilitate the import of materials for education, research, and culture.[37] At the start of the 1960s, the new research field of scientometrics used statistics to support the idea that rapid flow of information was a vehicle for social welfare: In his publication *Little Science, Big Science*, American scientific researcher Derek de Solla Price used captivating graphics to visualize not only the exponential growth of the "scientific community" and its journal publications but also the associated drop in the half-life of academic "papers" measured against the rapidly shortening citation phase for publications.[38] This strengthened the belief of American science policymakers that diffusion channels should accelerate and provided an argument for the value added by photocopies.

Scientific Publisher versus Research Library

In 1962, a study commissioned by the register of copyrights and the Council on Library Resources, Inc. presented an "optimal solution" to the conflict. This boiled down to licensing copies under the aegis of a "clearing house"[39] and was presented as the answer to a change in media usage that manifested itself in "on demand copying."[40] The increasing speed of communication and the decreasing half-life of information meant that media had to be produced on demand, not kept in stock. This was clearly inspired by an ASCAP-like solution: Anyone using media would now have to pay the copyright holder, even in the world of scholarship and libraries. The flow of money was to be organized in the old bureaucratic tradition of the clearing house (using the social science techniques of random samples and automatic data processors) without jeopardizing science's top priority in the Cold War (free flow of information).

Once the register of copyrights had presented his 1962 report on the revision of the law, the legal revision process (and thus the library copies conflict) entered the next phase.[41] Years of legal drafts, revisions, and hearings about copyright recommenced in Washington, DC; simultaneously, negotiations began before the court that this time (in the case of the photocopy) would come to a spectacular resolution.

In 1965, Lyle Lodwick, marketing director at Williams & Wilkins Co., and Francis Old of the company's legal department represented the medical publisher at a congressional hearing in Washington, DC.[42] Their argument used the comparison often cited in the Cold War between a free democratic system and state bureaucracy in dictatorships. Their message was that, if libraries were allowed to continue copying unimpeded, scientific journals and their publishers would soon vanish and, like opponents of the system, would need to be replaced by publishing houses financed and controlled by the state. Two years later, in 1967, William M. Passano, president of Williams & Wilkins Co., attended the hearing himself.[43] He repeated the demand for license fees and a clearing house for photocopies under the aegis of the Library of Congress.

Before the hearing concluded in April 1967, Passano wrote a letter to Martin M. Cummings, director of the National Library of Medicine (NLM): "Since the National Library of Medicine may . . . be requested to make copies of articles from journals published by the Williams and Wilkins Co., it seemed desirable that I explain to you, our policy in this matter. We are glad to give permission for the copying of articles which appear in our journals provided the person making the copy pays us royalty of 2 cents per page per copy for the privilege of copying the material on which we hold the copyright. In the absence of a royalty payment, no one has our permission to copy this material and any copying which should take place we would consider to be an infringement of our copyright. I trust that you will find this policy compatible with your operation."[44]

The publisher's letter to the renowned tuberculosis researcher, now the director of the largest state medical research agency, set out the arguments and driving factors behind the legal conflict, which would become the most famous Xerox case in history: The publisher claimed to be in the right and lay the fault with the research agency. He made the agency a contract offer (copies in exchange for license fees) while at the same time making a threat (referencing the law and expressing a willingness to go before the court—he had engaged Alan Latman, author of the 1960 fair use study commissioned by the Copyright Office, as an attorney).[45] The reply from the NLM's director was equally concise and determined: "We have given careful consideration to the request in your letter of April 27 that the National Library of Medicine reimburse Williams & Wilkins Co. for making photocopies of articles from journals in which you hold copyright. It is our opinion that this longstanding practice of making photocopies for scholarly purposes, represents a fair use of the copyright materials, and I am therefore, giving directions to the Library staff that our service be continued as in the past."[46] The top medical researcher also claimed to be right. He referenced common law (fair use) and history (the National Institute of Health had run a microfilm service since 1934, expanding it in 1957 to include a national and international photocopying service for medical literature in addition to interlending)[47] and also appeared willing to defend this right before the court.

When we consider that twenty thousand dollars per year of potential license fees were at stake here—an amount that the NLM could have paid without issue and an amount without which the small Baltimore publisher could probably have survived—this legal case can be read as negotiating how the flow of information (a highly charged concept within research policy) would be regulated in the future. As the theory goes, when people talked of Xerox, they were already thinking of computers.

Xerox as Precursor to the Computer

The 1960 American Bar Association (ABA) symposium on copyright revision included a presentation entitled *Technological Advances and Copyright*, which addressed the topic of information systems in connection with copyright for the first time.[48] IBM also presented the ABA symposium with a database system for case law: "In the not distant future the user of the library, instead of consulting a card file and requesting books, will seat himself at an electronic desk and operate a scanning and selector system monitored in the glass top of the desk."[49] The next sentence related this vision for the future to the current publishing system: "The impact on the publishing business of such a change is obvious."[50]

It now had to be decided whether the old publishing system would be protected via copyright or whether information systems in science and research would not be regulated. Should the development of a "substitute" or "parallel system" to traditional publishers be tolerated? Or should they be tied to publishers through a licensing system?

In 1964, computers suddenly became a central part of American copyright discourse when the Copyright Office decided that computer programs could also be registered for copyright protection.[51] A young law student named John F. Banzhaf III had submitted a simple computer program to the Copyright Office (on magnetic tape and in written form); previously, in 1961, North American Aviation Inc. had submitted magnetic tapes to the

Copyright Office with a corresponding (unsuccessful) request to register them for copyright protection.[52] BASF magnetic tapes were now being used to store digital data too, and in 1966 computer tapes made up 30 percent of BASF's turnover in the U.S.[53] The seventy-five publishers first addressed the new information systems at a 1964 conference in New York,[54] two years after Marshall McLuhan had composed a sort of swan song to the age of letterpress printing in *The Gutenberg Galaxy*.[55] Longstanding publishing houses were now confronted with the new discipline of information science. Representatives of MIT's Microreproduction Laboratory explained to them that "information retrieval" was a form of energy that was "vital to this country, needed for survival and for education." IBM representatives recommended that publishers acquire these devices themselves, because "the application of computers to information dissemination will be regarded much the same way as Gutenberg's invention of movable type is regarded today."[56]

Xerox and computers caused a sudden shift in the structure of the publishing and reproduction business. Allen Veaner, head librarian at Stanford University, even saw a new "economic complex" on the horizon that would encompass all facets of graphical communication—production, marketing, distribution, processing, and consumption.[57] He played on the fusions in the communications industry initiated when the Xerox Corporation purchased the microfilm company University Microfilm; this was followed by IBM's 1964 acquisition of school material manufacturer Science Research Associates, whereupon Xerox bought up American Education Publications Inc. Veaner also referred to the Interuniversity Communications Council (EDUCOM), a nonprofit organization founded in 1965 by eight American universities to accelerate the exchange of information via networks and data processing and, through a committee on copyright, to find a solution to the copyright problems of this ambitious major project.[58] EDUCOM secured two renowned legal professors for this purpose—Benjamin Kaplan of Harvard Law School and Arthur Miller of the University of Michigan Law School.

The question arose of how data input, storage, and output were to be classified within copyright categories. Were they copies? If so, when would the act of copying take place? Bella L. Linden first set out the legal consequences of programming procedures (INPUT, OUTPUT, STORAGE) in 1965:[59] Should entering information into databases (via punch cards, magnetic tapes, and other devices that can receive electrical impulses) be designated an act of copying? Or should they be tolerated as fair use? What about data output? And how should storage be handled?

In 1966, specialists in information systems and computer law were startled to hear of a draft law that treated every use of copyright-protected data as a breach of copyright.[60] As they understood it, only OUTPUT should be relevant to copyright, while INPUT ("prepare a substantial portion of a copyrighted works in a computer format or medium, e.g. punch cards") or STORAGE ("cause a computer to scan and store even temporarily within its memory a substantial portion of the work regardless of the input form or use of which the work was to be put") should be explicitly excluded.[61] Computers had enabled new forms of information acquisition (as stated by scholars) and works (as emphasized by publishers and authors) that could be deleted at any time without leaving a trace, and the law was to take account of these new practices.

In 1966, the NSF alone maintained 188 information systems; the Department of Defense had thirty-three and the Department of Health, Education and Welfare and the National Library of Medicine were developing their own national systems for medicine.[62] The NLM already had a "sophisticated computer" to access articles from medical journals for its specialist bibliography, the Index Medicus. The networking of these computers was still in the experimental stage, but it was only a matter of time before the computerized systems would be able to freely circulate scientific information between New York, Paris, and California. This data would be available not only to state-employed scientists but also to researchers in industrial laboratories.

As information systems appeared on the horizon, the copyright debate was heating up. In 1966, publisher Curtis Benjamin of the McGraw-Hill Book Company spoke up in the journal *Science*, saying that publishers were prepared to contribute to the national need for large-scale information systems and to make their materials available—"making sure, of course, that they receive adequate fees to compensate for the consequent loss of sales of printed copies."[63] Already considering new fields of business for publishers based on magnetic tapes, he warned the new system operators that their work was based on materials from the old publishers. A structural change was already becoming apparent in the publishing system, triggered by information researchers and the computer industry.

Regulating Information: Between Legislation, Courts, and Science Policy

1967: A Pivotal Year

From a historical perspective, 1967—the year in which William M. Passano and Martin M. Cummings first exchanged letters—was the year in which the Xerox discourse ceased to focus solely on photocopiers and entered the critical phase of conflicts about regulating future information systems. It had now become clear that the NLM not only had a long tradition of reproducing library documents but was already preparing for a national medical information system.

In 1967, the Federal Council for Science and Technology set up the Committee on Scientific and Technical Information (COSATI) with the involvement of national research agencies such as NASA, the NLM, the Department of Defense, the Library of Congress, and the Department of Justice. The committee's purpose was to discuss legal questions related to the setup of "national information systems."[64] The report was worded cautiously and mentioned the possibility of license systems and clearing houses as well as alternative, non-commercial forms for scientific and technical authors who "might be disposed to grant free licenses for the use of such materials."[65]

With regard to the INPUT/STORAGE/OUTPUT debate, the report argued for a moratorium on INPUT copyright fees for an unspecified period while the database systems were set up. It also recommended establishing a permanent committee to study such questions. In 1967, representatives of science and research successfully resisted restrictions on databases, information exchange systems, and computers in copyright drafts. Law professors Arthur Miller and Benjamin Kaplan played an important role in rejecting a quick, restrictive solution for computers.[66] In 1967 they opposed the draft laws in Congress and emphasized that these drafts would have kept things as they were in the mid-1950s, when the Copyright Office first began to prepare a legal revision. They explained that these drafts paid no attention to the "revolutions in communications technology" and their social impact and focused far more on the interests of publishers than on those of computer users.

This brings us back to the polemical paper by copyright specialist and Harvard lecturer Benjamin Kaplan mentioned in the introduction, which was also published in 1967 with the title *An Unhurried View of Copyright*.[67] Kaplan composed his swan song for copyright as work began to set up national data networks under the aegis of large research agencies like NASA, the Department of Defense, and the NLM. Visions of national computer systems for military-related research during the Cold War are therefore just as important to the historical context of this polemic as Marshall McLuhan's *Gutenberg Galaxy*, which Kaplan mentions.[68] As he envisaged the end of old copyright, Kaplan aligned himself with highly politicized researchers united against the restriction of still-young network technology: "I am suggesting that copyright or the larger part of its control will appear unneeded, merely obstructive, as applied to certain sectors of production and that here copyright law will lapse into disuse and may disappear."[69]

And that's not all: Two monographs on copyright were published in 1967 that addressed a wider audience. Naturally, they commented on the ongoing debate about Xerox and computers. *Copyright and Intellectual Property* was published by the Fund for the Advancement of Education.[70] Its author, Julius J. Marke, had campaigned for library copies back in the 1950s. He spoke out firmly against an ASCAP-like clearing house for library copies and was annoyed by attempts to control library copies, which he portrayed as an attack on librarians' "non-profit motivation."[71] Marke defended the copying practices of scientists, which did much more than substitute book purchases (as publishers suggested). On the last page of his book, he implied that scientists might be able to do without publishers in the future: "It is possible that information-system operators will make their own contracts with the authors and ask them to prepare their works especially for dissemination through the computer."[72]

The emancipation of librarians and technicians from publishers, contemplated within Binkley's circle in the 1930s in connection with microfilm, was further developed in the mid-1960s during the birth of computer-based networks. Furthermore, the old figure of the author was once again called into question by the blessings that the new machines were expected to bring: "Most of the materials will probably be developed through team effort. . . . Finally, it should be remembered that the machine itself will eventually be so programmed that it too can claim authorship of original works."[73]

In the pivotal year of 1967, Roland Barthes announced the "death of the author" in *Aspen* magazine, referencing modern poetic practices (which he claimed had long since buried the author) and arguing that reading, not authorship, should be the center of literary contemplation.[74] Librarians had also declared that the author was dead; this "death" referred to the legal concept of the author and their privileges (together with publishers) and was linked with the technocratic hope of a new era under the care of programmers.

The second publication from 1967 to address a wide audience was *Nearer to the Dust* by George A. Gipe. It was no coincidence that this was published by Williams & Wilkins.[75] *Nearer to the Dust* warned of the new technical potential to which Marke attached so much hope. It criticized the "automated unpersonal society that subordinates the needs of an information machine to the mind of a man"[76] and urged people to respect the needs of authors. Like Passano, Gipe called for photocopy license systems, either through a bureaucratic clearing house or—even better—by attaching counters to photocopiers.[77] This would allow the copying machine to count the fees itself; the bureaucratic apparatus would simply distribute them. With an estimated twelve million copies made in 1966, the considerable sum of 240 million dollars would be amassed in the U.S.; this was at least the projection presented to the Congress hearing by Lyle Lodwick, marketing director of Williams & Wilkins Co., in April 1967. Having founded their businesses on the basis of the printing press, publishers now wanted to earn money from photocopiers and information systems too.

When *Williams & Wilkins Co. v. United States of America* came before the Supreme Court in May 1974, there was plenty at stake: Not just royalties for photocopies but also the regulation of information systems still in their infancy and thus the role of publishers in the future information market. The case was considered highly relevant, as evidenced by the large number of expert reports submitted (twenty-one amicus curiae briefs submitted to the Court of Claim by scholars and publishers and fourteen additional reports to the Supreme Court).[78] The factions were not clear-cut; certain scientific societies that published their journals with Williams & Wilkins chose to support their publisher.

Ultimately, the court obstructed itself—one judge did not participate in the ruling—and on February 25, 1975, the Supreme Court announced that a decision had not been reached, confirming the verdict of the lower court in favor of the NLM. Nobody had expected that. Photocopying for research purposes would therefore remain unaffected by copyright restrictions. There may have been an element of chance here; the judge who recused himself had once acted as advisor to a medical center involved in the case. However, the two factions absolutely reflected the social constellation. The delayed decision also mirrored the situation on Capitol Hill, where legislators needed to decide on a new copyright.

Now the question of photocopies returned to legislators. However, Congress also postponed the decision about regulating photocopies and computers in copyright. While the draft laws for new copyright envisaged restrictive regulations for computers, Senator John L. McClellan had developed a political compromise during the 1967 copyright crisis, when the new national information systems suddenly took top priority within science policy. His solution was to set up a special commission that would attend to the question of copyright for Xerox copiers and computers.[79]

The National Commission on New Technological Uses of Copyrighted Works (CONTU) was established in December 1974 to avoid delaying or even jeopardizing the passage of the new Copyright Act of 1976. The commission was to provide Congress with recommendations on Xerox copiers and computers within three years.

Information Management

In 1970, information and knowledge management became the core issue of American science policy. The Committee on Science and Astronautics in the House of Representatives organized a high-caliber conference in January 1970 in which scientists and politicians discussed the future of information management. On Capitol Hill, sociologist Daniel Bell announced that the U.S. had become the world's first postindustrial country, a theory that he explained in detail three years later in a hefty monograph.[80] Unlike an agricultural or industrial society, a postindustrial society is no longer based primarily on raw materials but organizes itself using a complex system of knowledge and information. Stafford Beer, the British cyberneticist and management theorist, declared information management to be a matter of "self-regulation and self-organization."[81] According to Beer, only cybernetics could convey the "laws" of societies confronted with an explosion of information and increased complexity.

The early 1970s saw a new generation and a new type of scientist first weigh into the copyright debate. In 1974, the young political scientist Nicholas Henry, an assistant professor at the University of Georgia, published two articles in *Science* that made him the prototype of the new copyright expert. He criticized the institution of copyright for reasons of science and technology policy.[82] He could be considered a reformer of copyright in the tradition of Binkley and a promotor of new media. After all, he used Marshall McLuhan's dictum that everyone is a publisher in the Xerox age—most often quoted in these contexts—as a starting point to call for less copyright in the age of microfilm, Xerox, and computers.[83] However, his actions were much more complex: He placed great hope in CONTU, which he believed could create an "alternative agency for planning" and implement a "public policy for information."[84] Henry could also be viewed as a planning-crazy, cybernetic technocrat; his planning activities on behalf of "neo-publishing" took on gigantic proportions (as his five-volume edition of materials on the revision to the Copyright Act of 1976 tended to confirm).[85] In 1974, Henry appeared convinced that "more technology assessment, technological forecasting, and general research on new information technologies"[86] would generate better solutions than the expansion of copyright. Ultimately, Nicholas Henry's cybernetic access to knowledge management could be seen as a step toward a "pay-per-use society," to use Tarleton Gillespie's phrase.[87] Nicholas Henry's idea of 1974 was the same vision of future text dissemination through "information management" presented by cyberneticist Stafford Beer to legislators in Washington, DC, during the 1970 panel on Management of Information and Knowledge: Customers should be able to print their orders at home at the touch of a button once the provider had checked their ability to pay (also at the touch of a button).[88] When Henry spoke of neo-publishing, he also meant that publishers would have to carry out their own technical assessments in the future in order to secure their rights. This is exactly what publishers have now achieved with Digital Rights Management (DRM); access to data is controlled through technological means, not through the law. As British jurist Charles Clark encapsulated with his 1996 statement that "the answer to the machine is in the machine,"[89] the ideas of 1970 came to fruition in the computers of the 1990s.

Exceptions for copies within science and research were first enshrined in law in the U.S. Copyright Act of 1976 and defined in detail in CONTU's final report of 1978.[90] According to the report, it was not immediately necessary to extend the law to include photocopies because scientific journals—the branch of publishing most threatened by copies—did not appear to be in crisis.

The ASCAP-like regulation of library copies in the U.S. was finally off the table. Media use within U.S. science and research was not subject to payment due to the powerful position and high degree of organization within state-financed research during the Cold War. The demand for principles based on the reputation economy of science and not on the royalty economy of collecting societies had some powerful backers.

CHAPTER 10

Authors of Tradition

> This cultural legacy is not only a source of inspiration for the cultural and social development of the peoples of the various African nations, but also has the potential for an economic upturn that can be used to the benefit of citizens in every country.
>
> —Réunion africaine d'étude sur le droit d'auteur (1963)

After a part of cultural production was excluded from musical authors' rights, collectors and scholars adopted these traditional cultural assets back in the mid-nineteenth century. Jacob and Wilhelm Grimm—linguists, publishers of the German dictionary, and collectors of fairy tales—were the German-speaking region's most prominent representatives of this new academic field, which in the nineteenth century explored traditions and acquired authors' rights through its collecting and editing activities. An academic discipline was established that was termed *Volkskunde* in the German-speaking region and *folklore* in the Anglo-Saxon sphere, a name that would later become a metaterm for traditional music.

With the emergence of the phonograph, which opened up new sources of income for the people who held authors' rights, those areas of music production explicitly excluded from authors' rights attracted the attention of collectors at universities and in museums. Collections of folk music from all over the world were institutionalized as phonogram archives were founded in Europe and the U.S. Tellingly, the collection and nurture of traditional music flourished in the U.S. and Europe during the crises of modernization in the 1920s and 1930s. New arrangements of traditional music enjoyed a renaissance in entertainment venues. However, country and blues artists rarely registered their works with the U.S. Copyright Office or were thwarted by ASCAP's restrictive entry requirements.[1]

This chapter looks at the rebirth of tradition in copyright since the mid-twentieth century. As the concept of modernity was re-established in the nineteenth century, notions of the unalterable and eternal were emphatically rejected. For example, the conflict surrounding folklore shows how copyrights based on separating the modern from the traditional were fraught with ambiguities and contradictions. As time went on, these ambiguities and contradictions became apparent in various contexts. They initially emerged in the 1960s as folklore was enjoying a U.S. revival. This was a consequence of the decolonialization of former colonies of European member states of the Berne Convention; the former colonies demanded that folklore be integrated into the law, or they would walk away from international copyright. The ambiguities and contradictions again reared their heads in the 1990s within postcolonial discourse in cultural anthropology, which critically reviewed not only the standards and categories developed in the nineteenth century as modernization took hold but also concepts of nationalism in the decolonialized states. Finally, they also came to the fore in the present day during lengthy diplomatic efforts within the World Intellectual Property Organization (WIPO), founded in 1970, to integrate tradition into a new global legal structure with universal aspirations. Dipesh Chakrabarty suggested a review of the self-evident standards and categories that developed in the modern period and became pillars of modernization theories.[2] Copyright shows that European imperialism was just as involved in producing and reusing these cultural anchors as the nationalism of the Third World.

Private Property or Public Domain? Leadbelly or Lomax?

In 1957, the International Folk Music Council (founded in Britain in 1947) issued a declaration about copyright in folk music.[3] Folklore was not regulated by copyright, so there was plenty of scope for speculation. In the view of the Folk Music Council, "traditional tunes" belonged in "public domains." According to this international association of folk music experts, it was universally accepted that musicians were entitled to copyright for arrangements; however, not all countries recognized collectors' rights to written notation or mechanical recordings. The declaration explained why copyright was justified for collectors: First, committing oral renditions to paper takes a great deal of time and money and requires extensive knowledge. Second, notation requires "some measure of individual subjective interpretation on the part of the collector, owing partly to the frequent use of unfamiliar rhythms and intonations and partly to its inherent state of fluidity."[4] And third, by notating or recording, the collector gives the "authentic" its first definite form.

For this reason, the "first owner" should receive the same legal protection as for a conventional composition. The phrase "first owner" also implied the act of appropriating previously ownerless assets. Copyright was justified by notation, a de facto equivalent to composition. The extent to which folklorists had internalized the premises of authors' rights was reflected in the proposal for dealing with conflicts that arose when two identical sets of notation existed: Apparently, the existence of identical notation proved that one set of notation must be a duplicate; each set of notation would inevitably bear the collector's "individual, subjective" handwriting. Fourth, singers or instrument players could never demand copyright without the corresponding notation. Copyright was linked with an act of recording, equating the new media (sound recording and filming) to writing. In summary, the Folk Music Council stated that the collection of folk music should be protected by copyright, just like the composition of music.

When, in 1947, folklore researchers wanted to copyright their recording work, they were not far at all from the reasoning of Vesque von Püttlingen, who in 1864 wrote the first monograph on musical authors' rights and, in so doing, included the publishers of folk songs in authors' rights.[5] However, this position suffered when copyright practices for folk songs were criticized in American folklore journals in a brief yet intense debate in the early 1960s. This was prompted by the genre's revival in the 1950s, which led to many disputes regarding credits and royalties.[6]

This legal debate was triggered in 1960 by Irvin Silber in *Sing Out!*, the journal he co-founded in the "neo-folk" scene.[7] According to Silber, the problem of folk music copyright was caused by the introduction of compulsory licenses in the U.S. Copyright Act of 1909, which enabled the phonographic industry to reuse music material that went to the record press. He criticized the practices of a long list of producers, publishers, musicians, and collectors such as John and Allan Lomax, who had claimed coauthorship of "new additional material" (such as editions of songs by the blues musician Leadbelly) "including a number which were notated word for word and note for note from recordings made by Leadbelly in the years shortly before his death."[8] The claim by the legendary collectors that notating phonograph recordings made them authors went against the ethics of the neo-folk scene. On the other hand, certain folk artists owed their royalty payments to the Lomax family's collecting activities. In turn, many folklorists were incensed by these royalties for adaptions and arrangements, which ignored a song's long tradition: "Today the folk song world is in ferment over the problem of copyrights."[9] Silber proposed that royalties be wrested from the music industry by establishing a folk song foundation and that these royalties be used for folklore research, editing projects, and records. The fruits of ownership were to be shared, not distributed individually.[10] The aim was to offer noncommercial alternatives to ASCAP and BMI, the commercial collecting societies.

Bill Eitman spoke out in favor of copyrights for arrangements of songs in the public domain. Conversely, he also urged that all arrangements of folk songs would have to be permitted.[11] In the case of the Leadbelly/Lomax controversy, however, he believed it illegal and immoral that Lomax had "claim[ed] such ownership" to the material—Leadbelly was known as a "composer." To the neo-folk scene, which revered blues artists like Leadbelly and believed that it offered counter-models to the commercial music industry, Leadbelly was a composer.

Eitman called on the folk community to publicize false or exaggerated ownership claims by collectors and arrangers in magazines. He wanted the folk community to act as custodians and guardians of the folk tradition. New copyright ethics could be established by removing John Lomax's name from all editions and recordings of "Goodnight Irene": "Too many Negroes suffered too much to create Irene, and they would sleep more peacefully if Leadbelly, who brought Irene to womanhood, could have his name standing alone on the page, unaccompanied by the name of his generous benefactor."[12]

The neo-folk scene also presented itself as the savior of the "noble savages" deprived of their rights by an earlier generation of folklorists.

This neo-folk debate was taken up in *Western Folklore* magazine, which was founded in California in 1942. The American folklorist Gershon Legman took the view that the folklorists who had collected and published the songs with the support of the state and universities were the rightful owners of folklore, even though they had not created these songs themselves.[13] In a riposte, folklorist Charles Seeger questioned whether this right actually existed. He emphasized that traditional music belonged to the public domain and could not be legally claimed by any individual.[14] According to him, any legal claim to folk ignores "the continually changing succession of individual, mostly unknown, carriers of a bundle of traditions, millions of others dead or not yet born."[15] Laws and ethics had to be separated: Legal claims to copyright should be "penalized as fraudulent." However, there was an ethical duty to name sources and informants and include them in commercial income from folk music. His son, Pete Seeger, campaigned for a folk royalty foundation to further finance the collecting activities generously supported by the state during the economic crisis of the 1930s.[16] In a commentary first published in the *Wayne Law Review* in 1964, musicologist Barbara Klarman did not wish to leave the jurisdiction of this issue to the folk scene.

She advised private folk associations to work with the courts and teach them about the complex web within the folk tradition.[17]

Although traditional music handed down through generations had been excluded from modern copyright since it was founded, the figure of the collector linked this music with copyright. The collectors who became professional folklorists played no small part in this, appropriating the discourse on authors' rights and claiming copyrights for themselves. This position was criticized in the early 1960s within the folk music renaissance. Neo-folk representatives had an ambiguous relationship with copyright; while they fundamentally rejected copyrights and encouraged collective punishment for illegitimate claims, they also made a case for establishing joint foundations to tie folk research to the royalty economy.

Demand for Folklore Integration

At this time, young decolonialized African and Asian states also began to question the categories and concepts of authors' rights when the international community encouraged them to recognize international law agreements by joining the Berne Convention. International copyright agreements had changed in the meantime: By 1960, the Berne Convention (founded in 1886 under the aegis of Europe) and the Pan American Convention (founded in 1902) were no longer the only copyright agreements under international law. After World War II, the U.S. State Department had put the idea of embedding the U.S. into international copyright—an interest pursued in the 1930s and 1940s—back on the agenda. While the goal of joining the Berne Convention was pursued up until World War II, the State Department subsequently altered its policy. In the 1947 debate as to whether UNESCO should co-organize the Brussels conference on the revision of the Berne Convention, the Policy Committee on International Copyright in the State Department argued that this would continue "long established formulas and procedures": "A United Nations or UNESCO conference on Copyright Matter would be freer than the Brussels Conference sponsored by the Belgian Government."[18] The U.S. decided that, rather than pursue its interests in the tradition of the Berne Convention, it would organize its own international conference in the future. The goal would be to establish a new "universal" copyright agreement under the leadership of UNESCO. The foundation had been laid for the Universal Copyright Convention. The U.S. had emancipated itself from Europe once and for all, enabling itself and other states to conclude an alternative international copyright agreement. In the preamble, U.S. president Eisenhower announced a universal convention "appropriate to all nations of the world."[19] The previously particularistic U.S. had begun to establish universalistic copyright systems, albeit within a framework less strict than that of the Berne Convention.

A 1963 conference in what was then known as Congo-Brazzaville jointly organized by the old copyright organization (BIRPI) and UNESCO debated how this intended universalization could be implemented on African territory. Of the thirty young African nations invited, twenty took part in the conference. Two European "experts" from Germany and Sweden spoke about authors' rights.[20] The African delegates did not fundamentally question copyright; instead, they discussed ways to enshrine it in Africa. However, the African nations also suggested that the question of traditional music be discussed. This was the first time that folklore had been debated within the framework of international law. In the context of pan-Africanism, the African states saw folklore as a synonym for the cultural heritage of African countries and therefore considered it highly significant: "This cultural legacy is not only a source of inspiration for the cultural and social development of the peoples of the various African nations, but also has the potential for an economic upturn that can be used to the benefit of citizens in every country."[21] Discussions of authors' rights were discussions of the value and export of African culture and the hope—linked with authors' rights—of bringing it back to the continent, as expressed by the Ethiopian delegate: "The African music that has been greatly exported now tends to return to its continent of origin."[22] The young African states also explained to the European experts and observers from international organizations (which put the education and development of the "developing countries" above all else) that, as the Algerian delegate emphasized, African countries also produced "intellectual property."[23]

Following the conference, UNESCO and BIRPI developed a model copyright law for African countries. A Committee of African Experts met in Geneva in 1964 and passed a draft that, among other things, included a proposal to integrate folklore into authors' rights. However, a distinction between "works inspired by folklore" (which were to be included in authors' rights) and "works of folklore" (which continued to be excluded) would preserve the basic principles of copyright established in the eighteenth century.[24] A "work inspired by folklore" encompassed all compositions by an author produced "with the aid of elements which belong to the traditional African culture."[25] This wording meant that, as before, only individual creations (which could be inspired by tradition) received copyright protection. This was merely an old idea repackaged and had no impact; only the Tunisian copyright law of 1966 integrated folklore to protect the "exclusive rights in works inspired by folklore" from third parties who would exploit them for commercial gain.[26] Furthermore, such a law would have only a modest effect as long as it was enshrined only in national law. Other African countries such as Ghana, Zambia, and Malawi did not mention folklore in their laws in the 1960s.[27] Bolivia, Chile, Morocco, Algeria, and Senegal were among the nations to integrate folklore into their national laws in the 1970s.

In 1967, the Indian government commented that the model law could also be of interest to Asian countries, emphasizing that this could be the first step in protecting an export branch that would boom in the future: "The reason to protect folklore efficiently on an international basis would be, to add to works protected by copyright, on a national basis as well as by international copyright conventions, another great and important realm of artistic works, generally appreciated and largely distributed in industrialized countries too."[28] In doing so, the Indian government voiced an idea not previously considered by any African state: declining to sign the Berne Convention. The possibility that developing countries could exit the international copyright system had now been vocalized: "The influence certainly would not be the same and have the same importance in all countries. If such a step were to be considered, it should therefore be also explored, from which sources the gaps, created by such countermeasures could be filled and how the impact of such measures could be reduced."[29] However, this alternative scenario was not pursued and at most contributed to a separate, additional protocol with reduced requirements granted to the developing countries in Stockholm. Copyright had now entered the discourse on development.

In 1967, state officials from all continents converged on Stockholm to negotiate a revision to the Berne Convention that, in particular, was to incorporate the newly decolonialized countries into the agreement. Again, there were calls to integrate folklore. India proposed that folklore be explicitly mentioned in the Convention: "The question of protection of folklore had already been discussed at the East Asian Seminar on Copyright in 1967, which had decided that works of folklore might represent the creative efforts of a number of unidentified indigenous authors. They were therefore not only anonymous works in the sense of the Brussels text . . . of the Berne Convention, but also joint works, since in nearly all cases they were unfixed and represented a constantly changing pattern produced by successive performers and authors."[30] Australia agreed with the protection of folklore in principle but did so outside the Berne Convention, in a sui generis contract.[31] The former colony demanded wide-ranging exceptions for research. The Canadian representative emphasized that his country had a wealth of folklore that, in Canada's opinion, was part of the public domain. He resisted any legally specified restrictions on the public use of folklore. The Canadian delegate proved "deeply unwilling to enter into a discussion as to who owned or was entitled to use such material."[32]

It was therefore the new countries that wished to protect folklore using authors' rights. In principle, the demand to integrate folklore questioned the foundations of authors' rights and their international establishment in the Berne Convention. As the Australian representative aptly stated, authors' rights are based on authors: "The whole structure of the Convention was designed to protect the rights of identifiable authors. With a work of folklore there was no such author."[33] While the definition of an author had obviously been clarified, there was no common understanding of what constituted folklore. While the Czech representative took it for granted that these were "anonymous works with no publisher who could represent the author" and the French delegate spoke of "age-old anonymous works" as a matter of course, the Congolese representative fundamentally questioned this concept: "Folklore could be the product of a tribe, a family or even a particular person in that family; the definition of the term varied from country to country. Folklore could also be regarded as including a work which had been forgotten but which might have been the exclusive property of a family or a group."[34]

The recording and exclusive exploitation of folklore music by members of European states was compared to looting cultural assets for European museums. The developing countries saw themselves as the legitimate custodians of authorless music, which had to be treated as a phenomenon of the present, not of the past. The Congolese representative encapsulated the cultural biases on which these principles were based when he criticized the proposal to subsume folklore under the category of "anonymous works"; these works were not anonymous but rather the product of tribes, families, or individual members of these social groups.[35]

However, folklore remained a marginal issue at the Stockholm conference. The disputes between the new nations and the old signatories of the Berne Convention centered around exceptions for developing countries to support education, development, and culture (for example translations). The question of folklore was not discussed in further detail. The British delegate opined that there was no sense in debating it at that time because, for example, he saw no way of incorporating folklore into British law. Ultimately, folklore was not integrated into the agreement. This was just the first stage in the failure to incorporate the concerns of developing countries at the Stockholm revision conference. This failure finally became manifest when the member states did not ratify the agreed revision text and it was dropped and reworked (the industrial countries rejected the additional protocol with reduced requirements for developing countries, for which India had campaigned heavily). In 1967, the U.S. also declared that it could not enter into the Berne Convention under these conditions; the reason given was not the excessive requirements for the U.S. but the high concessions made for developing countries.[36] The U.S. slowly began to catch up with Europe. It would be merely a matter of time before the U.S. would surpass Europe with its ever-stricter copyright concepts.

The 1971 Paris version of the Berne Convention did not mention folklore either. Only the representative for Bolivia—a country that belonged neither to the Berne Convention nor to the Universal Copyright Convention—addressed the question of folklore again in Paris. In July 1971, he reminded the conference participants that it was important for international law to ensure that the people profiting from copyright were actually composers "and not mere usurpers of the creation of other people."[37] He explained that Bolivia had taken action against such practices by declaring traditional, anonymous folk music to be state property and called on the international community to use such nationalization measures to protect a country's "folk heritage" and thus to maintain and preserve the rights of the anonymous people who created this legacy.

A note in the minutes was all that remained of his contribution. Article 15 of the Paris version of the Convention states that in the case of anonymous works, the publisher named on the work shall represent the author "and in this capacity he shall be entitled to protect and enforce the author's rights."[38] It did not mention whether folklore was included in these anonymous works.

The basic assumption of authors' rights, which since the eighteenth century had distinguished between the individual works of single creators and collective creations passed down orally through the generations, remained valid until the end of the 1980s. This distinction is of fundamental economic importance: While the music of developing nations was an economic resource that authors could exploit, the creators of traditional music remained without legal protection. Third parties were free to use and exploit these works.

Reinventing Tradition

It was not until the end of the 1980s that legal discourse again addressed the exclusion of traditional cultural assets from authors' rights.[39] In 1985, a UNESCO/WIPO Working Group on the Intellectual Property Aspects of Folklore Protection developed a "model provision" as a guide for national laws to protect folklore against "illicit exploitation and other prejudicial actions."[40] If folklore had remained an expression of national heritage back in the 1960s, it was now a vessel for "social identity."[41] The UNESCO/WIPO commission recommended that this protection be enshrined outside of copyright because traditional and modern cultural creation employ inherently different concepts of time: "Traditional creations of a community . . . are generally much older than the duration of copyright so that, for this reason alone, a copyright-type protection, limited to the life of the author and a relatively short period thereafter, does not offer to folklore a long enough protection."[42] A new argument (folklore requires greater protection) had been found to leave the old copyright untouched.

In 1989, UNESCO issued a paper titled *Recommendation on the Safeguarding of Traditional Culture and Folklore*. Discourse had evolved in the meantime; traditional cultural assets were now reinterpreted and considered endangered and worthy of protection: "Recognizing the extreme fragility of the traditional forms of folklore, particularly those aspects relating to oral tradition and the risk that they might be lost."[43] Tradition was now elevated to the universal legacy of humanity, and legal protection for folklore was urgently recommended "in a manner inspired by the protection provided for intellectual productions." The point of reference for protection now shifted from the "nation" to "humanity." While the 1985 "model provision" still described folklore as the "living cultural heritage of the nation, developed and maintained by the communities within the nation,"[44] in 1989 folklore became a vehicle for international understanding, "part of the universal heritage of humanity," a "powerful means of bringing together different people and social groups."[45] It was clear that, in these new semantic contexts, folklore could attract more attention in international law.

The softening or even dissolution of central authors' rights distinctions enshrined in music copyright since the nineteenth century (recently observed in international law) is inconceivable without postcolonial discourse on traditional culture and folklore. In the 1990s, ethnomusicology scrutinized its own involvement in the music industry and criticized copyrights as ethnocentric and the integration of folklore into African legislation as nationalistic.[46] However, this general criticism of intellectual ownership of traditional culture did not go unquestioned itself; Michael Brown criticized this criticism as "romantic assumptions,"[47] and in his 1999 *Yearbook for Traditional Music*, Martin Scherzinger emphasized that copyright need not be ethnocentric a priori but that the concept itself contains an inherent ethnocentrism: "The same kind of thinking . . . separates human beings into non-Western groups, on the one hand, and Western individuals, on the other. It separated their stylized patterns of behavior into non-Western ritual as opposed to Western culture, their creative activity into non-Western craft as opposed to Western art and their music into non-Western social activity as opposed to Western aesthetic autonomy."[48] Simon Harrison also criticized the notion that traditional practices such as rituals are a priori the property of communities;[49] cultural anthropology research shows that specific groups and individuals are also granted the exclusive right to perform rituals, teach them, and pass them on to others. If we follow Harrison's argument, the distinction between modern individual authorship and traditional collectives is, in fact, fragile and cannot continue to be used as a legal basis without reflection.

When, in 1998, a new WIPO commission began to negotiate the integration of tradition into the international legal structure of authors' rights, the old concepts from the nineteenth century were no longer sacrosanct.[50] Old criteria such as the recording of a work in some form, individual authorship, and limited protection periods will likely be softened or abandoned in a future global legal framework. Folklore was now to be subsumed as a potential source of "innovation" and "creativity" under the concept of "traditional knowledge." Timelessness and a lack of author, two attributes that the modern era ascribed to tradition, will perhaps no longer be an obstacle to inclusion in the legal tradition. After all, tradition—at least in law—will at some time be modernized.

Conclusion

Legal Histories of Media Transformation

This project began with two present-day conflicts: First the Google Library copyright dispute, which had provoked a cultural struggle between Europe and the U.S. by 2005, when Jean-Noël Jeanneney, president of the National Library of France, realized that Google's copying project would bring about an American hegemony.[1] Second, the music file sharing dispute, which became a politically charged warzone when "internet activists" drew on political language to counter "copyright" with a "copyleft."

With my historical background, however, I quickly became skeptical of seemingly simple explanations. It cannot be denied that the internet endangered copyright. However, monocausal explanations, short time scales, and knee-jerk references to major epochal changes are just three good reasons for history scholars to counteract obvious facts with historically motivated questions. Duty bound to understand the present by exploring the past, I chose to study the regulation of library copies and music recordings in order to historicize Google Library and file sharing and place them in the context of social, economic, media, and legal developments.

One method employed by historical scholars is to use legal sources as seismographs while researching the history of other phenomena; these sources show how legal conflicts developed, yet can also be taken with a pinch of salt. My study therefore has three objectives, the first being to historicize the copyright conflict. This requires us to investigate a long time span beginning around 1850, when modern copyright laws were developed, and ending in 1980, before the advent of the internet. Second, copyright conflicts are to be taken as an opportunity to examine the social, economic, cultural, and political causes and consequences of media transformation. To achieve this, sources have been "repurposed" and read from a perspective that considers not only the law but also media in particular, as well as the economy, science and academia, and politics. Third, this book aims to indirectly reveal new perspectives on changes in the relationships between the Old World of Europe and the New World of the U.S. I also sought to examine how the reproduction practices of traditional cultural exporters differed from the copying norms of importers, how these various starting points changed over time, and to what degree they influenced each other.

Writing and Recording

When copyrights were invented in the eighteenth century, their aim was to regulate conflicts between publishers, reprinters, and authors regarding the reproduction of printed materials. The concept of a "work" was used to protect an "intangible asset"—a concept that shaped German copyright doctrine from the outgoing nineteenth century and the time of Josef Kohler—or "intellectual property," as this legal field was known in France. Economic considerations were central to music copyrights from the outset; they were one of the reasons why copyrights were developed in the first place and also influenced their composition. The way copyrights were formulated had a favorable impact on how music could be exploited. The doctrine prevailed that only composers, lyricists, and publishers could adapt and package musical works into marketable units. The expansion of copyright in the mid-nineteenth century had the opposite effect to free trade, restricting the free exchange of cultural assets. Copyrights also aided protectionist cultural policies and protected national music industries; ironically, copyrights grew stronger when integrated into free trade agreements.

The written form was a central criterion of mid-nineteenth-century musical copyright. Music not committed to writing and oral/community-based musical practices were excluded from copyright's legal structure. The concept of a written composition was developed ex negativo as the antithesis to tradition and orality even though, in practice, these distinctions were porous and triggered legal conflicts.

With the rise of the phonograph, writing lost its monopoly as the only medium for recording music. Once voices could be recorded via mechanical means, singing artists were incorporated into the law; this benefited com-posers, preserving their rights in the new era of the phonographic industry. The rights of performers remained tied to the rights of composers.

A reproduction concept developed that broke away from the notion of reprinting, put reproduction on an equal footing with exploitation, and thus offered ever-broader protection for intangible assets. The development of the phonographic industry challenged old author/publisher relationships and was accompanied by discussions of market power and monopolization in the U.S. and Germany. In both countries, a compulsory license was intro-duced when licenses for the media-based storage and distribution of music were enshrined in law. Authors' and publishers' work authority was relaxed and in some cases replaced with compensation systems based on monetary transactions.

In the nineteenth century, reproduction took on further social func-tions beyond economic exploitation; photographic reproduction techniques evolved to include the copying of manuscripts and printed materials in librar-ies. As notions of "global cultural heritage" developed, reproduction became a means of conservation and distribution and a vehicle for internationalist visions. Tied to a specific location, libraries were now regarded as a conser-vation risk and a hindrance to knowledge access, cosmopolitan attitudes, and progress. U.S. librarians and scholars became interested in acquiring copies of European library stocks. Copies could remedy a lack of tradition and could be used to acquire foreign cultural assets. Scholars discovered that photographic reproduction techniques could aid objectivity and rationaliza-tion, speed up their work, and soon provide an alternative to books. The option to bind copies, copy them again as required, and reproduce them via pictures rather than the pen freed scholars from transcription (tied to edit-ing projects) and from spatial and temporal restrictions. Until the end of the 1920s, authors and publishers remained certain that the new reproduction technologies would not jeopardize their interests or copyright but were a vehicle for scientific progress.

Collecting Societies and Research Materials

Music exploitation (based on license systems) via records, radio, and sound films was established and expanded between 1915 and 1945. The music royalty economy was based on collecting societies, which developed in nineteenth-century France in the tradition of bureaucratic agencies and expanded into other countries until they were usurped by national societies copying the French model. The collecting societies combined the interests of publishers, lyricists, and composers. Their admission rules and assessment criteria were based on the paradigm of writing developed in the nineteenth century and required members to have a certain number of compositions. Structured as cooperatives, the societies portrayed themselves as counterbalancing the commercially focused music industry. The societies liked to use prominent composers as figureheads in court and parliament and later played an influential role in composing and restructuring national laws and revising international agreements. In doing so, they evolved from collecting societies for license fees into powerful organizations that managed their own musical repertoire and, in the 1930s, began to look more and more like trusts and corporations. Parallels can be seen between the rhetoric used during the corporatist restructuring of the royalty economy in Germany's National Socialism era and that of the U.S.'s privately organized, monopolistic licensing. In both countries, there were resounding calls for strong, bureaucratically organized *visible hands* to handle the "chaos" of market forces and return some order to the complex situation. In the polarization crisis of the 1930s, media became symbols of social erosion and were stylized as a danger to cultural works, while copyright was appropriated as a means of protecting the artist from the media's destabilizing and corrosive impact on culture.

Authors and publishers had molded copyright discourse until the 1930s; as radio boomed, they found themselves challenged by new interest groups, which also formed international associations. The international regulations of the Berne Convention were joined by the contractual norms of international license agreements. Motivated by social policy and labor law, the International Labour Organization (ILO) also developed an interest in performers' rights during the economic crisis; performers had become more important thanks to the phonographic industry and radio, and they were dependent on these sources of income. Authors and publishers had traditionally used copyright to preserve their interests, so the ILO, the phonographic industry, and the broadcasting companies sought new legal norms (neighboring rights) outside of copyright.

In the crisis discourse of the 1930s, the new medium of radio was portrayed as the sole cause of the social and economic crisis—particularly in the U.S., where the collecting society ASCAP and the commercial radio companies fought for control of license fees and the music repertoire played on radio stations. ASCAP's restrictive admission rules (which offered membership only to established composers published on paper) proved to be its downfall, enabling radio stations to seek out an alternative music repertoire. Commercial radio stations discovered the traditional music passed down orally through the generations that had been excluded or neglected by ASCAP; this opened up the radio music market to the white rural folk tradition, Latin music, and African American music. For the empirical social researchers who emigrated from Germany to the U.S. during the National Socialist era, the radio war that escalated around 1940 provided social-science evidence for their theory that music renown is merely a consequence of radio advertising. The copyright conflict surrounding royalty fees became an argument within cultural industry criticism and thus part of the anti-American sentiment of the postwar period. At the same time, the radio war helped American performing artists to reach an audience beyond the East Coast and to offer European listeners appealing alternatives that would, in turn, be criticized as Americanization.

Academic and library copying practices differed significantly between the U.S. and Europe: In the U.S., this period was shaped by the development and analytical contemplation of alternative reproduction and organizational structures beyond the tradition of publishers, letterpress printing, and copyrights. In Europe, these issues were barely discussed. The interwar period was a time of internationalism and awakening for American scholarship. During the crisis years, a group of scholars and librarians funded by the state and sponsored by foundations realized that reproduction technologies could be used for research resources. They developed theories (extremely striking from a media history perspective) about the consequences of alternative reproduction media for publishers, authors, and scholars: Libraries would gradually revert to acting like publishers, as they had before letterpress printing was invented, and knowledge production and consumption would therefore also change. These developments occurred in connection with the New Deal, which encompassed much more than anticyclical economic policy and social reforms, and also inspired new forms of knowledge organization, avant-garde reflection on the media, and activities that questioned copyright in the academic environment. "Authors' interests" were criticized for obstructing scholarship, while copyright was denounced as an obsolete model tied to the publishing system and printing trade. America's Congress traditionally strove for particularist copyright in the interests of the country; in the 1930s, however, the Department of State became interested in copyright and advocated an internationalist policy that included the U.S. joining the Berne Convention. In contrast, during the Great Depression and the early war years, some scholars and librarians articulated a liberal American model based on the free circulation of ideas that opposed the European copyright model under the aegis of the Berne Convention.

Private Copies and Universal Norms

The postwar period was shaped by the development of new technologies (tape, Xerox, and computers), the U.S.'s emancipation from the Berne Convention's international copyright agreement hitherto influenced by Europe, the increasing social significance of the American scientific community, new home media practices using entertainment electronics, and, finally, criticism of copyright's foundations during a renaissance of oral music traditions excluded from authors' rights.

Designed by an exclusive group of lobbyists, copyright began attracting more and more criticism, not least due to new media that were to be used in new ways and increasingly challenged the legitimacy of copyright norms. By the time the internet was developed in the 1990s, copyright had been in crisis since the 1960s at the latest.

At first glance, this idea is disputed by the invention of device fees in Germany in the 1960s, which invalidated the previous specification that authors' rights restrictions would only apply to commercial reproduction. This continued a development, set in motion by the regulation of records, to link all media-based music storage or distribution with license fees for creators. However, the trend to link media usage with monetary transactions did not change the fact that a new generation of music consumers using magnetic tapes saw themselves as part of a new electronic revolution that no longer shared or respected copyright's underlying moral values.

The U.S. scientific community no longer identified with copyright either; their way had been paved in the 1930s by a generation of pioneers that used microfilm to establish informational infrastructures in research institutions. By the time Xerox enabled documents to be copied in seconds at the touch of a button, scholars did not want to give up their habitual practice. They emphasized that copies were more than just substitutes for buying a book or a journal—they were a new form of communication and knowledge transfer better suited to the information explosion and rapidly diminishing citation phases in academic journals than the practices established with old media. By 1967, Xerox debates had been eclipsed by plans for national information systems using networked computers. Fearing for their commercial futures, publishers wanted to apply their old privileges to the new media by introducing license fees; meanwhile, scientists, engineers, and science and technology policymakers sensed an opportunity to help establish autonomous communication for the sciences. Computers also challenged the established legal categories; the definition of reproduction had to be clarified in relation to computer-based data transfer. The scientific community resisted attempts by publishers and authors to draw the line at data input. Trumpeting the warning that strict computer regulation would impede scientific progress, scientists found themselves backed up by a mighty army of military-related and state-financed research institutions. The scientific community had huge political clout during the Cold War; as a consequence, copyrights for Xerox copies and databases were treated liberally in the U.S. in the 1960s and 1970s.

Another central foundation of musical authors' rights—the exclusion of oral traditions from copyright—also experienced difficulties in the 1960s. Long neglected by the music industry, this form of musical creation had been adopted by folklore researchers back in the nineteenth century. However, the practice established at this time—to grant collectors authors' rights that were not available to the musicians themselves—attracted criticism in the 1960s. When the new, decolonialized African and Asian national states were called upon to submit to international copyright, they also demanded that folklore be integrated into the legal structure. This demand was not met until the 1990s, reflecting the foundational distinction between oral tradition and modern, individual authorship. It was not until this distinction was re-analyzed within postcolonial criticism that the way was paved to rethink the integration of tradition into authors' rights. From a historical perspective, it is doubtful that copyright will actually become a universal global law protecting all forms of knowledge and cultural assets. It is far more likely that the numerous contradictions inherent in this legal area will regenerate and take on new forms as media, economics, politics, and technology develop and that copyright's credibility and enforceability will be consistently undermined.

Copyright was developed in the eighteenth century to regulate conflicts between publishers and reprinters, and the aesthetic and legal figure of the author was created to achieve this goal. The result was an alliance of convenience that in reality was liable to prolong these conflicts; this alliance will be consistently expanded to encompass new, rival media that since the nineteenth century have been disrupting the legal structure originally based on letterpress printing.

Yet this legal structure withstands every tremor, perhaps because it requires constant reinforcement. Copyright will always be at risk because it establishes ownership. It will be contested because it awards to some what it denies to others. It will be seen as unjust because it gives the individual an advantage over the collective with the aim of establishing corrective justice. Copyright was and remains a "loose-fish," to borrow Herman Melville's 1851 description of the laws of American whalers in *Moby Dick*.[2] How else can we explain the expansion of the © symbol, which originated in Anglo-Saxon law, into a global symbol, if not as an act of naming and preserving authors' constantly imperiled ownership of their works? How else can we describe the recurrent rhetoric about the murder of art by small-time piracy and mighty monopolies, if not as battle cries in intellectual property disputes? And what are attempts to link authors with works since the eighteenth century, if not aspirations to transform "loose-fish" into "fast-fish"?

At present, we cannot know whether digitalization and its technological means will put an end to this showdown by enabling one party to take ownership. The waters are choppy, we are all in their midst, and anyone who claims to understand and control them is sorely mistaken.

FURTHER READING

Bibliographic Essay

Ownership

In recent years, the theory and history of ownership have attracted increasing attention in the cultural sciences. Cultural anthropologist Marilyn Strathern and legal scholar Rosemary Coombe are pioneers in analyzing the development and cultural significance of tangible and intangible property.[1] Strathern emphasized the potentially stabilizing effect of owning ideas and things: "Ownership re-embeds ideas and products in an organism (whether a corporation, culture or individual author). Ownership gathers things together to a point by locating them in the owner, halting endless dissemination, effecting an identity."[2] Coombe, however, also highlights the destabilizing impact of proprietary rights and the unsettling effect of extending ownership to new fields: "The extension of proprietary rights to cultural forms has created immense new fields of potential economic value, engendered new industries, and raised a host of legal and ethical quandaries."[3] Historian Rebekka Habermas recently described the legal regulation of ownership as the incubator of modern law.[4] According to Habermas, modern German law developed from petty thefts in the mid-nineteenth century. Together, jurists, police officers, plaintiffs, defendants, witnesses, criminologists, social statisticians, and court reporters created a new, modern concept of ownership after old legal rights had been detached from social and emotional contexts and reduced to legally admissible issues.

Modern Copyright

Brad Sherman and Lionel Bently have theorized that the period around 1850 was a turning point in the history of copyright; it was at this point that "modern" copyright emerged.[5] Sherman and Bently use the term *modern* to refer to the international standardization of national law and the abstraction of concepts. Copyright was no longer restricted to literature but encompassed literature and art "in the widest sense."[6] In some respects, copyright still faces some of the challenges of the pre-modern era, as "the law still often finds itself in the uncomfortable situation where it must first distil the nature of the intangible property."[7] Sherman and Bently's suggestion that 1850 was a turning point and the start of "modern" copyright was the starting point of this book, despite criticism of their grand theory that the ongoing standardization and abstraction of copyright helped to modernize society.

In recent years, British legal history has strongly emphasized the cross-fertilization that occurs between the laws of different countries, revealing the *"copyright v. droit d'auteur/Urheberrecht* debates"[8] that dominated legal discourse in the nineteenth and twentieth centuries to be a myth cultivated in the age of nationalism. In contrast, German copyright study maintained a national focus; this includes Elmar Wadle's extensive oeuvre on the nineteenth century[9] and more recent legal history dissertations on legislation in the German empire,[10] the Weimar Republic,[11] and the revision process in the postwar society of the Federal Republic of Germany.[12]

For a long time, the analysis of copyright by US legal history scholars was a by-product of legislation.[13] In the 1990s, a field of research developed between legal and literary studies that looked at the "sprawling"[14] specialist field of intellectual property from a cultural science perspective.[15] Peter Jaszi, for example, pointed out that while the romantic concept of authorship established in the eighteenth century may have persisted in legislation and case law in nineteenth- and twentieth-century American copyright, the content of copyright and the legal definition of the author changed.[16]

One key conclusion from this recent research is that copyrights were not internationalized and standardized (with the exception of France) after national legislation; international regulations preceded national laws.[17] The history of international copyright was long restricted to the legal context; in the 1990s, historians such as Hannes Siegrist expanded the field to include social history. In Germany, Siegrist pioneered legal history with a social focus.[18] He put forward a theory of "propertization" in the wake of "liberalization, Europeanization, and globalization"[19] and discussed the increasing importance of intellectual property as a phenomenon of "possessive individualism"[20] in the "modern era" (since 1600) that could also be seen in agriculture, industry, and trade and accommodated demands from international markets for attribution of ownership.[21]

Overall, we have established that even the most recent research largely treats the US and Europe as two separate, monolithic blocks; until 1989 the US and Europe had two opposing international law systems, albeit with some overlaps. The transatlantic legal and media space is, however, important to attaining a historical understanding of the most recent developments in the recently concluded twentieth century. Branded as the book market's biggest pirate by Europe in the nineteenth century, the US began to outstrip

Europe—no longer as the custodian of the free international flow of ideas but as advocates of expanded copyright.

Technical Standards

Technology has been a fundamental part of copyright discourse since the nineteenth century. Legal historian Elmar Wadle went so far as to talk of the "development of copyright in response to technical innovations."[22] He argues that authors' rights first gained general recognition in the mid-nineteenth century (when new printing technologies were developed with photography and lithography) and thus freed themselves from the reprinting privileges of the early modern period. This set the legal process in motion, after which all technical innovations of the twentieth century could be easily integrated into the existing legal system. This is based on a positivist idea, absolutely comparable with scientific concepts, that law has constantly improved itself via technological catalysts. It was not until the "major development phases" of the outgoing twentieth century that problems occurred.

This argument fails to convince on multiple levels: A positivist legal concept ("improvement") interprets technology as an external factor ("these technical events") that disrupts the social order, which the law is to restore.[23] The American jurist Jessica Litman came to the opposite verdict in her analysis of twentieth-century copyright revisions (1909 and 1976).[24] According to Litman, the US legislative process, which is shaped by lobbyist negotiations, incorporates only established stakeholders. Negotiated compromises consider neither recent technological developments nor the flexibility required for future technological developments. Both of these analyses are impotent and unsatisfactory; they focus solely on the success or failure of a regulation strategy, do not ask what happens to technology when it is regulated, and, conversely, are not interested in examining how legal, economic, and scientific practices change when a new technology is integrated into the old law.

When new techniques were developed for regulating electronic media, the links between new technology and standardization became a focal area. Lawrence Lessig has emphasized that, alongside traditional laws, the internet introduced a new software- and hardware-based digital code.[25] These norms, ostensibly purely technological, have immense legal, political, social, and economic significance because, by means of standards, they favor regulations that are superior to traditional types of regulation: "This development will cause a shift in effective regulatory power—from law to code, from sovereigns to software. Just as there was a push toward a convergence on a simple set of network protocols, there will be a push toward convergence on a simple set of rules to govern transaction."[26] As a result of code-based regulation, norms are increasingly incorporated into technology. One example of these complex processes is the MP3 format, the standard for digital music.[27] As Jonathan Sterne and Tarleton Gillespie have shown, the MP3 was originally developed in the early 1990s as a standardized format for data exchange within the unplanned interaction between hackers, companies, and standardization organizations. What was initially conceived as an open system evolved into a new norm paradigm. The use of technology is no longer regulated through the law; instead, technology is produced and adapted in such a way that it can be regulated through the technology itself.

Miloš Vec has pointed out that nineteenth-century economics, technology, and knowledge not only encouraged the internationalization of law but also spawned fundamentally new forms of regulation that went beyond the scope of both the nation and the practices previously subsumed under law.[28] In doing so, he entered new legal history territory. His studies on technology normalization analyze the growing relevance of extralegal normalization and self-regulation in knowledge- and technology-based societies and the associated conflicts between legal and engineering cultures since the nineteenth century.

NOTES

Introduction

1. Kohler, *Das Autorrecht, eine zivilistische Abhandlung* (1880). On Josef Kohler's life and works, see Erler, "Josef Kohler" (1978); Adrian et al., *Josef Kohler und der Schutz des geistigen Eigentums in Europa* (1996).

2. "No. 506 Gesetz, betreffend das Urheberrecht an Schriftwerken, Abbildungen, musikalischen Kompositionen und dramatischen Werken. Vom 11. Juni 1870" (1870).

3. Before Josef Kohler, in the 1870s, some German jurists considered copyright from the perspective of jurisprudence; see Klostermann, *Das Urheberrecht an Schrift- und Kunstwerken, Abbildungen, Compositionen, Photographien, Mustern und Modellen, nach deutschem und internationalem Rechte systematisch dargestellt* (1876); Wächter, *Das Urheberrecht an Werken der bildenden Künste, Photographien und gewerblichen Mustern* (1877). For copyright theories in Germany in the nineteenth century, see Klingenberg, "Vom persönlichen Recht zum Persönlichkeitsrecht" (1979).

4. Kohler, *Das Autorrecht* (1880), 90.

5. Ibid., 2.

6. Ibid., 78.

7. Ibid., 98.

8. Ibid., 51–53.

9. Ibid., 53.

10. Stobbe, *Handbuch des deutschen Privatrechts* (1885), 2.

11. Niklas Luhmann has described this as historical semantics; in this case, "semantics" is independent of context. See Luhmann, *Gesellschaftsstruktur und Semantik* (1993), 1:19.

12. Kohler, *Recht und Persönlichkeit in der Kultur der Gegenwart* (1914), 268.

13. Kohler was one of the founders of the *Zeitschrift für vergleichende Rechtswissenschaft* (Journal of Comparative Law) in 1878.

14. Kohler also wrote about Islamic business law, Chinese penal law, Aztec law, Japanese law, vendettas, the prehistory of marriage, and totemism.

15. Kohler, *Das Autorrecht, eine zivilistische Abhandlung* (1880), 103.

16. Kohler, *Recht und Persönlichkeit in der Kultur der Gegenwart* (1914), 256–257. On the theory that new regulatory forms developed through the Industrial Revolution, see Vec, *Recht und Normierung in der Industriellen Revolution* (2006). On the development of international law in the nineteenth century, see Koskenniemi, *The Gentle Civilizer of Nations* (2002).

17. Kohler, *Recht und Persönlichkeit in der Kultur der Gegenwart* (1914), 264.

18. Ibid., 264.

19. Ibid., 266. Kohler's extensive library was sold to a Japanese buyer after his death in 1919 and later was destroyed by an earthquake and tsunami. This can be seen as a symbol of how universalistic jurisprudence resonated in the outgoing nineteenth century and how visions of global socialization evaporated after World War I.

20. *GRUR* 1, no. 1 (1896), 1–2.

21. Kohler, "Dichter und Erfinder" (1896).

22. *GRUR* 1, no. 1 (1896), 1.

23. Kaplan, *An Unhurried View of Copyright* (1967), in particular his third lecture: "Proposals and Prospects," 79–128.

24. Ibid., 116.

25. Ibid., 118.

26. McLuhan, *The Gutenberg Galaxy: The Making of Typographic Man* (1962).

27. Kaplan, *An Unhurried View of Copyright* (1967), 118.

28. Ibid., 119.

29. "Copyright Bill: Interest Groups Stymie Changes in Copyright Law" (1968).

30. Breyer, "The Uneasy Case for Copyright" (1970). For a dissenting view, see Tyerman, "The Economic Rationale for Copyright Protection for Published Books" (1971). Breyer's response can be found in "Copyright: A Rejoinder" (1972). Breyer was appointed a Supreme Court justice in 1994.

31. Breyer, "The Uneasy Case for Copyright" (1970), 321.

32. Ibid., 348.

33. Henry, "Copyright: Its Adequacy in Technological Societies" (1974); Henry, "Copyright, Public Policy, and Information Technology" (1974).

34. Barthes, "The Death of the Author" (1967), 185; Foucault, *Was ist ein Autor?* (2000 [1969]).

35. Edelman, *Le droit saisi par la photographie* (1980).

36. See Boyle, *Shamans, Software, and Spleens* (1997); Lessig, *Code and Other Laws of Cyberspace* (1999).

37. Vaidhyanathan, *Copyrights and Copywrongs* (2001).

38. Lessig, *Code and Other Laws of Cyberspace* (1999).

39. Vaidhyanathan, *Copyrights and Copywrongs* (2001), 149–184.

40. Peter Jaszi in Stockholm in 1997, cited in Vaidhyanathan, *Copyrights and Copywrongs* (2001), 229.

41. Boyle, *Shamans, Software, and Spleens* (1997), 191.

42. Blumenberg, *Aspekte der Epochenschwelle* (1976), 7–33.

43. McLuhan, *The Gutenberg Galaxy* (1962), 275.

44. Alongside Marshall McLuhan's "Toronto School," this approach is used in Germany by Friedrich Kittler and his students in particular. See Kittler, *Grammophon, Film, Typewriter* (1986); Kittler, *Aufschreibesysteme 1800/1900* (1995). For a critical appraisal of Friedrich Kittler, see Winthrop-Young, *Friedrich Kittler zur Einführung* (2005).

45. Bloch, *The Historian's Craft* (1992 [1949]), 59.

46. Benjamin, "Über den Begriff der Geschichte" (1991), 697.

47. On the copyright problem in the artistic avant-garde (not covered in this book), see Stokes, *Art and Copyright* (2001); Weibel, "Die Frage der Fotografie im Wiener Aktionismus als die Frage nach Autor und Autonomie in der Fotografie" (1993); Saint-Amour, ed., *Modernism and Copyright* (2011). On copyright for photog-

raphy, see Plumpe, *Der tote Blick* (1990), 53–95; for film: Gaines, "Early Cinema's Heyday of Copying" (2006) and Decherney, "Copyright Dupes: Piracy and New Media in Edison v. Lubin (1903)" (2007); for video: Hilderbrand, *Inherent Vice* (2009); for photography and film: Dommann, "Mobile Medien, reguliertes Eigentum" (2007).

48. Gumbrecht and Pfeiffer, *Materialität der Kommunikation* (1995).

49. On the history and theory of reproduction and copies, see Benjamin, *Das Kunstwerk im Zeitalter seiner technischen Reproduzierbarkeit* (1990); Schwartz, *The Culture of the Copy* (1996).

50. Luhmann, *Das Recht der Gesellschaft* (1995), 138.

51. Gaston Bachelard sees epistemes as exploring the "conditions of objective knowledge" and revealing the principles of "discursive objectivity." See Bachelard, *Die Bildung des wissenschaftlichen Geistes* (1987), 347–348.

52. This method is based on constructivist presuppositions and a preference for analyzing practices; see Latour, *Science in Action* (1987); Latour, *La fabrique du droit* (2002).

53. Grimm, *Recht und Staat der bürgerlichen Gesellschaft* (1987), esp. 399–427.

54. Fögen, "Die ungeliebten Kinder der Rechtswissenschaft" (2009), 92–93.

55. Wehler, *Deutsche Gesellschaftsgeschichte* (1987–2008), 1:9.

56. Grimm, "Die Bedeutung des Rechts in der Gesellschaftsgeschichte" (2000).

57. Willibald Steinmetz was one of the researchers in the German-speaking region to enter new empirical terrain in this field in the nineteenth century. See Steinmetz, *Begegnungen vor Gericht* (2002).

58. In the final third of the nineteenth century, the term *cultural technique* referred to techniques to cultivate, survey, and work the soil. More recently, the term has experienced a renaissance and metamorphosis within German media studies, referring to a concept for analyzing practices involved in the development of cultures. See Nanz and Siegert, eds., *ex machina* (2006); *Zeitschrift für Medien und Kulturforschung*, vol. 1 (2010): 101–219.

59. Vismann, *Akten* (2001); Vismann, "Tele-Tribunals: Anatomy of a Medium" (2003); Vismann, "Action Writing" (2002); Latour, *La fabrique du droit* (2002). On the mediality of the courts, see Gaiba, *The Origins of Simultaneous Interpretation* (1998); Downey, "Constructing 'Computer-Compatible' Stenographers" (2006); Vismann, *Medien der Rechtsprechung* (2011).

60. Teubner, "Global Bukowina" (1997).

61. Vec, "Aushöhlung des Staates?" (2000); Vec, "Verspäteter Gesetzgeber" (2002); Vec, *Recht und Normierung in der Industriellen Revolution* (2006), 293–377; Dommann, "08/15, QWERTY, PAL-SECAM, Paletten und MP3" (2009).

62. On the economic history of patents, see Machlup and Penrose, "The Patent Controversy in the Nineteenth Century" (1950); Fleischer, *Patentgesetzgebung und chemisch-pharmazeutische Industrie im deutschen Kaiserreich (1871–1918)* (1984); Tanner, "Property rights, Innovationsdynamik und Marktmacht" (1996). The only economic history study to examine patents and copyright as factors in US economic developments remains Khan, *The Democratization of Invention* (2005).

63. See, for example, Stiglitz, "Knowledge as a Global Public Good" (1999).

64. Hurt and Schuchman, "The Economic Rationale of Copyright" (1966), 432. This suggestion has been taken up in more recent works. Theoretical: Hutter, "On the Construction of Property Rights in Aesthetic Ideas" (1995). Empirical, using the

example of file sharing: Oberholzer-Gee and Strumpf, "The Effect of File Sharing on Record Sales" (2007). After analyzing log-ins on file-sharing servers, Oberholzer-Gee and Strumpf were unable to show that music downloads have any significant effect on sales of sound storage media.

65. North, *Institutionen, institutioneller Wandel und Wirtschaftsleistung* (1992).

66. Kevles, "Patents, Protections, and Privileges" (2007).

67. Biagioli, "Aporias of Scientific Authorship" (1999); Biagioli and Galison, eds., *Scientific Authorship* (2003); McSherry, *Who Owns Academic Work?* (2001); Johns, "Intellectual Property and the Nature of Science" (2006).

68. This theory is posited in Siegrist, "Die Propertisierung von Gesellschaft und Kultur" (2007), 49.

69. See Osterhammel, *Geschichtswissenschaft jenseits des Nationalstaats* (2001), 40. A history of transnational relationships does not aim to compare countries and civilizations; instead, it analyzes the movement of people, goods, and ideas as the transfer and acquisition of cultural assets.

70. "To study and compile data on the reproduction and use of copyrighted works of authorship in conjunction with automatic systems capable of storing, processing, retrieving and transferring information and by various forms of machine reproduction." National Commission on New Technological Uses of Copyrighted Works (CONTU), *Final Report* (1979), 5.

71. On the conceptual history of the "modern," see Gumbrecht, "Modern, Modernität, Moderne" (1978).

72. Berne Convention (since 1886) and Universal Copyright Convention (since 1952).

73. Brake, "Die Digital-Liberalen" (2006).

Chapter 1. Sheet Music

1. Foucault, "Die Wahrheit und die juristischen Formen" (2002), 736.

2. Foucault, "Was ist ein Autor?" (2000).

3. Ibid., 10. In the 1980s, this was expanded to become the key to understanding the civil society of the eighteenth century: See, for example, Sherman and Strowel, eds., *Of Authors and Origins* (1994).

4. For a dissenting view on the origin myth, see Coombe, "Challenging Paternity" (1994), 422.

5. On early modern printing privileges, see Loewenstein, "The Script in the Marketplace" (1985); Loewenstein, *The Author's Due* (2002); Long, "Invention, Authorship, 'Intellectual Property,' and the Origin of Patents" (1991); Long, *Openness, Secrecy, Authorship* (2001). On developments in Germany between the sixteenth and eighteenth centuries, see Vogel, "Deutsche Urheber- und Verlagsrechtsgeschichte zwischen 1450 und 1850" (1978). This study broke new ground by linking legal history and socio-historical perspectives. The antithesis of the privileged printer and author is the "pirate," a figure that Adrian Johns believes to have originated in Great Britain around 1660. See Johns, *Piracy* (2009).

6. On Germany, see Woodmansee, "The Genius and the Copyright" (1984). On France, see Hesse, "Enlightenment Epistemology and the Laws of Authorship in

Revolutionary France, 1777–1793" (1990); Scott, "Authorship, the Académie, and the Market in Early Modern France" (1998); Brown, "After the Fall" (1999). On Great Britain, see Rose, *Authors and Owners* (1993). For comparisons of Britain and Germany, see Biernacki, "The Social Manufacture of Private Ideas in Germany and Britain, 1750–1830" (2000).

7. Plumpe, "Eigentum—Eigentümlichkeit" (1979); Fleischhauer, "Eigentümlichkeit" (2006).

8. Barron, "Copyright Law's Musical Work" (2006).

9. Bosse, *Autorschaft ist Werkherrschaft* (1981).

10. On the U.S., see Solberg, ed., *Copyright Enactments, 1783–1900* (1900), 35–39.

11. For the Prussian law, see "No. 1840 Gesetz" (1837); Wadle, "Der Bundesbeschluss vom 9. November 1837 gegen den Nachdruck," in *Geistiges Eigentum: Bausteine zur Rechtsgeschichte* (1996/2003), 1:222–265.

12. On Great Britain, see Seville, *The Internationalisation of Copyright Law* (2009), 135–140; Copinger and Skone James, *Copinger and Skone James on the Law of Copyright* (1948), 11–12.

13. For the Austrian law, see *Patent vom 19. Oktober 1846* (1846).

14. See Blanc, *Traité de la contrefaçon en tous genres et de sa poursuite en justice* (1855), 243.

15. "No. 1840 Gesetz" (1837), 166.

16. Ibid., 165.

17. Ibid., 168.

18. Ibid., 375.

19. Ibid., 376.

20. Ibid.

21. *Bericht an die nieder-österreichische Handels- und Gewerbekammer* (1853).

22. Ibid., 5, 60.

23. Ibid., 60.

24. Ibid.

25. Ibid.

26. Püttlingen, *Das musicalische Autorrecht: Eine juristischmusicalische Abhandlung* (1864).

27. *Bericht an die nieder-österreichische Handels- und Gewerbekammer* (1853), 14.

28. Ibid., 15.

29. Ibid., 20–21.

30. Ibid., 15.

31. Püttlingen, *Das musicalische Autorrecht* (1864), 1.

32. Ibid., 2.

33. Richter, *Kunst und Wissenschaft und ihre Rechte im Staate* (1863). For information on Karl Richter, see Mischler, "Richter, Karl Thomas" (1889).

34. Richter, *Kunst und Wissenschaft und ihre Rechte im Staate* (1863), 157.

35. Ibid., 25.

36. Ibid., 96.

37. Ibid., 131.

38. Ibid., 155.

39. Ibid., 203–204.

40. Kohler, *Das Autorrecht, eine zivilistische Abhandlung* (1880), 72.

41. On free trade: Pollard, "Free Trade, Protectionism, and the World Economy" (2001); Osterhammel, "Anthropologisches zum Freihandel" (2007); Trentmann, *Free Trade Nation: Commerce, Consumption, and Civil Society in Modern Britain* (2008). On the genesis of commercial law norms in the German Empire in the context of nineteenth-century globalization, see Petersson, *Anarchie und Weltrecht* (2009). On the normalization of industrialization, see Vec, *Recht und Normierung in der Industriellen Revolution* (2006).

42. On the Berne Convention, see Löhr, *Die Globalisierung geistiger Eigentumsrechte* (2010).

43. "Urheber" (1746), 1133–1134.

44. "Tradition" (1745), 925.

45. "Tradition" (1854–1860 [1935]).

46. Gumbrecht, "Modern, Modernität, Moderne" (1978). See also Jauss, "Literarische Tradition und gegenwärtiges Bewusstsein der Modernität" (1970).

47. See Gumbrecht, "Modern, Modernität, Moderne" (1978), 110.

48. Püttlingen, *Das musicalische Autorrecht* (1864), 15.

49. Ibid., 16.

50. *BAR E 22 Nr. 2377.*

51. Bauer, *Das musikalische Urheberrecht* (1890), v.

52. Richter, *Kunst und Wissenschaft und ihre Rechte im Staate* (1863), 62.

53. Goehr, *The Imaginary Museum of Musical Works* (1992).

54. Püttlingen, *Das musicalische Autorrecht* (1864), 46–48.

55. Ibid., 70.

56. Ibid., 70–71.

57. Ibid., 76.

58. Ashley, *Richard Strauss* (1999), 37–38. Hansen, *Richard Strauss* (2003), 23–37. It is worth noting that this affair does not appear in Manuela Schmidt's extensive study of Richard Strauss's copyright activities. After all, Richard Strauss began to champion copyrights for composers in 1898, shortly after the dispute with Luigi Denza. See Schmidt, *Die Anfänge der musikalischen Tantiemenbewegung in Deutschland* (2005), 188 et seq.

59. On the history of music boxes, see Clark, *Musical Boxes* (1948); Ord-Hume, *Clockwork Music* (1973). On the music box industry in St. Croix, see Piguet, *Les faiseurs de musiques* (1996).

60. Bolley, *Berichte über die Betheiligung der Schweiz* (1868), 23. The smallest instruments cost forty francs, the larger ones 400 to 500 francs.

61. Ibid., 32.

62. Ibid., 32.

63. Ibid., 33.

64. Smith, *Theorie der ethischen Gefühle* (2004), 336–337.

65. Berg, "From Imitation to Invention" (2002).

66. Kaufmann, "Literarisches und künstlerisches Eigenthum" (1889); Röthlisberger, "Urheberrecht" ([1903–1911]); *Schweizerisches Bundesblatt XVI, Band 2* (1864), 24–26; *Traités et conventions entre la Suisse et la France* (1866).

67. *Schweizerisches Bundesblatt XVIII, Band 1, Nr. 20* (1866), 657–658. In May 1866, the French state passed a law stating that the playing of musical compositions did not violate literary and artistic property.

68. *Schweizerisches Bundesblatt 34, Band 1, Nr. 15* (1882), 712; *Ministère des affaires étrangères* (1882).

69. Ibid., 5. For the exception for music boxes, see Article 14, 9.

70. *RGZ 22* (1888), 174–183. See also "De la reproduction sonore des compositions musicales par des instruments mécaniques" (1890); *Le Droit d'auteur 4* (1891), 15, 81–83. *Le Droit d'auteur 5* (1895), 78–79.

71. *RGZ 22* (1888), 177.

72. *RGZ 22* (1888), 175–176.

73. *Ludolf Waldmann's gewonnene Prozesse* (1889).

74. Klier and Seemann, "Kunstlieder im Volksmunde" (1930).

75. See the website of the Arnold Schönberg Center, http://www.schoenberg.at.

76. Waldmann spoke of "corrupted composition." See *Ludolf Waldmann's gewonnene Prozesse* (1889), 9.

77. Ibid., 14.

78. Ibid., (1889), 13.

79. Ibid., 27.

80. *RGZ 27* (1891), 60–69, here 66.

81. Weber, *Wirtschaft und Gesellschaft* (1980), 382–385.

Chapter 2. Images of Books

1. Giry, *Manuel de diplomatique* (1925), 41–50.

2. See Prou, "L'état actuel des publications de fac-similé de chartes et autres documents d'archives" (1905), 62.

3. Talbot, *The Pencil of Nature* (1969). For Talbot's photo theory, see Geimer, *Theorien der Fotografie zur Einführung* (2009), 13–18.

4. See the dissertation by Saxer, *Die Schärfung des Quellenblicks* (2013).

5. Prou, "L'état actuel des publications de fac-similé de chartes et autres documents d'archives" (1905), 63. Berger, "Les fac-similés photographiques et les calques, résumé de la polémique entre MM. de Pfugk-Harttung et Sybel" (1885), 718–719.

6. On the concept of mechanical objectivity, see Daston and Galison, "The Image of Objectivity" (1992).

7. Chatelain, "La photographie dans les bibliothèques" (1891).

8. Treplin, "Das Bibliotheksrecht" (1933), 621–627. Estivals, *Le dépôt légal sous l'ancien régime de 1537 à 1791* (1961).

9. On Great Britain, see Seville, *The Internationalisation of Copyright Law* (2009), 47–63.

10. Solberg, *Copyright Enactments, 1783–1900* (1900), 40.

11. Johnston, *History of the Library of Congress* (1904), 439, general information on the Copyright Collection 440–450. The Librarian of Congress published statistics in the first annual report from 1866: Of the 7,251 new acquisitions, 5,603 documents were purchased and 836 came from the Copyright Collection.

12. Solberg, *Copyright Enactments, 1783–1900* (1900), 62–63.

13. See Saxer, *Die Schärfung des Quellenblicks* (2013). Marc, "Bibliothekswesen" (1911), 59. For example A.W. Sijthoff in Leiden, who published facsimiles of Greek and Latin texts from 1897.

14. Krumbacher, "Die Photographie im Dienste der Geisteswissenschaften" (1906), 613. In the case of Sijthoff, this was 150 copies.

15. Marc, "Bibliothekswesen" (1911), 60.

16. Chatelain, "La photographie dans les bibliothèques" (1891).

17. Ibid., 230.

18. Ibid., 239.

19. Krumbacher, "Die Photographie im Dienste der Geisteswissenschaften" (1906), 646.

20. Bergmans, "Les tentatives antérieures d'entente internationale pour la reproduction des manuscrits" (1905), 44.

21. Osterhammel, *Die Verwandlung der Welt* (2009), 33–36. Gumbrecht, "Modern, Modernität, Moderne" (1978).

22. *Actes du Congrès International pour la reproduction des manuscrits, des monnaies et des sceaux* (1905), 265.

23. Molsdorf, "Einige Ratschläge bei der Beschaffung photographischer Einrichtungen für Bibliothekszwecke" (1901).

24. Gayley, "The Reproduction of Manuscripts from the American Point of View" (1905), 214.

25. Ibid., 206.

26. Ibid., 209.

27. Ibid., 210.

28. See Herren, *Hintertüren zur Macht* (2000). Vec, *Recht und Normierung in der Industriellen Revolution* (2006).

29. *Actes du Congrès international pour la reproduction des manuscrits, des monnaies et des sceaux* (1905), 300.

30. Ibid., 300.

31. Ibid., 306.

32. Ibid., 332.

33. Fiebiger, "Internationale Photographische Ausstellung, Dresden 1909" (1909). Kögel, *Die Photographie historischer Dokumente nebst den Grundzügen der Reproduktionsverfahren wissenschaftlich und praktisch dargestellt* (1914).

34. See Krumbacher, "Die Photographie im Dienste der Geisteswissenschaften" (1906), 632. In 1906, Karl Krumbacher published the first comprehensive description of how photography was used in the humanities. This study was also received in the U.S. and discussed in *The Library Journal* in 1908. Fretwell, "Photographic Copying in Libraries" (1908).

35. Conventional photographs cost between fifty-seven and seventy-two pfennigs or between 1.08 and 1.33 marks for larger formats. A prism recording cost between twenty-five and thirty pfennigs, or thirty-seven pfennigs if a photographer was engaged. Krumbacher, "Die Photographie im Dienste der Geisteswissenschaften" (1906), 620.

36. Ibid., 630.

37. Chatelain, "La photographie dans les bibliothèques" (1891), 229.

38. Krumbacher, "Die Photographie im Dienste der Geisteswissenschaften" (1906), 620.

39. Ibid., 608.

40. Ibid., 619.

41. Ibid., 619.

42. Marc, "Bibliothekswesen" (1911), 63.

43. Ibid., 62.

44. Krumbacher, "Die Photographie im Dienste der Geisteswissenschaften" (1906), 652.

45. Ibid., 652–653, 657.

46. See "L'organisation de la documentation" (1908). Otlet, *Traité de Documentation* (1934); Dommann, "Dokumentieren" (2008).

47. *La Poste par pigeons voyageurs* (1870–1871).

48. Kittler, *Grammophon, Film, Typewriter* (1986), 149.

49. "Le livre microphotographique" (1911), 215.

50. "Micro-Photographs as Documentary Records" (1907).

51. On Paul Otlet, see Levie, *L'homme qui voulait classer le monde* (2006).

52. Goldschmidt and Otlet, "Sur une forme nouvelle du livre" (1907).

53. Ibid., 44. Hartmann, ed., *Vom Buch zur Datenbank* (2012).

54. Vander Haeghen, "Le Livre de Demain" (1907).

55. "Le livre microphotographique" (1911), 220.

56. Ibid., 221.

57. Ibid. Newspaper clippings are another technique for tailored reading: Heesen, *Der Zeitungsausschnitt* (2006).

58. Swingle and Swingle, "The Utilization of Photographic Methods in Library Research Work" (1916).

59. Ibid., 804.

60. Ibid.

61. Ibid., 802.

62. Ibid.

63. See Taylor, *The Principles of Scientific Management* (1911).

64. *Photostat* (1918).

65. *Photostat and War Collections Exhibited at Princeton* (1918), 271.

66. Swingle and Swingle, "The Utilization of Photographic Methods in Library Research Work" (1916), 802–803.

67. Otlet, "Le traitement de la littérature scientifique" (1918), 494.

68. *Le Droit d'Auteur* 24 (1911), 148.

Chapter 3. Voice Recorders

1. Talbot, *The Pencil of Nature* (1969).

2. On Great Britain, see Copinger and Skone James, *Copinger and Skone James on the Law of Copyright* (1948), 12. On the U.S., see Sanger, *The Statutes at Large, Treaties and Proclamations of the United States of America from December 1863 to December 1865* (1866), 540: "To the same extent, and upon the same conditions as to the authors of prints and engravings."

3. See Plumpe, *Der tote Blick* (1990), 55–95. Dommann, "Mobile Medien, reguliertes Eigentum" (2007). For the negative theory of photography of Talbot, Benjamin, and Barthes, see Geimer, *Theorien der Fotografie zur Einführung* (2009), 60–69.

4. *Der Schutz der Photographien gegen unbefugte Nachbildungen* (1878).

5. See Hansen, *Das Urheberrecht in der Praxis der Postkarten-Industrie* (1908); Kohler, *Kunstwerkrecht* (1908).

6. On the media and technological history of the phonograph and the gramophone in the U.S., see Read and Welch, *From Tin Foil to Stereo* (1977); Thompson, "Machines, Music, and the Quest for Fidelity" (1995); Siefert, "Aesthetics, Technology, and the Capitalization of Culture" (1995); Peters, "Helmholtz und Edison" (2002); Sterne, *The Audible Past* (2003). On talking machines in Germany, see Gauss, *Nadel, Rille, Trichter* (2009).

7. Peters, "Helmholtz und Edison" (2002), 303.

8. Emil Berliner, "The Gramophone: Etching the Human Voice," in *Journal of the Franklin Institute* (June 22, 1888), 425–247, quoted in Siefert, "Aesthetics, Technology, and the Capitalization of Culture" (1995), 447.

9. "Schellack" (1904).

10. See "Grammophon-Konzert im Beethovensaal" (1903), 277.

11. See "Amerikanische Phonographenfabriken in Deutschland" (1904); Maisonneuve, *L' invention du disque 1877–1949* (2009).

12. Pathé, *Premier Empire du Cinéma* (1994), 17–23.

13. Schuster, *Das Urheberrecht der Tonkunst in Österreich, Deutschland und anderen europäischen Staaten* (1891), 163–164.

14. Donle, *Der Phonograph und seine Stellung zum Rechte* (1897), 25.

15. On Germany, see Ihering, "Rechtsschutz gegen injuriöse Rechtsverletzungen" (1885); Keyssner, *Das Recht am eigenen Bilde* (1896). On the U.S., see Warren and Brandeis, "The Right to Privacy" (1890). See also Dommann, "Schutz vor Kodak!" (2013).

16. See Belting, *Faces* (2013).

17. *GRUR* 5, no. 4 (1900), 131–132.

18. Eger, *Der Phonograph und das Urheberrecht* (1900).

19. Ibid., 270.

20. Ibid.

21. Ibid., 276.

22. Ibid., 283.

23. *Stenographische Berichte über die Verhandlungen des Reichstags. X. Legislaturperiode. II. Session. 1900/1902, 76. Sitzung. Donnerstag 18. April 1901*, 2197. See also "Éditeurs de musique et fabricants d'instruments de musique mécaniques" (1903).

24. *Stenographische Berichte über die Verhandlungen des Deutschen Reichstags. X. Legislaturperiode. II. Session. 1900/1902. Erster Band* (1901), 520–567.

25. Ibid., 527.

26. "Der Phonograph im neuen Deutschen Urheberrecht-Gesetz" (1901).

27. Ibid.

28. *Stenographische Berichte über die Verhandlungen des Reichstags. X. Legislaturperiode. II. Session. 1900/1902. Dritter Band, 76. Sitzung. Donnerstag 18. April 1901* (1901), 2201. On Arnold Nieberding, see Vortmann, "Nieberding, Arnold" (1998).

29. *Stenographische Berichte über die Verhandlungen des Reichstags. X. Legislaturperiode. II. Session. 1900/1902. Dritter Band, 76. Sitzung. Donnerstag 18. April 1901* (1901), 2202.

30. "Phonographischer Wettstreit" (1901).

31. "Phonographen-Konzerte" (1903); "Grammophon-Konzert im Beethoven-saal" (1903).

32. On the history of the motif and production of the dog/gramophone image, see also Sterne, *The Audible Past* (2003), 301–307.

33. *Phonographische Zeitschrift* 9, no. 48 (1908), 1500.

34. "Der 'Phonographen-Ton'" (1902).

35. Bergfeld, "Phonograph und Publikum" (1902).

36. *Phonographische Zeitschrift* 2, no. 22 (1901), 267.

37. "Verschiedene Qualitäten für Phonographenwalzen" (1901).

38. "Unberechtigtes Kopieren von Phonographen-Walzen" (1904), 31.

39. "Akustische Schutzmarken" (1907).

40. *Phonographische Zeitschrift* 9, no. 43 (1908), 1327.

41. "Generalversammlung des Bundes der Sprechmaschinenhändler Deutschlands vom 25. März 1908" (1908), 471.

42. "Das Urheberrecht und der Phonograph" (1903).

43. Maugras and Guégan, *Le cinématographe devant le droit* (1908); Lefebvre, "Dr. Eugène-Louis Doyen und die Anfänge des Chirurgie-Films" (2005); Dommann, "Mobile Medien, reguliertes Eigentum" (2007).

44. "Cour d'appel de Paris, 1ère chambre" (1905), 36.

45. Ibid.

46. "Phonographen-Streik in Frankreich" (1905).

47. "Der Pariser Phonographen-Streik" (1905).

48. "Urheberrecht an Phonogrammen" (1908).

49. "Der Sprechmaschinen-Rekord und das Urhebergesetz" (1906), 622.

50. Ibid., 622.

51. Eisenmann, *Das Urheberrecht an Tonkunstwerken* (1907).

52. Ibid., 49.

53. Ibid., 42–43.

54. Ibid., 44.

55. Ibid., 52.

56. Ibid., introduction by Josef Kohler, 1.

57. Ibid., 14.

58. Ibid., 52.

59. Kittler, *Grammophon, Film, Typewriter* (1986), 131.

60. For example, see Lussy, *Die Kunst des musikalischen Vortrags* (1886).

61. Kohler, "Autorschutz des reproduzierenden Künstlers" (1909).

62. Ibid., 232.

63. "Albert Osterrieth zum Gedächtnis" (1927).

64. Osterrieth, "Das Urheberrecht an Phonogrammen nach dem deutschen Gesetz vom 19. Juni 1901" (1907), 1468.

65. *RGZ* 73, no. 77 (1910), 294–298. Cohn-Schmidt, "Die Entscheidung des Reichsgerichts in der Kopierfrage" (1910).

66. *RGZ* 73, no. 77 (1910), 297.

67. Lindemann, *Gesetz* (1910), Section 2, 39.

68. Ibid., Section 2, 41–42.

69. See Copyright Act 1911, Section 19.

70. Bosse, *Autorschaft ist Werkherrschaft* (1981), 7.

Chapter 4. Canned Music

1. Röthlisberger, "Gesamtüberblick über die Vorgänge auf urheberrechtlichem Gebiete (1902 und 1903)" (1904), 18.

2. Solberg, *Copyright Enactments, 1783–1900* (1900). For the history of American copyright and its internationalization in the 19th century, see Seville, *The Internationalisation of Copyright Law* (2009).

3. Quoted in Solberg, *Copyright Legislation* ([1929]).

4. The typescripts of the minutes were published during the preparation of the 1976 Copyright Act. Brylawski and Goldman, eds., *Legislative History of the 1909 Copyright Act* (1976), vols. 1–3; see also Litman, "Copyright Legislation and Technological Change" (1989).

5. Quoted in Solberg, *Copyright Legislation* ([1929]).

6. See Bowker and Solberg, *Copyright, Its Law and Its Literature* (1886), 31.

7. "Conference on Copyright, First Session, Second Session," in Brylawski and Goldman, eds., *Legislative History of the 1909 Copyright Act* (1976), 1:7–209, 2:3–5.

8. "Conference on Copyright, Third Session," in Brylawski and Goldman, eds., *Legislative History of the 1909 Copyright Act* (1976), 3:5.

9. "Conference on Copyright, Second Session, Seventh Meeting: 10.15 a.m. Saturday November 4, 1905," in Brylawski and Goldman, eds., *Legislative History of the 1909 Copyright Act* (1976), 2:241–244, here 2:242.

10. "Conference on Copyright, Second Session, Fifth Meeting: 10.55 a.m. Friday November 3, 1905," in Brylawski and Goldman, eds., *Legislative History of the 1909 Copyright Act* (1976), 2:166.

11. *Arguments Before the Committees on Patents of the Senate and House of Representatives, Conjointly on the Bills S. 6330 and H. R. 19853 to Amend and Consolidate the Acts Respecting Copyright. June 6, 7, 8 and 9, 1906* (1906), 3.

12. Bowker, *Copyright* (2002).

13. *Arguments Before the Committees on Patents of the Senate and House of Representatives, Conjointly on the Bills S. 6330 and H. R. 19853 to Amend and Consolidate the Acts Respecting Copyright. June 6, 7, 8 and 9, 1906* (1906), 3–26.

14. Ibid., 23.

15. Ibid., 24.

16. Ibid.

17. Ibid.

18. On John Philip Sousa, see Bierley, *The Incredible Band of John Philip Sousa* (2006), esp. 78–83; Warfield, "John Philip Sousa and 'The Menace of Mechanical Music'" (2009).

19. *Arguments Before the Committees on Patents of the Senate and House of Representatives, Conjointly on the Bills S. 6330 and H. R. 19853 to Amend and Consolidate the Acts Respecting Copyright. June 6, 7, 8 and 9, 1906* (1906), 141.

20. Sousa, "The Menace of Mechanical Music" (1906).

21. See Warfield, "John Philip Sousa and 'The Menace of Mechanical Music'" (2009); Sterne, *The Audible Past* (2003), 292–293.

22. Sousa, "The Menace of Mechanical Music" (1906), 281.

23. Ibid., 279.

24. Sinclair, *The Jungle* (1906).

25. Sousa, "The Menace of Mechanical Music" (1906), 279.

26. Ibid., 280.

27. Ibid., 284.

28. Eco, *Apokalyptiker und Integrierte* (1984).

29. Media scholar Jonathan Sterne also interpreted the phonograph as an instrument to embalm the voice. Sterne, *The Audible Past* (2003), 296–299.

30. Adorno and Horkheimer, "Kulturindustrie" (1944). See also the later summary: Adorno, "Résumé über Kulturindustrie" (1977).

31. Library of Congress. "National Jukebox," available at http://www.loc.gov/jukebox/, accessed August 7, 2011.

32. *White-Smith Music Publishing Company v. Apollo Company* (1908).

33. Ibid., 17.

34. Ibid.

35. Ibid., 20.

36. *To Amend and Consolidate the Acts Respecting Copyright. February 22, 1909. Report to accompany H. R. 28192. 60th session, 2nd Congress, House of Representatives, Report No. 2222* (1909).

37. *An Act to Amend and Consolidate the Acts Respecting Copyright* (1909).

38. Hubbell, *From Nothing to Five Million a Year* (n.d.), 5.

39. Bosse, *Autorschaft ist Werkherrschaft* (1981).

40. Röthlisberger, "Gesamtüberblick über die Vorgänge auf urheberrechtlichem Gebiet in den Jahren 1904, 1905 und 1906" (1907), 154.

41. Schmoeckel and Maetschke, *Rechtsgeschichte der Wirtschaft* (2008), 182–185.

42. Dorian, *Berliner Konferenz über Revision internationaler Urheberrechts-Gesetze* (1908), 40, 42; "Aus dem Verbande der Deutschen Sprechmaschinen-Industrie" (1907). Prenner, "Die Sprechmaschinenaufnahmen in ihrer Stellung zum Urheberrechte" (1907).

43. "Die Urheberrechts-Denkschrift des Verbandes der deutschen Sprechmaschinen-Industrie" (1908).

44. Union internationale pour la protection des oeuvres littéraires et artistiques, *Actes de la conférence réunie à Berlin du 14 octobre au 14 novembre 1908 avec les actes de ratification* (1910); Ladas, *The International Protection of Literary and Artistic Property* (1938), 1:419–438.

45. *BAR E 22 Nr. 2383. Convention de Berne revisée pour la protection des oeuvres litteréraires et artistique du 14 novembre 1908. Verschiedene Beschlüsse und Korrespondenzen. Akten der Konferenz. Band 1: Brief Justiz- und Polizei-Departement der schweizerischen Eidgenossenschaft an den Bundesrat, 29. Oktober 1908.*

46. On the Association littéraire et artistique internationale, see Ratisbonne, Lermina, and Pouillet, *Association littéraire & artistique internationale* (1889), 1878–1889.

47. See also Haase, *Übertragung von Werken der Tonkunst auf mechanische Musikinstrumente* (1914), 116–119.

48. "Das Ergebnis der internationalen Urheberrechts-Konferenz" (1908), 1461.

49. Volkmann, *Zur Neugestaltung des Urheberschutzes gegenüber mechanischen Musikinstrumenten* (1909), 16.

50. Cohn-Schmidt, "Die Weisheit der deutschen Regierung" (1910).

51. *"Das Urhebergesetz im Reichstag"* (1910); *Stenographische Berichte über die Verhandlungen des Reichstags. 1909/10. 12. Legislaturperiode, II. Session, 61. Sitzung. Dienstag 12. April 1910*, 2277–2291; Wilm, "Die Neugestaltung des Urheberrechts" (1910).

52. Lindemann, *Gesetz, betreffend das Urheberrecht an Werken der Literatur und der Tonkunst*Section 22, 78–82.

53. "Das Urhebergesetz im Reichstag" (1910); *Stenographische Berichte über die Verhandlungen des Reichstags. 1909/10. 12. Legislaturperiode, II. Session, 61. Sitzung. Dienstag 12. April 1910*, 2279.

54. Knoch, "Deutschlands und Amerikas Export- und Handelsbeziehungen in Sprechmaschinen" (1913). Rothgiesser, "Amerika und Deutschland als Konkurrenten auf dem Weltmarkt" (1913).

55. Fiesenig, *Urheberrecht und mechanische Musikinstrumente* (1916), 46.

56. Bowker, *Copyright* (2002), 212.

57. Ladas, *The International Protection of Literary and Artistic Property* (1938), 1:419–423, 429–433. Austria (1920), Bulgaria (1921), and Switzerland (1927) also introduced a compulsory license. See "Cour d'appel de Paris, 1ère chambre" (1905).

Chapter 5. Collecting Collectives

1. On the collecting societies from an economic perspective, see Wallis, et al., "Contested Collective Administration of Intellectual Property Rights in Music" (1999). Hutter, *Neue Medienökonomik* (2006), 85–94, "Die Rolle der Verwertergesellschaften."

2. Freely expanding on Pierre Bourdieu and Luc Boltanski's work on photography, "social uses" refers to the rules and conventions that influenced how musical recordings were used and treated. Bourdieu et al., *Eine illegitime Kunst* (1983).

3. For the history of SACEM, see Lemoine, *La Société des Auteurs, Compositeurs et Editeurs de Musique SACEM 1850–1950*; *Annuaire de la Société des auteurs et compositeurs dramatiques* (1950).

4. For the social and cultural history of French music between 1870 and 1940, see Pasler, *Composing the Citizen* (2009), 231–298.

5. On criticism in Belgium, see Kufferath, *Les Abus de la Société des Auteurs, Compositeurs et Editeurs de Musique* (1897). See also the written defense of the general agent in Switzerland: *Belehrende Mitteilungen an alle Vereine und Leute* (1896). On the debates in Great Britain, see Ehrlich, *Harmonious Alliance* (1989), 6–8, 12–15. In Switzerland, the Schweizer Hotelier-Verein (Swiss Hotel Association) petitioned the federal government to revise the law in order to put an end to SACEM's capriciousness. *Eingabe des Schweizer Hotelier-Vereins an den Schweizerischen Bundesrat betreffend das Urheberrecht der Autoren und Komponisten* (1901).

6. Kufferath, *Les Abus de la Société des Auteurs, Compositeurs et Editeurs de Musique* (1897), 59.

7. Ibid., 62.

8. See the publication to mark AKM's anniversary: *100 Jahre AKM* (1997).

9. On the origins of the Genossenschaft Deutscher Komponisten, see Schmidt, *Die Anfänge der musikalischen Tantiemenbewegung in Deutschland* (2005).

10. Genossenschaft Deutscher Komponisten, *Materialien zur Begründung einer Deutschen Centralstelle für die Verwertung musikalischer Aufführungsrechte* (1900), 10.

The GDT was attacked and criticized by music dealers, publishers, and associations. Genossenschaft Deutscher Tonsetzer, *Die Anstalt für Musikalisches Aufführungsrecht* (1904). Göhler, *Keine Konzert-Tantiemen!* ([1905?]).

11. Schuster, "Die Denkschrift der deutschen Komponisten über den Urheberrechtsentwurf" (1901), 19.

12. Göhler, *Keine Konzert-Tantiemen!* ([1905?]), 37.

13. Ibid., 26.

14. D'Albert, *Die Verwertung des musikalischen Aufführungsrechts in Deutschland* (1907), 85.

15. Ibid., 85.

16. Ibid., 3.

17. On "foreign" and "ethnic records" in the U.S., see Kenney, *Recorded Music in American Life* (1999), 65–87.

18. On the Vienna phonogram archive founded in 1899, see Pudor, "Das Phonogramm-Archiv der Wiener Akademie der Wissenschaften" (1901). See also Exner and Pöch, *Phonographische Aufnahmen in Indien und in Neu-Guinea* (1905); Hoffmann, "Vor dem Apparat" (2004); "Neues vom Phonogramm-Archiv der Wiener Akademie der Wissenschaften" (1902); Pollak, "Archives in Sound" (1925). On the phonogram archive in Berlin, see Stumpf, "Das Berliner Phonogrammarchiv" (1908); Ziegler, "Erich M. von Hornbostel und das Berliner Phonogramm-Archiv" (1998); Lange, "Archiv und Zukunft" (2010). On the history of American folklore, see Bendix, "Amerikanische Folkloristik" (1995).

19. "Deutsche Dialekt-Aufnahmen von Volksliedern" (1906).

20. Kenney, *Recorded Music in American Life* (1999), 135–157.

21. Southern, *The Music of Black Americans* (1983), 305.

22. On the confusing array of collecting societies in Germany, see Hinrichsen, *Die Übertragung des musikalischen Urheberrechts an Musikverleger und Musikverwertungsgesellschaften* (1934), 33–42.

23. Freiesleben, *Recht und Tonkunst* (1914), 74.

24. For AMMRE's viewpoint, see AMMRE, *Die Anstalt für mechanisch-musikalische Rechte und die Genossenschaft Deutscher Tonsetzer* ([1912]).

25. See "Institution pour la perception de droits sur les reproductions mécanique d'oeuvres musicales" (1912), 31; *Le Droit d'auteur* 25 (1912), 110; Lorenz, "Die sogenannten mechanisch-musikalischen Urheberrechte" (1913). *Le Droit d'auteur* 27 (1914), 107.

26. "Die Novitätenkonzerte der 'Ammre'" (1913).

27. "Novitäten-Abende der 'Ammre'" (1913), 427.

28. Cyril Ehrlich's history of the Performing Right Society (PRS) is extremely helpful. This is as yet the only historical study of a collecting society to approach the phenomenon from a historical/critical perspective through the eyes of a social and economic historian. Ehrlich, *Harmonious Alliance* (1989). We have much less to go on for the American Society of Composers, Authors and Publishers; the hagiographic reports and chance discoveries from the music departments of American libraries should be taken with a generous pinch of salt. See Mills, "What Is 'ASCAP'?" (1938); Hubbell, *From Nothing to Five Million a Year* (n.d.). Charles, "ASCAP—A Half Century of Progress" (1964).

29. See Johns, "Pop Music Pirate Hunters" (2002); Johns, *Piracy* (2009), 327–355; Ehrlich, *The Piano* (1976).

30. Hubbell, *From Nothing to Five Million a Year* (n.d.), 57.

31. *Herbert v. Shanley Co.*, 242, U.S. 591 (1917).

32. Hubbell, *From Nothing to Five Million a Year* (n.d.), 46.

33. Lemoine, *La Société des Auteurs, Compositeurs et Editeurs de Musique SACEM 1850–1950* (1950), 80–87.

34. Ibid., 90–99.

35. Ibid., 105–108, 170–180; *GEMA-Nachrichten* 23 (April 20, 1929), 8–10.

36. *GEMA-Nachrichten* 4 (April 30, 1927), 5.

37. Genossenschaft Deutscher Tonsetzer, *Geschäfte gegen die Schaffenden* (1933), 11.

38. *GEMA-Nachrichten* 7 (November 5, 1927), 1.

39. *GEMA-Nachrichten* 9 (March 1, 1928), 7.

40. For the ASCAP classification rules, see *GEMA-Nachrichten* 41 (June 4, 1931), 12–14; Hubbell, *From Nothing to Five Million a Year* (n.d.), 60–63. In his excellent study on the conflict between ASCAP and the radio stations, John Ryan has collated a great deal of information on ASCAP's business policy from unpublished dissertations and gray literature from the U.S. Congress and from documents on court proceedings against ASCAP. Ryan, *The Production of Culture in the Music Industry* (1985), 28, 54–75.

41. Hubbell, *From Nothing to Five Million a Year* (n.d.), 60.

42. *GEMA-Nachrichten* 41 (June 4, 1931), 13; Ryan, *The Production of Culture in the Music Industry* (1985), 28.

43. *GEMA-Nachrichten* 41 (June 4, 1931), 13.

44. *GEMA-Nachrichten* 9 (March 21, 1928), 5, 8.

45. Board of Trade, *Copyright Royalty (Mechanical Musical Instruments) Inquiry* (1928).

46. Ibid., 9.

47. See Ehrlich, *Harmonious Alliance* (1989), 38–42; *The P.R. Gazette* V, no. 3 (1935), 57; V, no. 4 (1935), 71; and V, no. 10 (1936), 220–222.

48. On the Hollerith machines, see Heide, *Punched-Card Systems and the Early Information Explosion 1880–1945* (2009), 164–180.

49. *The P.R. Gazette* V, no. 9 (1936), 200–203.

50. Ibid., 203.

51. Weber, *Wirtschaft und Gesellschaft* (1980), ch. III.2.

52. *GEMA-Nachrichten* 15 (October 15, 1928), 6.

53. *GEMA-Nachrichten* 33 (March 7, 1930), 2–10.

54. See *GEMA-Nachrichten* 30 (December 27, 1929), 3–8; 37 (August 22, 1930), 2–3; Genossenschaft Deutscher Tonsetzer, *Grundordnung der Anstalten für Musikalische Urheberrechte* [1931].

55. Plugge and Roeber, *Das musikalische Tantiemerecht in Deutschland* (1930); see also *GEMA-Nachrichten* 33 (March 7, 1930), 8–10; 37 (August 22, 1930), 4.

56. Plugge and Roeber, *Das musikalische Tantiemerecht in Deutschland* (1930), 132.

57. [Reichskartell der Musikveranstalter Deutschlands], *Die Neugestaltung des deutschen Urheberrechts* ([1932]), 2 (list of supporting associations).

58. See *GEMA-Nachrichten* 56 (April 5, 1933), 2–15; 59 (July 21, 1933), 2–11; *Stagma-Nachrichten*, 1933–1944. On National Socialist copyright, see Hoffmann, *Ein deutsches Urheberrechtsgesetz* (1933); Hefti, "Das Urheberrecht im Nationalsozialismus" (1988);

Vogt, *Die urheberrechtlichen Reformdiskussionen in Deutschland während der Zeit der Weimarer Republik und des Nationalsozialismus* (2004).

Chapter 6. Celluloid Circulations

1. On the history of Photo Copie GmbH, see "25 Jahre Photo Copie GmbH" in *Der Mikrofilm: Mitteilungen der Photo Copie GmbH und der Mikrofilm GmbH* 2, no. 2 (1952), 1–7. On its founder, Robert Koch-Hesse, see "Koch-Hesse, Robert," *Munzinger Online/Personen*.

2. *Zentralblatt für Bibliothekswesen* 48 (1931), 95.

3. Schwartzkoppen, "Die rechtliche Zulässigkeit der Photokopie im Rechte des Auslandes und nach dem Entwurf zu einem neuen Urheberrechtsgesetz" (1934), 300.

4. Binkley, *Methods of Reproducing Research Materials* (1931).

5. Parts of this chapter are based on the following publications, which also deal with further aspects: Dommann, "Papierstau und Informationsfluss" (2008); Dommann, "Recording Prints, Reading Films" (2010).

6. See "Copia."

7. Binkley, *Manual on Methods of Reproducing Research Materials* (1936), 161–176. For a list of companies, see Schürmeyer and Loosjes, "Literatur über die Anwendung von photographischen Reproduktionsverfahren in der Dokumentation" (1937). For example: Cinescopie and Photoscopie in Brussels; E.K.A. in France; Leica and Leitz in Germany; and Folmer Graflex and Recordak in the U.S.

8. For example: Internationale Camera Gesellschaft (ICA) in Dresden (Famulus), Optische Anstalt von C. P. Goertz in Berlin (Kontophot), Photo Copie GmbH in Berlin (Photokopist), and the American companies Photostat and Rectigraph (Photostat). On technical developments, see *Der Photostat* (1927); Wentzel, "Amerikanische Vervielfältigungsgeräte auf photographischer Grundlage (Photostat, Rectigraph, Photostat-Recorder)" (1929); Schürmeyer, "Die Photographie im Dienste der bibliothekarischen Arbeit" (1933); Van Asperen, "Neuzeitliche photographische Reproduktionsverfahren" (1934).

9. Wentzel, "Amerikanische Vervielfältigungsgeräte auf photographischer Grundlage (Photostat, Rectigraph, Photostat-Recorder)" (1929), 143.

10. "Siemens Reproduktions-Automat" (1936), 5.

11. Elster, "Zur Photokopie-Frage" (1931), 1118, 1122.

12. "Siemens Reproduktions-Automat" (1936), 5.

13. Sevensma, "Die Bibliothek des Völkerbunds" (1931).

14. Intellectual collaboration had intensified in the final third of the nineteenth century during World's Fairs; see Fuchs, "Der Völkerbund und die Institutionalisierung transnationaler Beziehungen" (2006). Paul Otlet also publicized the documentation techniques in the International Research Council; see Schuster, ed., *International Research Council* (1920), 124–145.

15. See Völkerbund, *Das internationale Institut für geistige Zusammenarbeit* (1927).

16. Carpenter, "Toward a New Cultural Design" (2007).

17. Holbrook, *Survey of Activities of American Agencies in Relation to Materials for Research in the Social Sciences and the Humanities* (1932).

18. Binkley, *Methods of Reproducing Research Materials* (1931).

19. "Le livre microphotographique" (1911).

20. Otlet, "Le livre photomicrographique" (1934), 19–20. On the history of documentation, see Dommann, "Dokumentieren" (2008).

21. LOC, Records of the Joint Committee on Materials for Research (JCMR), Container 54, Folder Film Copying: Apparatus: Projector Recordak. John K. Boeing, Recordak, *Journal of Documentary Reproduction* 3, no. 3 (1940), 153–168.

22. Binkley, *Manual on Methods of Reproducing Research Materials* (1936).

23. Ibid., 160.

24. Ibid.

25. Binkley, "New Tools for Men of Letters" (1935), 522.

26. Ibid., 519.

27. Ibid., 529.

28. Binkley, *Manual on Methods of Reproducing Research Materials*, 196–197.

29. McLuhan, *The Gutenberg Galaxy* (1962). See also Eli Bronstein's 1966 interview with Marshall McLuhan: McLuhan, *Das Medium ist die Botschaft* (2001), 126–128 (German translation of *The Medium is the Massage*).

30. LOC, Records of the Joint Committee on Materials for Research (JCMR), Container 52, Folder Film Copying, Reprint: Fox, Louis, F., Films for Folios, Reprint: *The Library Journal* (May 1, 1937).

31. LOC, Records of the Joint Committee on Materials for Research (JCMR), Container 49, Film Copying a) General Correspondence, Charles E. Rush, Summary Account: Investigation of Continental Micro-photographic Methods.

32. *Exposition internationale des arts et techniques appliqués à la vie moderne, Paris 1937* (1937).

33. LOC, Records of the Joint Committee on Materials for Research (JCMR), Container 52, Film Copying a) Paris Exhibition: Letter from Robert Binkley to James Shotwell, January 15, 1936.

34. LOC, Records of the Joint Committee on Materials for Research (JCMR), Container 52, Film Copying a) Paris Exhibition: Letter from Robert Binkley to William Warner Bishop, June 8, 1936.

35. LOC, Records of the Joint Committee on Materials for Research (JCMR), Container 52, Film Copying a) Paris Exhibition: Letter from Robert Binkley to David Stevens, Rockefeller Foundation, November 10, 1936; Rockefeller Foundation, *Annual Report 1937*, New York Rockefeller Foundation (1938), 56.

36. LOC, Records of the Joint Committee on Materials for Research (JCMR), Container 52, Film Copying a) Paris Exhibition: Letter from Robert Binkley to Charles E. Rush, November 10, 1936.

37. LOC, Records of the Joint Committee on Materials for Research (JCMR), Container 52, Film Copying a) Paris Exhibition: Letter from Llewellyn Raney to Robert Binkley, January 7, 1937.

38. Raney, *American Trends in Textual Reproduction* (1939).

39. LOC, Records of the Joint Committee on Materials for Research (JCMR), Container 52, Film Copying a) Paris Exhibition: Letter from Llewellyn M. Raney to David Stevens, Rockefeller Foundation, February 1, 1937.

40. LOC, Records of the Joint Committee on Materials for Research (JCMR), Container 50, Film Copying, a) General Film Stability: Research at National Bureau of Standards on Reproduction of Records. JCMR, Container 52, Folder

Film Copying: Gunderson, Frank N., "As a Matter of Record," *Modern Plastics* 15, no. 7 (1938).

41. Binkley, *Manual on Methods of Reproducing Research Materials* (1936), 106.

42. Decades later, Nicholson Baker furiously decried the destruction of documents by libraries. Baker, *Double Fold* (2001).

43. See also Shera, "Herman Howe Fussler" (1983).

44. Raney, "The Decision of Paris" (1938), 158.

45. LOC, Records of the Joint Committee on Materials for Research (JCMR), Container 59, Order Blank, Bibliofilm Service of Science Service. LOC, JCMR, Container 59, Bibliofilm Service, Circular of Information.

46. Seidell, "A Plan for the Dissemination of Scientific Literature by Means of Microfilms" (1937). Seidell, "The Utilization of Microfilms in Scientific Research" (1939), 33.

47. Seidell, "Microfilm Copying of Scientific Literature" (1939), 220.

48. Marwitz, "Das Photokopierverfahren" (1931).

49. Ibid., 950.

50. Elster, "Zur Rechtsfrage der Photokopie" (1932), 88; see also Elster, "Zur Photokopie-Frage" (1931), the first article *GRUR* ever published on the subject of photocopies.

51. Elster, "Zur Rechtsfrage der Photokopie" (1932), 88.

52. Diesch, "Eine Entgegnung zur Frage der Photokopie" (1932), 140.

53. See Hillig, "Zur Frage der Photokopie" (1933).

54. Treplin, "Das Bibliotheksrecht" (1933), 627–634; *Zentralblatt für Bibliothekswesen* 50 (1933), 590–594; Schreiber, "Pflicht und Recht der Bibliotheksphotokopie" (1934).

55. *Reproduktion* (April 1933), 63–64 ("I hereby explicitly declare that I am the lawful owner of the reproduction rights . . . and am liable for all claims").

56. Bourgeois, "La reproduction des documents en relation avec les droits d'auteur & d'editeur" (1932), 38.

57. See Schwartzkoppen, "Die rechtliche Zulässigkeit der Photokopie im Rechte des Auslandes und nach dem Entwurf zu einem neuen Urheberrechtsgesetz" (1934), 306–307.

58. Ostertag, "Die Photokopie im Lichte des Urheberrechts" (1935).

59. Binkley, "Techniques and Policies of Documentary Reproduction" (1939), 15.

60. LOC, Records of the Joint Committee on Materials for Research (JCMR), Box 73, Folder Agenda Material, Memorandum from Robert C. Binkley, February 6, 1939.

61. Ibid.

62. Johann Heinrich Zedler equates *credit* to renown, favor, grace, power, manifold validity, belief, and fidelity. See "Credit" in Zedler, *Grosses vollständiges Universal-Lexicon aller Wissenschaften und Künste* (1733), vol. 6, 1599.

63. LOC, Records of the Joint Committee on Materials for Research (JCMR), Container 57, File Memorandum. Correspondence and Agreement on the Photographic Copying by Libraries of Copyrighted Material.

64. See Schreiber, "Photokopie und Bibliotheken" (1936).

65. "The Gentlemen's Agreement and the Problem of Copyright," *The Journal of Documentary Reproduction* 2, no. 1 (1939), 29–36.

66. Rockefeller Foundation, *Annual Report 1938*, 345 et seq.

67. NARA RG 59, Entry 5211, Box 4, 71st Congress, Senate, Confidential. Convention and Protocol Relating to the Protection of Literary and Artistic Work. Message From the President of the United States, January 21, 1931. RG 59, Entry 5211, Box 4, International Convention of the Copyright Union. Hearings Before a Subcommittee of the Committee on Foreign Relations United States Senate, 75th Congress First Session on Executive E., 73th Congress, Second Session International Convention of the Copyright Union, Revised at Rome, June 22, 1928. April 12 and 13, 1937. Washington, D.C.: 1937.

68. LOC, Records of the Joint Committee on Materials for Research (JCMR), Container 58, Copyright General Correspondence, Letter from Robert C. Binkley to Edith Ware, Executive Secretary, Committee for the Study of Copyright, February 24, 1938.

69. LOC, Records of the Joint Committee on Materials for Research (JCMR), Container 58, Copyright General Correspondence, Letter from Robert C. Binkley to James Shotwell, January 12, 1938.

70. LOC, Records of the Joint Committee on Materials for Research (JCMR), Container 58, Copyright General Correspondence, Letter from Robert C. Binkley to Edith Ware, Executive Secretary, Committee for the Study of Copyright, June 8, 1938.

71. LOC, Records of the Joint Committee on Materials for Research (JCMR), Container 58, Copyright General Correspondence, Robert C. Binkley: Memorandum on Copyright, July 8, 1938.

72. LOC, Records of the Joint Committee on Materials for Research (JCMR), Container 58, Copyright General Correspondence, Robert C. Binkley to Edith Ware, August 23, 1938.

73. LOC, Records of the Joint Committee on Materials for Research (JCMR), Container 59, General Correspondence 1940, Memorandum from Richard E. Manning to Robert C. Binkley and H. M. Lydenberg, March 7, 1940.

74. American Bar Association (ABA). *Section of Patent, Trade Mark and Copyright Law. Committee Report to be Presented at the Annual Meeting 1940.*

75. On the various reasons for rejecting entry into the Berne Convention between 1920 and 1940, see Goldman, *The History of U.S.A. Copyright Law Revision from 1901 to 1954* (1960), 11.

76. LOC, Records of the Joint Committee on Materials for Research (JCMR), Container 59, General Correspondence 1940, Homer T. Bone, US Senate Committee on Patents, April 4, 1940.

77. LOC, Records of the Joint Committee on Materials for Research (JCMR), Container 59, Copyright General, Letter from Robert C. Binkley to Richard E. Manning, July 30, 1939.

78. Power, *Edition of One* (1990), 139–146.

79. Raney, "American Trends in Textual Reproduction" (1939), 79.

80. Donker Duyvis, "La photocopie micrographique sur papier" (1935).

81. Hijmans, "Fotokopie oder Mikrokopie für die Dokumentation" (1937).

82. Bush, "As We May Think" (1945). Due to the "retrieval problem in photography," attempts were made in the early 1930s to search microfilms using machines. Buckland, *Emanuel Goldberg and His Knowledge Machine* (2006).

Chapter 7. Performing Artists

1. On the history of electroacoustics, see Thompson, *The Soundscape of Modernity* (2002), 229–315.

2. *The P.R. Gazette* II, no. 4 (April 1926), 85.

3. On the history of radio in Germany, see Dahl, *Radio* (1983); Dussel, *Deutsche Rundfunkgeschichte* (2010). For a legal history perspective on radio law in the Weimar Republic, see Fessmann, *Rundfunk und Rundfunkrecht in der Weimarer Republik* (1973). For media studies perspectives on Germany and the U.S., see Hagen, *Das Radio* (2005).

4. On the history of radio in Great Britain, see Briggs, *The Birth of Broadcasting*, Vols. 1 & 2 (1961); Crisell, *An Introductory History of British Broadcasting* (1997).

5. Giesecke, "Der Zusammenschluss der europäischen Rundfunkgesellschaften" (1927).

6. *1re Congrès juridique international de T.S.F.* (1925), 57–65.

7. RGZ, I, 422/1925 and RGZ, I, 287/1925. Cited in *GRUR* 31, no. 7 (1926), 343–349.

8. Homburg, "Die Probleme des Funkrechtes und das Comité International de la T.S.F." (1927), 32.

9. On the history of sound film in the U.S., see Crafton, *The Talkies* (1997).

10. Hoffmann, "Das Urheberrecht des nachschaffenden Künstlers" (1927), 69.

11. Cahn-Speyer, "Rundfunk, Schallplatte und ausübender Künstler" (1927).

12. Lion, "Das Recht des wiedergebenden Künstlers" (1927).

13. Elster, "Die wettbewerbliche und die immanente Begrenzung des Urheberrechts" (1926), 499.

14. Smoschewer, "Zur Frage des Urheberschutzes der wiedergebenden Künstler" (1927), 52.

15. Smoschewer, "Einige Gedanken über die Zusammenarbeit von Urhebern und Sendestellen" (1927), 138.

16. *1re Congrès juridique international de T. S.F.* (1925), 66.

17. Ibid., 66.

18. Rome Convention of October 26, 1961, for the Protection of Performers, Producers of Phonograms and Broadcasting Organizations. See Ulmer, *Der Rechtsschutz der ausübenden Künstler, der Hersteller von Tonträgern und der Sendegesellschaften in internationaler und rechtsvergleichender Sicht* (1957), 2–9.

19. Elster, "Die wettbewerbliche und die immanente Begrenzung des Urheberrechts" (1926), 501.

20. *Foundation of an International Institute for the Unification of Private Law (Offer of the Italian Government). League of Nations. Geneva, September 30, 1924. A. 134 (1) 1924. V. Institut international pour l'unification du droit privé. Offre du gouvernement italien. Société des Nations. Genève, le 29 April 1926. C.262.M.101.1926 V.*

21. Smoschewer, "Zur Frage der Regelung des Rundfunks durch die Berner Konvention" (1927).

22. "Die Vorschläge der italienischen Regierung und des Internationalen Büros zum Schutze der Werke der Literatur und Kunst zum Funk-Urheberrecht" (1927).

23. Ladas, *The International Protection of Literary and Artistic Property* (1938), 1:101.

24. On the concept of work authority, see Bosse, *Autorschaft ist Werkherrschaft* (1981).

25. WIPO (Geneva), Historical Collection E 2380n 6133 B.I.R.P.I. Conférence de Rome 1928. Procès Verbaux des Sous Commissions.

26. WIPO (Geneva), Historical Collection E 2380n 6133 B.I.R.P.I. Conférence de Rome 1928. Procès Verbaux des Sous Commissions. Deuxième Sous Commission: Radiophonie. 1ère séance, 8 mai 1928, 6.

27. See Crafton, *The Talkies* (1997). On the work situation for musicians in the U.S. entertainment industry after 1926, see Kraft, "Musicians in Hollywood" (1994).

28. See *P.R. Gazette* IV, no. 6 (October 1932), 111; V, no. 7 (January 1933), 127–128.

29. Baum, *Rundfunk und Schallplatte* (1932); Giannini, *Rechtsprobleme der Schallplatte* (1934), 271.

30. International Labour Office, *International Labour Conference* (1939), 31, 125.

31. On the ILO, see Hughes and Haworth, *The International Labour Organization (ILO)* (2011). See also the list of work agreements and recommendations in *Die Internationale Arbeitsorganisation* (1950), 175–189.

32. International Labour Office, *International Labour Conference* (1939), 79.

33. See chapter 6.

34. International Labour Office, *International Labour Conference* (1939), 21.

35. Ibid., 26–27.

36. Ibid., 90.

37. Ibid., 81–87.

38. Ibid., 111–112.

39. Literature on the history of copyright in the music industry is sparse and relates mainly to the recent past. For example, see Laing, "Copyright and the International Music Industry" (1993). On the U.S., see Jones, "Music and Copyright in the USA" (1993); Cummings, "From Monopoly to Intellectual Property" (2010).

40. See BIEM, *Bureau International des Sociétés gérant les Droits d'Enregistrement et de Reproduction Mécanique 1929–1979* (1980); *GEMA Nachrichten* 21 (1954), 7–8.

41. Unfortunately, there is no critical historical study of the IFPI; only fragmentary sources and flattering commemorative publications remain. See Giannini, "Rechtsprobleme der Schallplatte" (1934); Thalheim, "Der erste internationale Kongress der phonographischen Industrie in Rom und die Gründung der internationalen Vereinigung der phonographischen Industrie" (1934); International Federation of the Phonographic Industry, *The Industry of Human Happiness* ([1959]); Borwick and Stuart-Hunt, *International Federation of Producers of Phonograms and Videograms* (1983).

42. International Federation of the Phonographic Industry, *The Industry of Human Happiness* ([1959]), 98.

43. Giannini, "Rechtsprobleme der Schallplatte" (1934), 284–286.

44. The bibliographic information is as follows: Benito Mussolini, *La nuova politica dell'Italia: Discorsi e dichiarazioni a cura di Amedeo Giannini* (Milan, 1923). On Amedeo Giannini, see Melis, "Giannini, Amedeo," (2000).

45. Giannini, "Rechtsprobleme der Schallplatte" (1934), 284.

46. Wolf, "Mussolini und die Filesharing-Jäger" (2008).

47. *Legge 22 aprile 1941 n. 633, Protezione del diritto d'autore e di altri diritti connessi al suo esercizio. (G.U. n.166 del 16 luglio 1941).* See also Straschnov, *Le Droit d'auteur et les droits connexes en radiodiffusion* (1948), 155.

48. Ibid., 154.

49. International Federation of the Phonographic Industry, *The Industry of Human Happiness* [1959], 122–124; Baum, "Die Urteile in den Prozessen zwischen Rundfunk und Schallplattenindustrie und ihre Kritik" (1937/1938).

50. Ulmer, *Der Rechtsschutz der ausübenden Künstler, der Hersteller von Tonträgern und der Sendegesellschaften in internationaler und rechtsvergleichender Sicht* (1957), 2–10; Straschnov, *Le Droit d'auteur et les droits connexes en radiodiffusion* (1948).

51. Baum, "Die Brüsseler Konferenz zur Revision der Revidierten Berner Übereinkunft" (1949).

52. On the history of radio in the U.S., see Sterling and Kittross, *Stay Tuned* (1990).

53. Unless stated otherwise, the following remarks are based on: Gitlin, *Radio Infringement of Music Copyright* (1938). Ryan, *The Production of Culture in the Music Industry. The ASCAP-BMI Controversy* (1985). Sterling and Kittross, *Stay Tuned* (1990), 131–132, 193–194; Streeter, "Broadcast Copyright and the Bureaucratization of Property" (1994), 313–317.

54. Bamberger Case, Jerome H. Remick & Co. v. American Automobile Accessories Co.

55. *To Amend the Copyright Act. Hearings before a Subcommittee of the Committee on Patents, United States, Senate, 68th Congress, 1st Session on S. 2600, a Bill to Amend Section 1 of an Act Entitled "An Act to Amend and Consolidate the Acts Respecting Copyright," Approved March 4, 1909. April 9, 17, and 18, 1924* (1924).

56. Ibid., 173.

57. *S. 2328 and H. R. 10353 Bills to Amend Section I of an Act Entitled "An Act to Amend and Consolidate the Acts Respecting Copyright," Approved March 4. 1909, As Amended by Adding Subsection F. Joint Hearings Before the Committees on Patents Congress of the United States 69th Congress, First Session. April 5, 6, 7, 8, and 9, 1926* (1926). On further unsuccessful bills in Congress in the 1930s, see Simpson, "The Copyright Situation as Affecting Radio Broadcasting" (1931).

58. NYPL, NYC, M-Clipping Copyright 1920s–1930s, *NY Times*, May 15, 1932.

59. NYPL, NYC, M-Clipping Copyright 1920s–1930s, *NY Herald Tribune*, August 25, 1932.

60. Sterling and Kittross, *Stay Tuned* (1990), 132.

61. Gitlin, "Radio Infringement of Music Copyright" (1938), 83.

62. American Society of Composers, Authors and Publishers, *The Murder of Music* [1933].

63. American Society of Composers, Authors and Publishers, *How the Public Gets Its New Music* (1933).

64. Ibid., 6.

65. American Society of Composers, Authors and Publishers, *Who Uses Music and Why* (1934), 9.

66. *ASCAP Journal* (November 1937), 5.

67. On the discourse in Great Britain, see *Radio and the Composer* (1935), 4.

68. Chandler, *The Visible Hand* (1977).

69. *Copyright Law Symposium* 1 (1938), 5.

70. Ibid., 5.

71. American Society of Composers, Authors and Publishers, *The Story of ASCAP* [1946], 13–15.

72. Ibid., 14.

73. Ibid.

74. *ASCAP Journal* (October 1937), 24. NYPL, NYC, M-Clipping, ASCAP, Allen, Leonhard, "The Battle of Tin Pan Alley," in *Harper's Magazine*, October 1940 [reprint without page reference].

75. NYPL, NYC, M-Clipping Copyright 1920s–1930s, *New York Post* (February 21, 1936); *New York Herald Tribune* (August 2, 1936).

76. NYPL, NYC, M-Clipping Copyright 1920s–1930s, *New York Times* (August 9, 1936).

77. On the conflict between ASCAP and the NAB, see Ryan, *The Production of Culture in the Music Industry* (1985); Streeter, "Broadcast Copyright and the Bureaucratization of Property" (1994), 314–317; Sterling and Kittross, *Stay Tuned* (1990), 193.

78. NYPL, NYC, M-Clipping Copyright 1920s–1930s, August 4, 1939 [newspaper information not given]: "Broadcasters Fight on Music Fees."

79. NYPL, NYC, M-Clipping, "Broadcasting System—ASCAP-BMI Agreements, Portrait of a Protector" ([1941]).

80. NYPL, NYC, M-Clipping, ASCAP, *New York Herald Tribune* (November 15, 1940).

81. NYPL, NYC, M-Clipping, ASCAP, 1930–1939, *New York Herald Tribune* (December 31, 1940).

82. See Kenney, *Recorded Music in American Life* (1999), 186–196; Southern, *The Music of Black Americans* (1983), 519–520.

83. NYPL, NYC, M-Clipping, ASCAP, Allen, Leonhard, "The Battle of Tin Pan Alley," in *Harper's Magazine* (October 1940) [reprint without page reference].

84. On Paul Lazarsfeld's radio research, see Schrage, *Psychotechnik und Radiophonie* (2001), 309–319; Hagen, *Das Radio* (2005), 288–295; Peters, "The Uncanniness of Mass Communication in Interwar Social Thought" (1996).

85. "John Gray Peatman, Radio and Popular Music," in Lazarsfeld and Stanton, eds., *Radio Research 1942–1943* (1944), 360.

86. *Billboard* (December 13, 1941), cited in ibid., 362.

87. *Broadcasting Magazine* (September 29, 1941), cited in "John Gray Peatman, Radio and Popular Music," in Lazarsfeld and Stanton, eds., *Radio Research 1942–1943* (1944), 362.

88. Adorno and Horkheimer, "Kulturindustrie" (1944); Adorno, "Résumé über Kulturindustrie" (1977).

89. "John Gray Peatman, Radio and Popular Music," in Lazarsfeld and Stanton, eds., *Radio Research 1942–1943* (1944), 362.

Chapter 8. Fees for Devices

1. On the experimental use of sound recording devices, see Butzmann, "Was nicht in der Bedienungsanleitung stand" (1994).

2. See Nesper, *Nimm Schallplatten selber auf!* (1932), esp. 7–9; Kluth, *Jeder sein eigener Schallplattenfabrikant* (1932).

3. Nesper, *Nimm Schallplatten selber auf!* (1932), 70.

4. Kluth, *Jeder sein eigener Schallplattenfabrikant* (1932), 93.

5. There has as yet been no critical study of the economic or company history of Grundig AG. Historical research is also restricted because the Grundig AG archive has not been accessible since the company became insolvent in 2003. Biographies of Max Grundig are extremely hagiographic: Bronnenmeyer, *Max Grundig* (1999); Mayer, *Grundig und das Wirtschaftswunder* (2008).

6. See WWZ H + I Bg 1185 Grundig Aktien Gesellschaft Fürth Bayern. Dokumentensammlung: *ZEIT Magazin* 19 (May 5, 1978).

7. Here I have drawn on what is so far the only social and economic history study to deal marginally with Max Grundig as well: Woller, *Gesellschaft und Politik in der amerikanischen Besatzungszone* (1986), 281–287; on Ludwig Erhard, see 240 et seq., 267 et seq., 306 et seq.

8. The following information is based on a company brochure from 1960; see WWZ H + I Bg 1185 Grundig Aktien Gesellschaft Fürth Bayern. Dokumentensammlung: *Grundig und sein Werk, ein Leistungsbericht*, Nuremberg (1960).

9. Kittler, *Grammophon, Film, Typewriter* (1986), 169.

10. BASF, *Heiteres Tonband-Brevier* [1960], 8; *Tape Recording and Reproduction Magazine* 4, no. 3 (1960), 22–23. For the history of plastic in the Federal Republic of Germany, see Westermann, *Plastik und politische Kultur in Westdeutschland* (2007).

11. Kittler, *Grammophon, Film, Typewriter* (1986), 166.

12. See WWZ H + I Bg 1185 Grundig Aktien Gesellschaft Fürth Bayern. Dokumentensammlung: *Grundig und sein Werk, ein Leistungsbericht*, Nuremberg (1960), 47.

13. Ibid., 66; Woller, *Gesellschaft und Politik in der amerikanischen Besatzungszone* (1986), 240 et seq., 267 et seq., 306 et seq.

14. See WWZ H + I Bg 1185 Grundig Aktien Gesellschaft Fürth Bayern. Dokumentensammlung, *NZZ*, no. 1028 (April 11, 1956).

15. Erhard, *Wohlstand für alle* (1957).

16. *GEMA Nachrichten* 8 (1950), 12–16. Here too, the only works on the history of GEMA come from GEMA's closest circle; see Schulze, *Geschätzte und geschützte Noten* (1995).

17. *Verhandlungen des Deutschen Bundestages und des Bundesrates, 205. Sitzung, Mittwoch den 23. April 1952*, 8844–8851. Also: *Drucksache Nr. 3251* and *Nr. 3252*.

18. *GEMA Nachrichten* 15 (1952), 18.

19. *GEMA Nachrichten* 14 (1952), 5–7.

20. See Habermas, *Diebe vor Gericht* (2008).

21. *GEMA Nachrichten* 14 (1952), 5.

22. Gesellschaft für musikalische Aufführungs- und mechanische Vervielfältigungsrechte (GEMA, previously STAGMA), *Magnettongeräte und Urheberrecht* (1952), 7.

23. *GEMA Nachrichten* 9 (1950), 10.

24. For Alfred Baum's legal opinion, see Gesellschaft für musikalische Aufführungs- und mechanische Vervielfältigungsrechte (GEMA, previously STAGMA), *Magnettongeräte und Urheberrecht* (1952), 32.

25. Schulze, *Das deutsche Urheberrecht an Werken der Tonkunst und die Entwicklung der mechanischen Musik* (1950), 39.

26. Callon, "Die Sozio-Logik der Übersetzung" (2006).

27. Runge, "Rechtsfragen um das Magnetophon" (1951), 236.

28. Erffa, "Die neuere technische Entwicklung und ihr Einfluss auf das Urheberrecht" (1951), 223.

29. Gentz, "Überspielungsfreiheit zum persönlichen Gebrauch?" (1952), 499.

30. Gesellschaft für musikalische Aufführungs- und mechanische Vervielfältigungsrechte (GEMA, previously STAGMA), *Magnettongeräte und Urheberrecht* (1952), 56.

31. Mediger, "Magnetton und Urheberercht" (1951), 385.

32. Haeger, *Zur Gefahr der Urheberrechtsverletzung durch Tonband-Vervielfältigung gemäss § 15 Abs. 2 LUG* (1954), 54.

33. Ibid., 56.

34. See Schulze, "Geschäfte mit Musik" (1956).

35. Diefenbach, *Tonband-Hobby* (1962), 143–147.

36. *Tape Recording and Reproduction Magazine* 4, no. 3 (February 10, 1960), 13.

37. *Tape Recording and Reproduction Magazine* 3, no. 10 (October 1959), 35.

38. *GEMA Nachrichten* 21 (1954), 15–18.

39. Schulze, *Geschäfte mit Musik* (1956), 17.

40. Ibid., 18.

41. See, for example, Richter, *Tonaufnahme für alle* (1958); Brauns, *Stereotechnik* (1961); Diefenbach, *Tonband-Hobby* (1962).

42. Mayer and Conly, *Hi-Fi* (1956), 119.

43. Gardner and Arnison, *Tape Recording as a Pastime* (1959), 44.

44. Ibid., 44.

45. Mayer and Conly, *Hi-Fi* (1956), 120.

46. Hirschman, *Shifting Involvements* (1982); on long-lasting consumer goods, see 46–66.

47. Diefenbach, *Tonband-Hobby* (1962), 70–74.

48. BASF, *Heiteres Tonband-Brevier* [1960], 33.

49. Diefenbach, *Tonband-Hobby* (1960); Gardner and Arnison, *Tape Recording as a Pastime* (1959).

50. Siegfried, *Time Is on My Side* (2006), 103–107. The transistor radio is a parallel phenomenon for use outside the home. See Fickers, *Der "Transistor" als technisches und kulturelles Phänomen* (1998).

51. Gardner and Arnison, *Tape Recording as a Pastime* (1959), 13.

52. Ibid., 14.

53. Ibid.

54. Pfaller, *Die Illusionen der anderen* (2002), 35–43.

55. *Tape Recording and Reproduction Magazine* 1, no. 2 (1957), 4.

56. *Tape Recording and Reproduction Magazine* 3, no. 1 (January 1959), 38–39.

57. Purves, *The Grundig Book* (1962), 46–60.

58. See, for example, GRUR 56, nos. 7/8 (1954), 363–369: "Urteil des Kammergerichts vom 6. Oktober 1953. Aktz. 5 U 1122/53"; GRUR 57, no. 10 (1955), 492–502: "Urteil des Bundesgerichtshofs vom 18. Mai 1955. Aktz. I ZR 8/54 (Kammergericht)."

59. GRUR 57, no. 10 (1955), 492–502: "Urteil des Bundesgerichtshofs vom 18. Mai 1955. Aktz. I ZR 8/54 (Kammergericht)," here 494.

60. *GRUR* 57, no. 10 (1955), 492–502: "Urteil des Bundesgerichtshofs vom 18. Mai 1955. Aktz. I ZR 8/54 (Kammergericht)," here 499.

61. *GRUR* 57, no. 2 (1955), "Deutsche Vereinigung für gewerblichen Rechtsschutz und Urheberrecht. Urheberrechtliche Arbeitssitzung am 30. September 1954," 79.

62. WWZ Basel, H + I Bg 1185 Grundig Aktien Gesellschaft Fürth Bayern. Dokumentensammlung. *Deutsche Zeitung Stuttgart* 191 (August 19–20, 1961); Leinveber, "Die wichtigsten Neuerungen der deutschen Urheberrechtsreform" (1966), 135.

63. *GRUR* 57, no. 2 (1955), "Deutsche Vereinigung für gewerblichen Rechtsschutz und Urheberrecht: Urheberrechtliche Arbeitssitzung am 30. September 1954," 79.

64. Fack, "Mehr Schutz für das Geistige Eigentum" (1961), 11; *GEMA Nachrichten* 54 (June 1962), 8; see also Haeger, "Der Einbruch von Nutzungsrechten in die Privatsphäre" (1963), 351–352.

65. See "Denkschrift des Gesamtverbandes der Tonträger-Hersteller zur Regelung der Tonbandfrage durch das neue Urheberrechtsgesetz: Stellungnahme des Arbeitskreises der deutschen Schallplattenindustrie zur Tonbandfrage," *GEMA Nachrichten* 54 (June 1962), 17–19.

66. *GEMA Nachrichten* 54 (June 1962), 9.

67. Ibid., 9.

68. *GEMA Nachrichten* 64 (June 1965), 2–5; 65 (September 1965), 1–23.

69. Leinveber, "Die wichtigsten Neuerungen der deutschen Urheberrechtsreform" (1966), 135.

70. *Tape Recording Fortnightly* 5, no. 3 (February 8, 1961).

71. M**r, P**l, "Confessions of an Illicit Tape Recordist" (1963), 109.

72. On Great Britain, see *Tape Recording and Reproduction Magazine* 1 (March 1957), 9–10; 1, no. 8 (September 1957), 13; 3, no. 5 (May 1959), 18–19. On the U.S., see *HiFi Stereo Review* 4, no. 3 (March 1960), 52; Barsley, *Tape Recording* (1967), 53–55.

73. *Tape Recording and Reproduction Magazine* 3, no. 7 (July 1959), 32–33; *Tape Recording Fortnightly* 5, no. 13 (June 28, 1961); 5, no. 14 (July 12, 1961), 20; 5, no. 20 (October 4, 1961); 6, no. 7 (July 1962).

74. *Tape Recording and Reproduction Magazine* 3, no. 10 (October 1959), 32.

75. Ibid., 32.

76. *Tape Recording and Reproduction Magazine* 13, no. 11 (1969), 365.

77. Ibid., 369.

78. "An Interview with Marshall McLuhan," *The Structurist* (January 1, 1966), 68.

Chapter 9. Flow of Information

1. Bush, *Science, the Endless Frontier* (1990 [1945]); for the political and scientific context, see the foreword by Daniel Kevles, ix–xxxiii.

2. Ibid., 112.

3. Kastenmeier, "The Information Explosion and Copyright Law Revision" (1967), 195. This chapter benefited significantly from editions of important documents by political scientist Nicholas Henry in the highly politicized copyright discourse of the 1970s. Henry, *Copyright, Congress, and Technology* (1978–1980).

4. Luce, *The American Century* (1941).

5. On the interaction of science, technology, and law in the U.S., see Jasanoff, *Science at the Bar* (1995), esp. 1–23.

6. Krige, *American Hegemony and the Postwar Reconstruction of Science in Europe* (2006).

7. American Library Association, Board on Resources of American Libraries and International Relations Board, *Conference on International Cultural, Educational, and Scientific Exchanges. Princeton University November 25–26, 1946* (1947), 43–54.

8. On war research in Great Britain, see Edgerton, *Warfare State* (2006).

9. See *American Documentation* 1 (1952), 112–115: "Fair Copying Declaration."

10. Board of Trade, *Report of the Copyright Committee* (1952), 16–22.

11. Wilson, *Copyright and the Scientist* (1952). The French law of 1957 did not deal with photocopies; in the view of one commentator, however, it was probably tolerated for private use. See *Le Droit d'auteur* 72 (1959), 185–186.

12. de Boor, "Vervielfältigung zum persönlichen Gebrauch?" (1954), 447.

13. Reimer, "Die Rechte der Autoren und Verleger bei Vervielfältigung von Zeitschriften im Wege der Mikrophotographie" (1948).

14. Winter, *Vorschläge für eine Vereinbarung über den redlichen Verkehr mit photomechanischen Vervielfältigungen* (1957), 14–19. On documentation in the Welt-Wirtschafts-Archiv (Global Economic Archive) in Hamburg, see Heesen, *Der Zeitungsausschnitt* (2006).

15. Winter, *Vorschläge für eine Vereinbarung über den redlichen Verkehr mit photomechanischen Vervielfältigungen* (1957), 17.

16. *Annual Report of the Librarian of Congress for the Fiscal Year 1955–56*, 60; 1957, 65–66; 1958, 65.

17. *Annual Report of the Librarian of Congress for the Fiscal Year 1959*, 2.

18. Goldman, *The History of U.S.A. Copyright Law Revision from 1901 to 1954* (1960), iii.

19. Latman, "Fair Use of Copyrighted Works" (1960).

20. Varmer, "Photoduplication of Copyrighted Material by Libraries" (1960).

21. On the scientific and corporate history of Xerox, see Owen, *Copies in Seconds* (2004); Mort, *The Anatomy of Xerography* (1989); Gundlach, "Retrospective on Xerography and Chester F. Carlson" (1990); Zannos, *Chester Carlson and the Development of Xerography* (2002).

22. *American Documentation* 2 (1951), 115.

23. See Ballou, "Developments in Copying Methods—1958" (1959); Veaner, "Xerox Copyflo at Harvard University Library" (1962), 13.

24. Ballou, "Developments in Copying Methods—1958" (1959), 88.

25. Striedl, *Der xerographische Rollendruck als bibliothekarisches Hilfsmittel unter Berücksichtigung von Erfahrungen an der bayerischen Staatsbibliothek* (1959).

26. "Out to Crack Copying Market" (1959); Stevens, "Library Experience with the Xerox 914 Copier" (1962); Crawford, "Notes of a Librarian on Contemplating Her Xerox Machine" (1963).

27. Stevens, "Library Experience with the Xerox 914 Copier" (1962), 26.

28. Hawken, "Reprographic Technology: Present and Future" (1964), 48.

29. Crawford, "Notes of a Librarian on Contemplating Her Xerox Machine" (1963), 398.

30. Shepard, "Library Service and Photocopying" (1966), 331.

31. Benjamin, *Das Kunstwerk im Zeitalter seiner technischen Reproduzierbarkeit. Drei Studien zur Kunstsoziologie* (1990), 13.

32. "Joint Libraries Committee on Fair Use in Photocopying, Report on Single Copies" (1961).

33. "Survey of Copyrighted Material Reproduction Practices in Scientific and Technical Fields" (1963).

34. Ibid., 84.

35. Luhmann, *Die Realität der Massenmedien* (2004), esp. 10–11.

36. Zieger, *Vervielfältigen—aber wie?* (1965), 103.

37. *Bulletin of the Copyright Society of the U.S.A.* 4, no. 6 (1957), 194–195: "UNESCO. Free Flow of Information."

38. Price, *Little Science, Big Science* (1963), 62–91.

39. "First Annual Report of the Committee to Investigate Problems Affecting Communication in Science and Education" (1962).

40. Hattery and Bush, *Reprography and Copyright Law* (1964), esp. "Alternative Solutions," 131–147.

41. *Annual Report of the Librarian of Congress for the Fiscal Year 1962*, 1.

42. "Copyright Law Revision. Hearings before Subcommittee No. 3 of the Committee on the Judiciary, House of Representatives, 89th Congress, First Session, on H.R. 4347, H. R. 5680, H.R. 6831, H.R. 6835, Bills for the General Revision of the Copyright Law, 1965. Washington 1965." Henry, *Copyright, Congress, and Technology* (1978–1980), 1:383–387.

43. "Copyright Law Revisions. Hearings, 1967 before the Subcommittee on Patents, Trademarks and Copyright of the Committee on the Judiciary, United States Senate, 90th Congress, 1th Session, Pursuant to S. Res. 37 on S. 597, Washington 1967." Published in: Henry, *Copyright, Congress, and Technology* (1978–1980), 2:124–132.

44. National Library of Medicine, (NLM) MS C 421 *Williams & Wilkins Co. v. The United States* (1938–1982) Container 3, Folder 19: Letter from William M. Passano to Martin M. Cummings, April 27, 1967.

45. In his outline of the history of American copyright, Paul Goldstein also spoke with both protagonists. Goldstein, *Copyright's Highway* (2003), 63–103.

46. NLM, MS C 421 *Williams & Wilkins Co. v. The United States* (1938–1982), Container 3, Folder 19: Letter from Martin M. Cummings to William M. Passano, May 2, 1967.

47. NLM, MS C 421 *Williams & Wilkins Co. v. The United States* (1938–1982), *Medical Librarianship, A Mid Century Survey. A Symposium. The Loan Policy of the National Library of Medicine, May 6–10, 1957.*

48. MacDonald, "Technological Advances and Copyright" (1960).

49. Ibid., 4.

50. Ibid.

51. *Bulletin of the Copyright Society of the U.S.A.* 11 (1964), 361, "Copyright Registration for Computer Programs. Announcement from the Copyright Office." See also Banzhaf, "Copyright Protection for Computer Programs" (1964).

52. Cary, "Copyright Registration and Computer Programs" (1964), 363.

53. *Datamation* 12 (1966), 69.

54. "Copyright Implications in the New Science of Data Storage and Retrieval" (1964).

55. McLuhan, *The Gutenberg Galaxy* (1962), introduction.

56. "Copyright Implications in the New Science of Data Storage and Retrieval" (1964), 22.

57. Veaner, "Developments in Copying Methods and Graphic Communication" (1966), 199.

58. See Miller, "EDUCOM" (1966).

59. Linden, "The Law of Copyright and Unfair Competition" (1965).

60. "Copyright Amendment Passes House Committee" (1966).

61. "Copyright Amendment Passes House Committee" (1966), 69.

62. Federal Council For Science and Technology, Ad Hoc Task Force on Legal Aspects Involved in National Information, *The Copyright Law as It Relates to National Information Systems and National Programs* (1967), 8–9.

63. Benjamin, "Computers and Copyrights" (1966).

64. Federal Council For Science and Technology, Ad Hoc Task Force on Legal Aspects Involved in National Information (1967).

65. Ibid., 12.

66. Miller, "Computers and Copyright Law" (1967); Kaplan and Miller, "Computers and the Copyright Bill" (1967).

67. Kaplan, *An Unhurried View of Copyright* (1967), introduction.

68. Ibid., 118.

69. Ibid., 121.

70. Marke, *Copyright and Intellectual Property* (1967).

71. Ibid., 82.

72. Ibid., 105.

73. Ibid.

74. Barthes, "The Death of the Author" (1967).

75. Gipe, *Nearer to the Dust* (1967).

76. Ibid., 261–262.

77. Ibid., 249–250.

78. *Williams & Wilkins Co. v. United States*, U. S. Supreme Court, Records and Briefs, 420 US 376 (1973–1974).

79. CONTU, *Final Report* (1979); on the background and mandate, see 3–8.

80. Panel on Science and Technology, *Eleventh Meeting*, 19–20; Bell, *The Coming of Post-Industrial Society* (1973).

81. Panel on Science and Technology, *Eleventh Meeting*, 54.

82. Henry, "Copyright" (1974); Henry, "Copyright, Public Policy, and Information Technology" (1974); see also Henry, *Copyright, Information Technology, Public Policy: Part II* (1976); Henry, "The New Copyright Act" (1977).

83. Henry, "Copyright" (1974), 993.

84. Henry, "Copyright, Public Policy, and Information Technology" (1974), 390–391.

85. Henry, *Copyright, Congress, and Technology* (1978–1980).

86. Henry, "Copyright" (1974), 1002.

87. Gillespie, *Wired Shut* (2007), 274.

88. Panel on Science and Technology, *Eleventh Meeting* (1970).

89. Clark, "The Answer to the Machine Is in the Machine" (1996).

90. CONTU (1979). On photocopies: "Machine Reproduction—Photocopying," 47–78.

Chapter 10. Authors of Tradition

1. Kenney, *Recorded Music in American Life* (1999); Meade, "Copyright" (1971).

2. Chakrabarty, "Europa provinzialisieren" (2010).

3. Karpeles, "Communication on Copyright" (1963), 188–189.

4. Ibid., 188.

5. Püttlingen, *Das musicalische Autorrecht* (1864), 70.

6. Folk singer and composer Oscar Brand dedicated a chapter of his monograph about folk to the "legal tangle." Brand, *The Ballad Mongers* (1962), 201–215. On the history of folklore in the U.S., see Bendix, *Amerikanische Folkloristik* (1995).

7. Silber, "Folk Songs and Copyrights" (1960).

8. Ibid., 36.

9. Ibid.

10. Cynthia Gooding has elaborated the same position. Gooding, "Concerning Copyrights" (1961).

11. Eitman, "Copyrights and Collectors" (1960).

12. Ibid., 22.

13. Legman, "Who Owns Folklore?" (1962), originally published in *Wayne Law Review* 72 (1964).

14. Seeger, "Who Owns Folklore?" (1962).

15. Ibid., 96.

16. Seeger, "The Copyright Hassle" (1963–1964).

17. Klarman, "Copyright and Folk Music" (1965).

18. NARA RG 59, Entry 5211, Box 10, Policy Committee on International Copyright, The Proposed Brussels Conference on Copyright. The Sponsorship of a Conference on Copyright for the drafting of a universal convention, July 1, 1947 [Confidential]. See also NARA RG 59, Entry 5211, Box 8: July 1, 1947 Policy Committee on International Copyright. NARA RG 59, Entry 5211, Box 7 Draft: Policy Statement of Copyright [Confidential]. NARA RG 59, Entry 52 11, Box 10: United States Delegation. The Second Session of a General Conference, UNESCO, Mexico City 1947, November 6 1947, Working Committee E, Copyright.

19. *Copyright: Convention and Protocols Between the United States of America and Other Governments* (1955), 3.

20. Kaminstein, "Global Copyright" (1964).

21. UNESCO and BIRPI, "Réunion africain d'étude sur le droit d'auteur (Brazzaville, 5–10 août 1963)" (1963), 153.

22. Ibid., 252.

23. Ibid.

24. UNESCO and WIPO, "Records of the Committee of African Experts to Study a Draft Model Copyright Law, Geneva, 30 November to 4 December 1964," *Copyright Bulletin* XVIII (1965), 9–47, 14, 20.

25. Ibid., 20.

26. WIPO, *Records of the Intellectual Property Conference of Stockholm, June 11 to July 14, 1967* (1971), 876.

27. Moreira da Silva, "Folklore and Copyright" (1967), 58.

28. Ministry of Education, Government of India, *International Copyright* (1967), 85.

29. Ibid.

30. WIPO, *Records of the Intellectual Property Conference of Stockholm, June 11 to July 14, 1967* (1971), 876.

31. Ibid.

32. Ibid., 877–878.

33. Ibid., 877.

34. Ibid., 914.

35. Ibid.

36. This is according to a report by a legal advisor to the Department of State on the revision conferences in Paris and Geneva. Hadl, "Toward International Copyright Revision" (1970): 186 ("The Register of Copyrights announced . . . in December 1967, that it would be impossible for the United States to join the Berne Convention if it had to accept the Stockholm Protocol and that he viewed with very great concern the confusion and erosion in standards of international copyright protection.").

37. WIPO, *Records of the Diplomatic Conference for the Revision of the Berne Convention (Paris, July 5 to 24, 1971)* (1974), 141.

38. Ibid., 188.

39. Chaves, "Le folklore brésilien et sa protéction" (1980); Gavrilov, "La protection juridique des oeuvres du folklore" (1984); Niedzielska, "Les aspects propriété intellectuelle de la protection du folklore" (1980); Epacka, "La question collective du droit d'auteur" (1987); Ndoye, "La protection des expressions du folklore au Sénégal" (1989).

40. UNESCO and WIPO, *Model Provision for National Laws on the Protection of Expressions of Folklore against Illicit Exploitation and Other Prejudicial Actions* (1985).

41. Ibid., 3.

42. Ibid.

43. UNESCO, *Recommendation on the Safeguarding of Traditional Culture and Folklore* (1989).

44. UNESCO and WIPO, *Model Provision for National Laws on the Protection of Expressions of Folklore Against Illicit Exploitation and Other Prejudicial Actions* (1985), 9.

45. UNESCO, *Recommendation on the Safeguarding of Traditional Culture and Folklore* (1989), 238.

46. Mills, "Indigenous Music and the Law" (1996).

47. Brown, "Can Culture Be Copyrighted?" (1998), 193.

48. Scherzinger, "Music, Spirit Possession, and the Copyright Law" (1999), 111.

49. Harrison, "Ritual as Intellectual Property" (1992).

50. WIPO, *Intellectual Property Needs and Expectations of Traditional Knowledge Holders* (2001); Wendland, "Intellectual Property, Traditional Knowledge and Folklore" (2002).

Conclusion

1. Jeanneney, *Googles Herausforderung* (2006).
2. Melville, *Moby-Dick; or, the Whale* (1851), 440.

Bibliographic Essay

1. Strathern, "Potential property" (1996); Strathern, *Property, Substance and Effect* (1999); Coombe, "Challenging Paternity: Histories of Copyright" (1994); Coombe, *The Cultural Life of Intellectual Properties* (1998).
2. Strathern, "Potential property" (1996), 30.
3. Coombe, *The Cultural Life of Intellectual Properties* (1998), 7.
4. Habermas, "Von Anselm von Feuerbach zu Jack the Ripper" (2003). Habermas, "Eigentum vor Gericht" (2006); Habermas, *Diebe vor Gericht* (2008).
5. Sherman and Bently, *The Making of Modern Intellectual Property Law* (1999).
6. Ibid., 119.
7. Ibid., 192. For nineteenth-century copyright in an international context, see also Seville, *The Internationalisation of Copyright Law* (2009); Alexander, *Copyright Law and the Public Interest in the Nineteenth Century* (2010).
8. Sherman and Bently, *The Making of Modern Intellectual Property Law* (1999), 212. Sherman and Bently emphasize the cross-fertilization and transfer between legal categories. Elmar Wadle takes the opposite standpoint of national legal traditions. Wadle, "Entwicklungsschritte des Geistigen Eigentums in Frankreich und Deutschland" (1999).
9. Wadle, *Geistiges Eigentum* (2003 [1996]); Wadle, "Entwicklungsschritte des Geistigen Eigentums in Frankreich und Deutschland" (1999).
10. Bandilla, *Urheberrecht im deutschen Kaiserreich* (2005).
11. Vogt, *Die urheberrechtlichen Reformdiskussionen in Deutschland während der Zeit der Weimarer Republik und des Nationalsozialismus* (2004).
12. Maracke, *Die Entstehung des Urheberrechtsgesetzes von 1965* (2003). One exception to this is Matthias Wiessner's study on GDR copyright in an international context. Wiessner, "Die DDR und das internationale Urheberrechtsregime" (2007).
13. First in connection with the Copyright Act of 1909: Bowker, *Copyright* (no year [1912]). On the history of Anglo-Saxon copyright, see Patterson, *Copyright in Historical Perspective* (1968). For a quick overview of developments in the U.S. with a focus on problems, see Goldstein, *Copyright's Highway* (2003).
14. See Fisher, "Geistiges Eigentum—ein ausufernder Rechtsbereich" (1999).
15. This field of research is well documented in Woodmansee and Jaszi, eds., *The Construction of Authorship* (1994). In the spirit of critical theory: Bettig, *Copyrighting Culture* (1996). For a literary studies perspective on the literary property debate surrounding work by American writers in the nineteenth century, see Buinicki, *Negotiating Copyright* (2006).
16. Jaszi, "Toward a Theory of Copyright" (1991); Jaszi, "On the Author Effect" (1994). Oren Bracha recently made a similar argument based on an analysis of nineteenth-century case law. Although the concept of authorship, which was the key

point of reference at the end of the eighteenth century, was challenged in the nineteenth century as companies and corporations became increasingly important to cultural production, the erosion caused by economic forces did not bring about a legal paradigm shift. Bracha, "The Ideology of Authorship Revisited" (2008).

17. Dölemeyer, "Wege der Rechtsvereinheitlichung" (2002). The development of international law has now been well documented; from the bilateral agreement in the nineteenth century, to the Berne Convention of 1886, right up to the Universal Copyright Convention (UCC) of 1955 established by the U.S. under the auspices of UNESCO. For a concise overview of international copyright up to the end of the 1930s, see Ladas, *The International Protection of Literary and Artistic Property* (1938). For a look at the history of law and the institution on the 100th birthday of the Berne Convention, see Ricketson, *The Berne Convention for the Protection of Literary and Artistic Works: 1886–1986* (1987). The self-satisfied commemorative publication is Schulze, *Hundert Jahre Berner Konvention* (1987). A critical study of the World Intellectual Property Organization (WIPO), founded in 1970, which also manages the Berne Convention can be found in May, *The World Intellectual Property Organization* (2007).

18. For an international study on the social history of the attorney profession, see Siegrist, *Advokat, Bürger und Staat* (1996).

19. Siegrist and Sugarman, eds., *Eigentum im internationalen Vergleich (18.–20. Jahrhundert)* (1999), 30.

20. Siegrist, "Geschichte und aktuelle Probleme des geistigen Eigentums (1600–2000)" (2004), 323.

21. Siegrist, "Geistiges Eigentum im Spannungsfeld von Individualisierung, Nationalisierung und Internationalisierung" (2005). For the history of the Berne Convention, see in particular an essay on the subject by Isabella Löhr, who viewed the internationalization of intellectual property as a key driving force behind new forms of international collaboration for international cultural markets: Löhr, "Der Völkerbund und die Entwicklung des internationalen Schutzes geistigen Eigentums in der Zwischenkriegszeit" (2006). See also Löhr, *Die Globalisierung geistiger Eigentumsrechte* (2010).

22. Wadle, "Die Entfaltung des Urheberrechts als Antwort auf technische Neuerungen" (1985).

23. Dommann, "Rechtsinstrumente" (2005).

24. Litman, "Copyright Legislation and Technological Change" (1989).

25. Lessig, *Code and Other Laws of Cyberspace* (1999).

26. Ibid., 206.

27. Sterne, "The Mp3 as Cultural Artifact" (2006); Gillespie, *Wired Shut* (2007).

28. Vec, *Recht und Normierung in der Industriellen Revolution* (2006); Vec, "Kurze Geschichte des Technikrechts" (2003); Vec, "Weltverträge für Weltliteratur" (2008). Seckelmann, *Industrialisierung, Internationalisierung und Patentrecht im Deutschen Reich 1871–1914* (2006).

Bibliography

1. Archives

Library of Congress, Washington, D.C.

mm 78028043 Joint Committee on Material for Research (approx. 1930–1940) (JCMR)

NARA, Collegepark, MD

RG 59, Entry 5211, Box 1–11

National Library of Medicine, Bethesda, MD

MS C 421 Williams & Wilkins Co. v. The United States (1938–1982)

New York Public Library Performing Arts, Music, New York City

M-Clippings Broadcast Music Inc.—BMI—ASCAP Dispute
M-Clippings Columbia Broadcasting System—ASCAP-BMI Agreements
M-Clipping Copyright 1920s–1930s
M-Clipping Copyright 1940s–1950s
M-Clippings ASCAP 1930–1939
M-Clippings ASCAP 1940–1950
M-Clippings ASCAP 1951–1956
M-Clippings ASCAP 1957–1960
M-Clippings ASCAP 1961–1963
M-Clippings ASCAP "Undated" (Folder 1 & 2)

Rundfunkmuseum Fürth, Max-Grundig-Stiftungs-Archiv, Fürth, Germany

GRUNDIG-Tonbandgeräte: Prospekte, Werbematerialien

Schweizerisches Bundesarchiv, Bern

BAR E 22 Nr. 2377 Berner Übereinkunft zum Schutze von Werken der Literatur und Kunst. Bestrebungen vor der Berner Übereinkunft (1858–1983).
BAR E 22 Nr. 2378 Berner Übereinkunft zum Schutze von Werken der Literatur und Kunst. Konferenz in Bern 1884 (1884–1885).
BAR E 22 Nr. 2379 Berner Übereinkunft zum Schutze von Werken der Literatur und Kunst in Bern 1884 (1885–1886).
BAR E 22 Nr. 2380 Berner Übereinkunft zum Schutze von Werken der Literatur und Kunst. Konferenz in Bern 1884 (1886–1887).
BAR E 22 Nr. 2383 Berner Übereinkunft zum Schutze von Werken der Literatur und Kunst. Internationale Konferenz in Berlin vom 14.10.–14.11.1908.

Schweizerisches Sozialarchiv, Zurich

Zeitungsausschnitte 24.4 Urheberrecht 1943–2006

Schweizerisches Wirtschaftsarchiv, Basel

Bv G 136 World Intellectual Property Organization. Dokumentensammlung.
Vo H II 3b CH Urheberrecht. Dokumentensammlung. Zeitungsartikel.
H + I Bg 1185 Grundig Aktien Gesellschaft Fürth Bayern. Dokumenten-
sammlung.
H + I Bg 1254 Xerox Corporation, Stamford Conn. Dokumentensammlung.

World Intellectual Property Organization (WIPO), Geneva

Historical Collection E 2380n 6133 B.I.R.P.I. Conférence de Rome 1928.
Procès Verbaux des Sous Commissions.

2. Periodicals

American Bar Association (ABA). Section of Patent, Trade Mark and Copyright
    Law, *Committee Reports to be Presented at the Annual Meeting* (1931–1974)
*American Documentation: A Quarterly Review of Ideas, Techniques, Problems, and
    Achievements in Documentation* (1950–1969)
Annuaire de la Société des auteurs et compositeurs dramatiques (1866–1956)
Annual Report of the Librarian of Congress (1866–1980)
ASCAP Journal (1937–1938)
Bulletin de l'Institut international de bibliographie (1895–1914)
Bulletin of the Copyright Society of the U.S.A. (1953–1980)
Congrès juridique international de T.S.F. (1925–1930)
United Nations Educational, Scientific and Cultural Organization (UNESCO),
    Copyright Bulletin (1948–1966)
Copyright Law Symposium (1938–1980)
Datamation (1960–1970)
Der Mikrofilm: Mitteilungen der Photo Copie GmbH und der Mikrofilm GmbH (1951–
    1968)
Entscheidungen des Reichsgerichts in Zivilsachen (RGZ) (1880–1945)
Geistiges Eigentum (1935–1938)
GEMA Nachrichten (1927–1933, 1949–1980)
GEMA News (1964–1982)
Gewerblicher Rechtsschutz und Urheberrecht (GRUR) (1896–1979)
HiFi Stereo Review (1960–1968)
*I.I.D. Communicationes: Communications trimestrielles de l'Institut International de
    Documentation* (1934–1938)
The Journal of Documentary Reproduction (1938–1942)
*Le Droit d'auteur: Organ officiel du Bureau de l'Union internationale pour la protection
    des oeuvres littéraires et artistiques* (1888–1980)
Library Journal (1876–1980)

Library Resources and Technical Services (LRTS) (1957–1980)
MULL: Modern Uses of Logic in Law: Quarterly Newsletter of the Electronic Data
    Retrieval Committee of the American Bar Association (1959–1966)
Nachrichtenblatt der Photo Copie GmbH Berlin (1936–1939)
The Performing Right Gazette (1922–1939)
Phonographische Zeitschrift (1900–1933)
Reproduktion: Monatszeitschrift für photomechanische Reproduktionsverfahren,
    1930–1938
Reprographie (1961–1971)
Rockefeller Foundation, Annual Reports (1913–1980)
Schweizerisches Bundesblatt/Bundesblatt der Schweizerischen Eidgenossenschaft
    (1848–1900)
Sing Out! (1950–1970)
STAGMA Nachrichten (1933–1944)
Stenographische Berichte über die Verhandlungen des Reichstags (1895–1918)
Tape Recording and Reproduction Magazine (London, 1957–1970)
Tape Recording Fortnightly (London, 1960–1961)
Verhandlungen des Deutschen Bundestages und des Bundesrates [microform]: Proto-
    kolle, Drucksachen, Register (1949–1980)
Zentralblatt für Bibliothekswesen (1884–1944)

3. Printed Sources

100 Jahre AKM: Autoren, Komponisten, Musikverleger. Vienna: 1997.
An Act to Amend and Consolidate the Acts Respecting Copyright. Approved, March 4, 1909.
    60th Congress, 2nd session. [Washington]: 1909. Available at http://www.
    copyright.gov/history/1909act.pdf, accessed August 7, 2011.
Actes du Congrès international pour la reproduction des manuscrits, des monnaies et des
    sceaux: tenu à Liége, les 21, 22 et 23 août 1905. Brussels: 1905.
Adorno, Theodor W. "Résumé über Kulturindustrie." In Kulturkritik und Gesellschaft
    I: Prismen. Ohne Leitbild, edited by Theodor Adorno, 337–345. Frankfurt am
    Main: 1977.
Adorno, Theodor W., and Max Horkheimer. "Kulturindustrie: Aufklärung als Mas-
    senbetrug." In Dialektik der Aufklärung, edited by Theodor Adorno and Max
    Horkheimer, 144–198. Nimeguen: 1944.
"Akustische Schutzmarken." Phonographische Zeitschrift 8, no. 45 (1907), 1257–1258.
"Albert Osterrieth zum Gedächtnis." GRUR 32, no. 9 (1927), 589–598.
American Library Association. Board on Resources of American Libraries and Interna-
    tional Relations Board, Conference on International Cultural, Educational, and Sci-
    entific Exchanges. Princeton University, November 25–26, 1946: Preliminary Memo-
    randa by Edwin Everitt Williams and Ruth Verrill Noble. Recommendations Adopted,
    Summary of Discussion. Chicago: 1947.
American Society of Composers, Authors, and Publishers. How the Public Gets Its New
    Music: A Statement of Some of the Reasons for the Copyright Law, Its Operation and
    How It Benefits the Public. New York: 1933.

———. *The Murder of Music*. New York: [1933].

———. *The Story of ASCAP: An American Institution. More Than 30 Years of Service*. [New York]: [1946].

———. *Who Uses Music and Why*. New York: 1934.

"Amerikanische Phonographenfabriken in Deutschland." *Phonographische Zeitschrift* 5, no. 19 (1904), 335–336.

Anstalt für mechanisch-musikalische Rechte, GmbH (AMMRE). *Die Anstalt für mechanisch-musikalische Rechte und die Genossenschaft Deutscher Tonsetzer: Ein Wort zur Aufklärung!* Berlin: [1912].

Arguments before the Committees on Patents of the Senate and House of Representatives, Conjointly on the Bills S. 6330 and H. R. 19853 to Amend and Consolidate the Acts Respecting Copyright. June 6, 7, 8, and 9, 1906. Washington, D.C.: 1906.

"Aus dem Verbande der Deutschen Sprechmaschinen-Industrie." *Phonographische Zeitschrift* 8, no. 27 (1907), 670–671.

Ballou, Hubbard W. "Developments in Copying Methods—1958." *Library Resources and Technical Services (LRTS)* 3, no. 2 (1959), 86–97.

Banzhaf, John F. III. "Copyright Protection for Computer Programs." *Columbia Law Review* 64, no. 7 (1964), 1274–1300.

Barsley, Michael. *Tape Recording*. London: 1967.

Barthes, Roland. "The Death of the Author." *Aspen Magazine* 5/6 (1967). Available at http://www.ubu.com/aspen/aspen5and6/index.html, accessed April 3, 2018.

BASF. *Heiteres Tonband-Brevier: Ein Streifzug um alles, was mit Magnetophonband BASF zusammenhängt*. [Ludwigshafen]: [1960].

Bauer, Josef. *Das musikalische Urheberrecht: Nebst der internationalen Berner Litterarkonvention vom 9. September 1886 und den zwischen Deutschland und den ausländischen Staaten zum Schutz von Litteratur und Kunst geschlossenen Verträgen unter Anziehung der sämtlichen einschlägigen Entscheidungen des Reichsgerichts und des Reichsoberhandelsgerichts für den praktischen Gebrauch*. Leipzig: 1890.

Baum, Alfred. "Die Brüsseler Konferenz zur Revision der Revidierten Berner Übereinkunft." *GRUR* 51, nos. 1, 2 (1949), 1–44.

———. "Rundfunk und Schallplatte." *GRUR* 37, no. 3 (1932), 259–270.

———. "Die Urteile in den Prozessen zwischen Rundfunk und Schallplattenindustrie und ihre Kritik." *Geistiges Eigentum* 3 (1937/1938), 239–266.

Belehrende Mitteilungen an alle Vereine und Leute, die sich in der Schweiz mit dem Urheberrecht an Werken der Litteratur und Kunst beschäftigen: Antwort an die beleidigenden Zeitungsangriffe durch E. Knosp in Bern. Generalagent für die Schweiz der Société des Auteurs, Compositeurs et Editeurs de Musique. Bern: 1896.

Bell, Daniel. *The Coming of Post-Industrial Society: A Venture in Social Forecasting*. New York: 1973.

Benjamin, Curtis G. "Computers and Copyrights: Restrictions on Computer Use of Copyrighted Material Would Protect Authors, Publishers, and even Users." *Science* 152 (April 8, 1966), 181–184.

Berger, Elie. "Les fac-similés photographiques et les calques, résumé de la polémique entre MM. de Pflugk-Harttung et Sybel." *Bibliothèque de l'Ecole des Chartes* XLVI (1885), 718–719.

Bergfeld, Julius. "Phonograph und Publikum." *Phonographische Zeitschrift* 8, no. 10 (1902), 119–121.

Bericht an die nieder-österreichische Handels- und Gewerbekammer, erstattet von der Commission, welche über das a. h. Patent vom 19. Oktober 1846 zum Schutze des literarisch-artistischen Eigenthums zu berathen hatte. Vienna: 1853.

Bergmans, Paul. "Les tentatives antérieures d'entente internationale pour la reproduction des manuscrits." In *Actes du Congrès international pour la reproduction des manuscrits, des monnaies et des sceaux: tenu à Liége, les 21, 22 et 23 août 1905,* 41–56. Brussels: 1905.

BIEM. *Bureau International des Sociétés gérant les Droits d'Enregistrement et de Reproduction Mécanique 1929–1979.* Paris: 1980.

Binkley, Robert C. *Manual on Methods of Reproducing Research Materials: A Survey Made for the Joint Committee on Materials for Research of the Social Science Research Council and the American Council of Learned Societies.* Ann Arbor: 1936.

——. *Methods of Reproducing Research Materials: A Survey Made for the Joint Committee on Material for Research of the Social Science Research Council and the American Council of Learned Societies.* Ann Arbor: 1931.

——. "New Tools for Men of Letters." *The Yale Review* 24 (1935), 519–537.

——. "Techniques and Policies of Documentary Reproduction." *F. I. D. Communicationes* 6 (1939), 12–15.

Blanc, Etienne. *Traité de la contrefaçon en tous genres et de sa poursuite en justice. Concernent: Les oeuvres littéraires, dramatiques, musicales et artistiques; les dessins et les marques de fabrique; les titres d'ouvrages et les noms d'auteurs; les invention brevetées, les enseignes; les désignation de marchandises, les étiquettes et les noms de commerçants, avec le texte des lois et décrets et les principaux monuments de jurisprudence sur la matière.* Paris: 1855.

Board of Trade. *Copyright Royalty (Mechanical Musical Instruments) Inquiry: Report of Committee. Presented by the President of the Board of Trade to Parliament by Command of His Majesty, June 1928.* London: 1928.

——. *Report of the Copyright Committee: Presented by the President of the Board of Trade to Parliament by Command of Her Majesty, October 1952.* London: 1952.

Bolley, Pompejus Alexander. *Berichte über die Betheiligung der Schweiz an der internationalen Ausstellung von 1867 (in Paris), sammt Katalog.* Bern: 1868.

Boor, [first name not given] de. "Vervielfältigung zum persönlichen Gebrauch?" *GRUR* 6, no. 10 (1954), 440–447.

Borwick, John, and Peta Stuart-Hunt. *International Federation of Producers of Phonograms and Videograms: The First Fifty Years. Celebrating the Fiftieth Anniversary of IFPI, International Federation of Phonogram and Videogram Producers.* London: 1983.

Bourgeois, P. "La reproduction des documents en relation avec les droits d'auteur & d'editeur." In *Vorträge der 11. Konferenz. I. I. D., Brussels 1932, Vol. 1,* edited by I. I. D., Internationales Institut für Dokumentation (Institut International de Bibliographie), 37–47.

Bowker, Richard Rogers. *Copyright: Its History and Its Law.* Buffalo, N.Y.: 2002 [1912].

Bowker, R. R., and Thorvald Solberg. *Copyright, Its Law and Its Literature.* London and New York: 1886.

Boyle, James. *Shamans, Software, and Spleens: Law and the Construction of the Information Society.* Cambridge, Mass. and London: 1997.

Brake, Michael. "Die Digital-Liberalen." *Die Tageszeitung* (September 11, 2006), 14.

Brand, Oscar. *The Ballad Mongers: Rise of the Modern Folk Song.* New York: 1962.

Brauns, Heinrich. *Stereotechnik: Ein Buch für Techniker, Amateure und Hi-Fi-Tonband-und Schallplattenfreunde.* Stuttgart: 1961.

Breyer, Stephen. "Copyright: A Rejoinder." *UCLA Law Review* 20, no. 1 (1972), 75–83.

———. "The Uneasy Case for Copyright: A Study of Copyright in Books, Photocopies, and Computer Programs." *Harvard Law Review* 84, no. 2 (1970), 281–351.

Brown, Michael F. "Can Culture Be Copyrighted?" *Current Anthropology* 39, no. 2 (1998), 193–222.

Brylawski, E. Fulton, and Abe Goldman, eds. *Legislative History of the 1909 Copyright Act, Vol. 1–6.* South Hackensack, N.J.: 1976.

Bush, Vannevar. "As We May Think." *Atlantic Monthly* (1945). Available at http://www.theatlantic.com/doc/194507/bush.

———. *Science, the Endless Frontier: A Report to the President on a Program for Postwar Scientific Research, Foreword by Erich Bloch; preface by Daniel J. Kevles.* Washington, D.C.: 1990 [1945].

Cahn-Speyer, Rudolf. "Rundfunk, Schallplatte und ausübender Künstler." *Blätter für Funkrecht. Herausgegeben im Auftrag der Reichs-Rundfunkgesellschaft m.b.H. in Berlin von Rechtsanwalt Willy Hoffmann* 6 (1927), 85–89.

Cary, George D. "Copyright Registration and Computer Programs." *Bulletin of the Copyright Society of the U.S.A.* 11 (1964), 361–368.

Charles, Ruth. "ASCAP—A Half Century of Progress." *Bulletin of the Copyright Society of the U.S.A.* 11, no. 3 (1964), 133–143.

Chatelain, Émile. "La photographie dans les bibliothèques." *Revue des bibliothèques* 1 (1891), 225–241.

Chaves, Antonio. "Le folklore brésilien et sa protéction." *Le Droit d'Auteur* 93 (1980), 109–112.

Clark, Charles. "The Answer to the Machine Is in the Machine." In *The Future of Copyright in a Digital Environment: Proceedings of the Royal Academy Colloquium organized by the Royal Netherlands Academy of Sciences (KNAW) and the Institute for Information Law, (Amsterdam, 6–7 July 1995),* edited by P. Bernt Hugenholtz, 139–145. The Hague: 1996.

Cohn-Schmidt, J. "Die Entscheidung des Reichsgerichts in der Kopierfrage." In *Phonos* 2, no. 8 (1910), 145–146.

———. "Die Weisheit der deutschen Regierung." In *Phonos* 2, no. 3 (1910), 33–36.

"Copia." In *Grosses vollständiges Universal-Lexicon aller Wissenschaften und Künste,* edited by Johann Heinrich Zedler, vol. 6, 1200. Halle and Leipzig: 1733.

Copinger, Walter Arthur, and Frances Edmund Skone James. *Copinger and Skone James on the Law of Copyright: Including International and Colonial Copyright, with the Statutes Relating thereto and Forms and Precedents.* London: 1948.

Copyright Act 1911 (Great Britain). Available at http://www.legislation.gov.uk/ukpga/Geo5/1-2/46, accessed August 7, 2011.

"Copyright Amendment Passes House Committee." *Datamation* 12, no. 12 (1966), 69–70.

"Copyright Bill: Interest Groups Stymie Changes in Copyright Law." In *Legislative and the Lobbyists,* edited by Congressional Service Quarterly, Washington, D.C. (May 1968), 82–84.

"Copyright Implications in the New Science of Data Storage and Retrieval." *Publishers Weekly* (November 30, 1964), 20–23.

Copyright: Convention and Protocols between the United States of America and Other Governments. Dated at Geneva September 6, 1952. Washington, D.C.: 1955.

"Cour d'appel de Paris, 1ère chambre: Audience de 1er février 1905.—Enoch et Cie. c. Société des phonographes et grammophones." *Le Droit d'Auteur* 18 (1905), 35–36.

Crawford, Helen. "Notes of a Librarian on Contemplating Her Xerox Machine." *Bulletin of the Medical Library Association* 51, no. 3 (1963), 397–399.

Cunha, Xavier da. "La législation portugaise sur la reproduction des manuscrits." In *Actes du Congrès International pour la Reproduction des Manuscrits, des Monnaies et des Sceaux tenu à Liége, les 21, 22 et 23 août 1905*, 2–10. Brussels: 1905.

D'Albert, Wolfgang. *Die Verwertung des musikalischen Aufführungsrechts in Deutschland.* Jena: 1907.

"Das Ergebnis der internationalen Urheberrechts-Konferenz." *Phonographische Zeitschrift* 9, no. 47 (1908), 1461–1462.

"Das Urhebergesetz im Reichstag." *Phonographische Zeitschrift* 11, no. 15 (1910), 387–388.

"Das Urheberrecht und der Phonograph." *Phonographische Zeitschrift* 4, no. 11 (1903), 161.

"De la reproduction sonore des compositions musicales par des instruments mécaniques." *Le Droit d'Auteur* 3 (1890), 15–16.

Der Lesesaal von morgen . . . Advertising brochure from Photo-Copie GmbH. Berlin: [1931].

"Der Pariser Phonographen-Streik." *Phonographische Zeitschrift* 6 (1905), 274.

"Der Phonograph im neuen Deutschen Urheberrecht-Gesetz." *Phonographische Zeitschrift* 2, no. 8 (1901), 88.

"Der 'Phonographen-Ton.'" *Phonographische Zeitschrift* 3, no. 34 (1902), 344–345.

"Der Photostat." *Photographische Korrespondenz* 63 (1927), 187–188.

Der Schutz der Photographien gegen unbefugte Nachbildungen: Gesetz vom 10. Januar 1876. Mit den Ergänzungs- und Vollzugs-Bestimmungen der Reichs- und Landes-Gesetzgebung. Nach den Materialien des Reichstages dargestellt von einem Mitgliede desselben. Berlin: 1878.

"Der Sprechmaschinen-Rekord und das Urhebergesetz." *Phonographische Zeitschrift* 7, no. 30 (1906), 621–622.

"Deutsche Dialekt-Aufnahmen von Volksliedern." *Phonographische Zeitschrift* 7, no. 32 (1906), 665–666.

Die Internationale Arbeitsorganisation: Dreissig Jahre Kampf für soziale Gerechtigkeit, 1919–1949. Geneva: 1950.

"Die Novitätenkonzerte der 'Ammre.'" *Phonographische Zeitschrift* 14, no. 19 (1913), 427–428.

"Die Urheberrechts-Denkschrift des Verbandes der deutschen Sprechmaschinen-Industrie." *Phonographische Zeitschrift* 9, nos. 26, 27, 30 (1908), 766–767, 792–793, 870–874.

"Die Vorschläge der italienischen Regierung und des Internationalen Büros zum Schutze der Werke der Literatur und Kunst zum Funk-Urheberrecht." *Blätter für Funkrecht: Herausgegeben im Auftrag der Reichs-Rundfunkgesellschaft m.b.H. in Berlin von Rechtsanwalt Willy Hoffmann* 1, no. 4 (1927), 50–51.

Diefenbach, Werner W. *Tonband-Hobby: Praktikum für Tonbandfreunde.* Berlin-Tempelhof: 1962.

Diesch, Carl. "Eine Entgegnung zur Frage der Photokopie." In *Minerva-Zeitschrift* 9 (1932), 138–140.

Donker Duyvis, Frits. "La photocopie micrographique sur papier." *I.I.D. Communicationes* 2, no. 2 (1935), 16–23.

Donle, Friedrich. *Der Phonograph und seine Stellung zum Rechte.* Neuburg a.D.: 1897.

Dorian, M. *Berliner Konferenz über Revision internationaler Urheberrechts-Gesetze: Instrumente zur mechanischen Hervorbringung von Musikstücken. Geschichte der Bewegung und Analysis der vorgeschlagenen Gesetzgebung, Verband der deutschen Sprechmaschinen-Industrie.* [1908].

Edelman, Bernard. *Le droit saisi par la photographie: Eléments pour une théorie marxiste du droit.* Paris: 1980 [1973].

"Éditeurs de musique et fabricants d'instruments de musique mécaniques." *Le Droit d'Auteur* 16 (1903), 70.

Eger, Leo. "Der Phonograph und das Urheberrecht." *Archiv für bürgerliches Recht* 18 (1900), 264–290.

Eingabe des Schweizer Hotelier-Vereins an den Schweizerischen Bundesrat betreffend das Urheberrecht der Autoren und Komponisten. Beau-Rivage: 1901.

Eisenmann, Ernst. *Das Urheberrecht an Tonkunstwerken: Grundlagen zur Beurteilung der neuen Instrumente zu Musikvorführungen (Phonograph, Theatrophon, Pianola).* Berlin and Leipzig: 1907.

Eitman, Bill. "Copyrights and Collectors." *Sing Out!* 10, no. 3 (1960), 20–22.

Elster, Alexander. "Die wettbewerbliche und die immanente Begrenzung des Urheberrechts." *GRUR* 31, no. 11 (1926), 493–502.

——. "Zur Photokopie-Frage." *GRUR* 36, no. 9 (1931), 952–955.

——. "Zur Rechtsfrage der Photokopie." *Minerva-Zeitschrift* 9 (1932), 86–88.

Epacka, Yves D. "La question collective du droit d'auteur: l'expérience pratique d'une société africaine." *Le Droit d'Auteur* 100 (1987), 390–396.

Erffa, Margarethe Freiin von. "Die neuere technische Entwicklung und ihr Einfluss auf das Urheberrecht." *GRUR* 53, no. 5 (1951), 226–230.

Erhard, Ludwig. *Wohlstand für alle, bearbeitet von Wolfram Langer.* Düsseldorf: 1957.

Exner, F. M., and R. Pöch. *Phonographische Aufnahmen in Indien und in Neu-Guinea.* Vienna: 1905.

Exposition internationale des arts et techniques appliqués à la vie moderne, Paris 1937: Album officiel. Photographies en couleurs. Paris: 1937.

Fack, Fritz Ullrich. "Mehr Schutz für das Geistige Eigentum: Eine Übersicht über das geplante neue Urheberrecht." *Frankfurter Allgemeine Zeitung,* no. 295 (December 20, 1961), 11.

Federal Council for Science and Technology. *The Copyright Law as it Relates to National Information Systems and National Programs: Committee on Scientific and Technical Information (COSATI).* Washington, D.C.: 1967.

Fiebiger, Otto. "Internationale Photographische Ausstellung, Dresden 1909: Die Photographie im Dienste des Bibliothekswesens." *Centralblatt für Bibliothekswesen* 26 (1909), 451–456.

Fiesenig, Wolfgang. *Urheberrecht und mechanische Musikinstrumente.* Bayreuth: 1916.

"First Annual Report of the Committee to Investigate Problems Affecting Communication in Science and Education." *Bulletin of the Copyright Society of the USA* 10, no. 1 (1962), 1–25.

Foucault, Michel. "Was ist ein Autor?" In *Texte zur Theorie der Autorschaft*, edited by Fotis Jannidis, Gerhard Lauer, Matias Martinez, and Simone Winko, 198–229. Stuttgart: 2000 [1969].

Foundation of an International Institute for the Unification of Private Law (Offer of the Italian Government): League of Nations. Geneva, September 30th, 1924. A. 134 (1) 1924. V.

Freiesleben, Gerhard. *Recht und Tonkunst: Eine Gemeinverständliche Darstellung des Musikalischen Urheber- und Verlagsrechts.* Leipzig: 1914.

Fretwell, John. "Photographic Copying in Libraries." *The Library Journal* 33, no. 6 (1908), 223–224.

Gardner, Douglas, and Ian Arnison. *Tape Recording as a Pastime.* London: 1959 [1958].

Gavrilov, E. P. "La protection juridique des oeuvres du folklore." *Le Droit d'Auteur* 97 (1984), 75–79.

Gayley, Charles Mills. "The Reproduction of Manuscripts from the American Point of View." In *Actes du Congrès international pour la reproduction des manuscrits, des monnaies et des sceaux: tenu à Liége, les 21, 22 et 23 août 1905*, 203–215. Brussels: 1905.

"Generalversammlung des Bundes der Sprechmaschinenhändler Deutschlands vom 25. März 1908." *Phonographische Zeitschrift* 9, no. 15 (1908), 470–473.

Genossenschaft Deutscher Komponisten. *Materialien zur Begründung einer Deutschen Centralstelle für die Verwertung musikalischer Aufführungsrechte.* Berlin: 1900.

Genossenschaft Deutscher Tonsetzer. *Die Anstalt für Musikalisches Aufführungsrecht. Zur Aufklärung und Abwehr: Denkschrift der Genossenschaft Deutscher Tonsetzer.* Berlin: 1904.

——. *Geschäfte gegen die Schaffenden: Eine Stellungnahme zu der Denkschrift der Arbeitsgemeinschaft der Verbreiter von Geisteswerken.* Berlin: 1933.

——. *Grundordnung der Anstalten für Musikalische Urheberrechte.* Berlin: [1931].

Gentz, Günther. "Überspielungsfreiheit zum persönlichen Gebrauch?" *GRUR* 54, no. 11 (1952), 495–500.

Gesellschaft für musikalische Aufführungs- und mechanische Vervielfältigungsrechte (GEMA, previously STAGMA). *Magnettongeräte und Urheberrecht: Eine Sammlung von Rechtsgutachten.* Munich and Berlin: 1952.

Giannini, Amadeo. "Rechtsprobleme der Schallplatte." *UFITA* 7 (1934), 267–288.

Giesecke, Heinrich. "Der Zusammenschluss der europäischen Rundfunkgesellschaften." In *Blätter für Funkrecht: Herausgegeben im Auftrag der Reichs-Rundfunkgesellschaft m.b.H. in Berlin von Rechtsanwalt Willy Hoffmann* 1, no. 2 (1927), 20–30.

Gipe, George A. *Nearer to the Dust: Copyright and the Machine.* Baltimore: 1967.

Giry, A. *Manuel de diplomatique.* Paris: 1925 [1894].

Gitlin, Paul. "Radio Infringement of Music Copyright." *Copyright Law Symposium* 1 (1938), 61–90.

Göhler, Georg. *Keine Konzert-Tantiemen! Ein Aufruf an alle Freunde der deutschen Musikpflege.* Altenburg: [1905?].

Goldman, Abe A. *The History of U.S.A. Copyright Law Revision from 1901 to 1954: Copyright Law Revision. Studies Prepared for the Subcommittee on Patents, Trademarks, and Copyrights of the Committee on the Judiciary United States Senate Eighty-Sixth Congress, First Session Pursuant to S. Res. 53, Study No. 1, Committee Print. July 1955.* Washington, D.C.: 1960.

Goldschmidt, Robert, and Paul Otlet. "Sur une forme nouvelle du livre." *Bulletin de l'Institut international de bibliographie* 12 (1907), 61–69.

Gooding, Cynthia. "Concerning Copyrights." *Sing Out!* 11, no. 1 (1961), 24–25.

"Grammophon-Konzert im Beethovensaal." *Phonographische Zeitschrift* 4, no. 15 (1903), 219, 221.

Haase, Eckart. *Übertragung von Werken der Tonkunst auf mechanische Musikinstrumente: Dissertation Rechts- und staatswissenschaftliche Fakultät der Kaiser-Wilhelms-Universität zu Strassburg.* Borna, Leipzig: 1914.

Hadl, Robert D. "Toward International Copyright Revision." *Bulletin of the Copyright Society of the U.S.A.* 18, no. 3 (1970), 183–228.

Haeger, Siegfried. "Zur Gefahr der Urheberrechtsverletzung durch Tonband-Vervielfältigung gemäß § 15 Abs. 2 LUG." *GRUR* 56, no. 2 (1954), 52–57.

———. "Der Einbruch von Nutzungsrechten in die Privatsphäre." In *Persönlichkeit und Technik im Lichte des Urheber-, Film-, Funk- und Fernsehrechts: Ehrengabe für Ernst E. Hirsch,* edited by Georg Roeber, 329–356. Baden-Baden: 1963.

Hansen, Fritz. *Das Urheberrecht in der Praxis der Postkarten-Industrie: Nach einem Vortrage, gehalten auf der Mitglieder-Versammlung des Schutzverbandes für die Postkarten-Industrie (E. V.) in Leipzig 1908.* Berlin: 1908.

Harrison, Simon. "Ritual as Intellectual Property." *Man* (New Series) 27, no. 2 (1992), 225–244.

Hattery, Lowell H., and George P. Bush, eds. *Reprography and Copyright Law.* Washington, D.C.: 1964.

Hawken, William R. "Reprographic Technology: Present and Future." *Reprography and Copyright Law,* edited by Lowell H. Hattery and George P. Bush, 39–49. Washington, D.C.: 1964.

Henry, Nicholas, ed. *Copyright, Congress, and Technology: The Public Record, Vol. I–V.* Phoenix: 1978–1980.

———. *Copyright, Information Technology, Public Policy: Part II: Public Policies–Information Technology.* New York and Basel: 1976.

———. "Copyright: Its Adequacy in Technological Societies." *Science* 186, no. 4168 (December 13, 1974), 993–1004.

———. "Copyright, Public Policy, and Information Technology." *Science* 183, no. 4123 (1974), 384–391.

———. "The New Copyright Act, or How to Get into a Heap of Trouble Without Really Trying." *PS* 10, no. 1 (1977), 6–8.

Herbert v. Shanley Co. 242, U. S. 591 (1917). Available at http://supreme.justia.com/us/242/591/case.html, accessed August 17, 2011.

Hijmans, K. "Fotokopie oder Mikrokopie für die Dokumentation." *I.I.D. Communicationes* 4, no. 1 (1937), 7–9.

Hillig. "Zur Frage der Photokopie." *Börsenblatt für den Deutschen Buchhandel* 100, no. 80 (1933), 244–245.

Hinrichsen, Hans Joachim. *Die Übertragung des musikalischen Urheberrechts an Musikverleger und Musikverwertungsgesellschaften.* Leipzig: 1934.

Hoffmann, Willy. "Das Urheberrecht des nachschaffenden Künstlers." *GRUR* 32, no. 2 (1927), 69–72.

———. *Ein deutsches Urheberrechtsgesetz: Entwurf eines Gesetzes über das Urheberrecht mit Begründung.* Berlin: 1933.

Holbrook, Franklin F. *Survey of Activities of American Agencies in Relation to Materials for Research in the Social Sciences and the Humanities: Compiled for the Joint Committee on Materials for Research of the American Council of Learned Societies and the Social Science Research Council.* Washington, D.C., and New York: 1932.

Homburg, Robert. "Die Probleme des Funkrechtes und das Comité International de la T.S.F." *Blätter für Funkrecht: Herausgegeben im Auftrag der Reichs-Rundfunkgesellschaft m.b.H. in Berlin von Rechtsanwalt Willy Hoffmann* 1, no. 3 (1927), 30–32.

Hubbell, Raymond. *From Nothing to Five Million a Year: The Story of ASCAP by a Founder.* Washington, D.C.: 1937.

Hurt, Robert M., and Robert M. Schuchman. "The Economic Rationale of Copyright." *American Economic Review* 56, no. 2 (1966), 421–432.

Ihering, Rudolf von. "Rechtsschutz gegen injuriöse Rechtsverletzungen." *Jahrbücher für die Dogmatik des heutigen römischen und deutschen Privatrechts.*, 23 = N.F Bd. 11 (1885), 155–338.

Institut international pour l'unification du droit privé. *Offre du gouvernement italien: Société des Nations. Genève, le 29 April 1926. C.262.M.101.1926 V.*

"Institution pour la perception de droits sur les reproductions mécanique d'oeuvres musicales." *Le Droit d'Auteur* 25 (1912), 31–32.

International Federation of the Phonographic Industry, ed. *The Industry of Human Happiness: Published as a Book of Commemoration by the International Federation of the Phonographic Industry.* London: [1959].

International Labour Office. *International Labour Conference: Twenty-Sixth Session, Geneva. Rights of Performers in Broadcasting, Television and the Mechanical Reproduction of Sounds. Fourth Item on the Agenda.* Geneva: 1939.

"An Interview with Marshall McLuhan." *The Structurist* (January 1, 1966), 61–69.

Jeanneney, Jean-Noël. *Googles Herausforderung: Für eine europäische Bibliothek.* Berlin: 2006 [2005].

"Joint Libraries Committee on Fair Use in Photocopying, Report on Single Copies." *Bulletin of the Copyright Society of the U.S.A.* 9, no. 1 (1961), 79–84.

Kaminstein, Abraham L. "Global Copyright: Recent International Copyright Conferences in Africa, Europe, and Asia." *Bulletin of the Copyright Society of the U.S.A.* 11, no. 4 (1964), 225–233.

Kaplan, Benjamin. *An Unhurried View of Copyright.* New York and London: 1967.

Kaplan, Benjamin, and Arthur R. Miller. "Computers and the Copyright Bill." *Educom* 2, no. 3 (1967), 3–11.

Karpeles, Maud. "Communication on Copyright." *Western Folklore* 22, no. 3 (1963), 187–189.

Kastenmeier, Robert W. "The Information Explosion and Copyright Law Revision." *Bulletin of the Copyright Society of the U.S.A.* 14, no. 3 (1967), 195–204.

Kaufmann. "Literarisches und künstlerisches Eigenthum." *Volkswirtschafts-Lexikon der Schweiz (Urproduktion, Handel, Industrie, Verkehr etc.)*, Vol. II, edited by A. Furrer, 342–354. Bern: 1889.

Keyssner, Hugo. *Das Recht am eigenen Bilde.* Berlin: 1896.

Klarman, Barbara Friedman. "Copyright and Folk Music—A Perplexing Problem." *Bulletin of the Copyright Society of the U.S.A.* 12 (1965), 277–292.

Klier, Karl, and Erich Seemann. "Kunstlieder im Volksmunde: Nachweise." *Jahrbuch für Volksliedforschung* 2 (1930), 156–160.

Klostermann, Rudolf. *Das Urheberrecht an Schrift- und Kunstwerken, Abbildungen, Compositionen, Photographien, Mustern und Modellen, nach deutschem und internationalem Rechte systematisch dargestellt.* Berlin: 1876.

Kluth, Heinrich. *Jeder sein eigener Schallplattenfabrikant.* Berlin: 1932.

Knoch, Arthur. "Deutschlands und Amerikas Export- und Handelsbeziehungen in Sprechmaschinen." *Phonographische Zeitschrift* 14, no. 22 (1913), 475–477.

Kögel, P. R. *Die Photographie historischer Dokumente nebst den Grundzügen der Reproduktionsverfahren wissenschaftlich und praktisch dargestellt.* Leipzig: 1914.

Kohler, Josef. "Autorschutz des reproduzierenden Künstlers." *GRUR* 14, no. 6 (1909), 230–232.

——. *Das Autorrecht, eine zivilistische Abhandlung: Zugleich ein Beitrag zur Lehre vom Eigenthum, vom Miteigenthum, vom Rechtsgeschäft und vom Individualrecht. Separatdruck aus Ihering's Jahrbuch.* Jena: 1880.

——. "Dichter und Erfinder." In *GRUR* 1, no. 1 (1896), 3–4.

——. *Kunstwerkrecht (Gesetz vom 9. Januar 1907).* Stuttgart: 1908.

——. *Recht und Persönlichkeit in der Kultur der Gegenwart.* Stuttgart and Berlin: 1914.

Krumbacher, Karl. "Die Photographie im Dienste der Geisteswissenschaften." In *Sonderabdruck: Neue Jahrbücher für das klassische Altertum* 17 (1906), 601–660.

Kufferath, Maurice. *Les Abus de la Société des Auteurs, Compositeurs et Editeurs de Musique.* Brussels: 1897.

"L'organisation de la documentation." *Bulletin de l'Institut international de bibliographie* 13 (1908), 184–191.

La Poste par pigeons voyageurs: Souvenir du siège de Paris. Spécimen identique d'une des pellicules de dépêches portées a Paris par pigeons voyeurs. Photographiées par Dagron. Seul photographe du Gouvernement pour toutes les dépêches officielles et privées sur pellicule. Notice sur le voyage du ballon Le Niepce. Emportant M. Dagron et ses collaborateurs. Détails sur la mission qu'ils avaient à remplir. Tour–Bordeaux: 1870–1871.

Latman, Alan. "Fair Use of Copyrighted Works." In *Copyright Law Revision: Studies Prepared for the Subcommittee on Patents, Trademarks, and Copyrights of the Committee on the Judiciary United States Senate Eighty-Sixth Congress, Second Session, Pursuant to S. Res. 240, Study 14, Committee Print,* edited by the Library of Congress Copyright Office, 1–44. Washington, D.C.: 1960.

Lazarsfeld, Paul F., and Frank Stanton, eds. *Radio Research 1942–1943.* New York: 1944.

"Le livre microphotographique: Le Bibliophote ou livre à projection." *Bulletin de l'Institut international de bibliographie* 16 (1911), 215–222.

Legge 22 aprile 1941 n. 633, Protezione del diritto d'autore e di altri diritti connessi al suo esercizio. (G.U. n.166 del 16 luglio 1941). Available at http://www.interlex.it/testi/l41_633.htm, accessed September 2, 2011.

Legman, G. "Who Owns Folklore?" *Western Folklore* 21, no. 1 (1962), 1–12.

Leinveber, Gerhard. "Die wichtigsten Neuerungen der deutschen Urheberrechtsreform." *GRUR* 68, no. 3 (1966), 132–137.

Lemoine, Jean-Jacques. *La Société des Auteurs, Compositeurs et Editeurs de Musique SACEM 1850–1950.* Bar-sur-Aube, France: 1950.

Lessig, Lawrence. *Code and Other Laws of Cyberspace.* New York: 1999.

Library of Congress. "National Jukebox." Available at http://www.loc.gov/jukebox/, accessed August 7, 2011.

Lindemann, Otto. *Gesetz, betreffend das Urheberrecht an Werken der Literatur und der Tonkunst: Vom 19. Juni 1901. In der Fassung des Gesetzes vom 22. Mai 1910.* Berlin: 1910.

Linden, Bella L. "The Law of Copyright and Unfair Competition: The Impact of the New Technology on the Dissemination of Information." *MULL* (June 1965), 44–52.

Lion. "Das Recht des wiedergebenden Künstlers." *GRUR* 32, no. 5 (1927), 296–300.

Lorenz, H. "Die sogenannten mechanisch-musikalischen Urheberrechte." *Phonographische Zeitschrift* 14, no. 27 (1913), 586.

Luce, Henry R. "The American Century." *Life* 10, no. 7 (February 17, 1941), 61–65.

Ludolf Waldmann's gewonnene Prozesse gegen die Fabrikanten der "mechanischen Musik-Instrumente": Lösung einer hochwichtigen sozialen Frage. Von höchstem Interesse für die ganze musikalische Welt! Berlin: 1889.

Lussy, Mathis. *Die Kunst des musikalischen Vortrags: Anleitung zur ausdrucksvollen Betonung und Tempoführung in der Vocal- und Instrumentalmusik. Nach der fünften französischen und ersten englischen Ausgabe von Lussys "Traité de L'Expression musicale" mit Autorisation des Verfassers übersetzt und bearbeitet.* Leipzig: 1886 [Paris: 1873].

M**r, P**l. "Confessions of an Illicit Tape Recordist." *High Fidelity: The Magazine for Music Listeners* 13, no. 8 (1963), 38–40, 109.

MacDonald, Joseph. "Technological Advances and Copyright." *Bulletin of the Copyright Society of the U.S.A.* 8, no. 1 (1960), 3–5.

Marc, Paul. "Bibliothekswesen." In *Angewandte Photographie in Wissenschaft und Technik*, edited by K. W. Wolf-Czapek, 57–76. Berlin: 1911.

Marke, Julius J. *Copyright and Intellectual Property.* New York: 1967.

Marwitz. "Das Photokopierverfahren." *Börsenblatt für den Deutschen Buchhandel* 98, no. 252 (1931), 949–950.

Maugras, E., and M. Guégan. *Le cinématographe devant le droit.* Paris: 1908.

Mayer, Martin, and John M. Conly. *Hi-Fi: How to Pick the Best Components for Every Budget.* New York: 1956.

McLuhan, Marshall. *Das Medium ist die Botschaft*, edited and translated by Martin Baltes, Fritz Boehler, Rainer Höltschl, and Jürgen Reuss. Dresden: 2001.

———. *The Gutenberg Galaxy: The Making of Typographic Man.* [Toronto]: 1962.

———. *Understanding Media: The Extensions of Man.* New York: 1964.

Meade, Guthrie T. "Copyright: A Tool for Commercial Rural Music Research." *Western Folklore* 30, no. 3 (1971), 206–214.

Mediger, Harald. "Magnetton und Urheberrecht." *GRUR* 53, no. 8/9 (1951), 382–386.

Melville, Herman. *Moby-Dick: oder: Der Wal. Roman.* German translation by Friedhelm Rathjen. Frankfurt am Main: 2012 [1851].

"Micro-Photographs as Documentary Records." *The British Journal of Photography* (January 18, 1907), 39.

Miller, Arthur R. "Computers and Copyright Law." *Michigan State Bar Journal* 46, no. 4 (1967), 11–18.

Miller, James G. "EDUCOM: Interuniversity Communications Council." *Science* 154, no. 3748 (1966), 483–488.

Mills, E. C. "What Is 'ASCAP'?" *Copyright Law Symposium* 1 (1938), 193–195.

Mills, Sherylle. "Indigenous Music and the Law: An Analysis of National and International Legislation." *Yearbook for Traditional Music* 28 (1996), 57–86.

Ministère des affaires étrangères: *Convention conclue le 23 février 1882, entre la France et la Confédération Suisse pour la garantie réciproque de la propriété littéraire et artistique.* Paris: 1882.

Ministry of Education Government of India. *International Copyright: Needs of Developing Countries.* New Delhi: 1967.

Molsdorf. "Einige Ratschläge bei der Beschaffung photographischer Einrichtungen für Bibliothekszwecke." *Zentralblatt für Bibliothekswesen* 18, nos. 1, 2 (1901), 23–31.

Moreira da Silva, Mario. "Folklore and Copyright." *EBU review/B* 101 (1967), 53–59.

Mussolini, Benito. *La nuova politica dell'Italia: Discorsi e dichiarazioni a cura di Amedeo Giannini.* Milan: 1923.

National Commission on New Technological Uses of Copyrighted Works (CONTU). *Final Report.* Washington, D.C.: 1979.

Ndoye, Babacar. "La protection des expressions du folklore au Sénégal." *Le droit d'auteur* 102 (1989), 396–401.

Nesper, Eugen. *Nimm Schallplatten selber auf! Eine Anleitung zur Selbstherstellung von Schallplatten.* Stuttgart: 1932.

"Neues vom Phonogramm-Archiv der Wiener Akademie der Wissenschaften." *Phonographische Zeitschrift* 3, no. 32 (1902), 331–332.

Niedzielska, Marie. "Les aspects propriété intellectuelle de la protection du folklore." *Le droit d'auteur* 93 (1980), 279–286.

"No. 506 Gesetz, betreffend das Urheberrecht an Schriftwerken, Abbildungen, musikalischen Kompositionen und dramatischen Werken. Vom 11. Juni 1870." *Bundes-Gesetzblatt des Norddeutschen Bundes*, no. 19 (1870), 339–354.

"No. 1840 Gesetz zum Schutze des Eigenthums an Werken der Wissenschaft und Kunst gegen Nachdruck und Nachbildung. Vom 11. Juni 1837." In *Gesetz-Sammlung für die Königlichen Preußischen Staaten 1837*, 165–171.

"Novitäten-Abende der 'Ammre.'" *Phonographische Zeitschrift* 14, no. 18 (1913), 412.

Organisation des nations unies pour l'éducation, la science et la culture (UNESCO) et Bureaux internationaux reunis pour la protection et la propriété intellectuelle (BIRPI). "Réunion africain d'étude sur le droit d'auteur (Brazzaville, 5–10 août 1963)." *Inter-auteurs* 152 (1963), 151–155.

Osterrieth, Albert. "Das Urheberrecht an Phonogrammen nach dem deutschen Gesetz vom 19. Juni 1901." *Phonographische Zeitschrift* 8, nos. 50, 51 (1907), 1434–1436, 1466–1468.

Ostertag, F. "Die Photokopie im Lichte des Urheberrechts." In *Rapports Conference de documentation Copenhague 1935*, edited by Internationales Institut für Dokumentation (Institut International de Bibliographie), Os.1–Os.8. Brussels: 1935.

Otlet, Paul. "Le livre photomicrographique." In *I.I.D. Communicationes* 1, no. 2 (1934), 19–20.

——. "Le traitement de la littérature scientifique." *Revue général des sciences* 29 (1918), 494–502.

——. *Traité de Documentation: Le livre sur le livre. Théorie et pratique.* Brussels: 1934.

"Out to Crack Copying Market." *Business Week* (September 19, 1959), 86–93.

Panel on Science and Technology. *Eleventh Meeting, The Management of Information and Knowledge. Proceedings before the Committee on Science and Astronautics, U.S. House of Representatives, Ninety-First Congress, Second Session, January 27, 28 and 29, 1970, Washington 1970, No. 15.*

"Patent vom 19. Oktober 1846. Gesetz zum Schutze des literarischen und artisthischen Eigenthumes gegen unbefugte Veröffentlichung, Nachdruck und Nachbildung." In *Justizgesetzsammlung (1846)*, 375–386. Available at http://alex.onb.ac.at/cgi-content/anno-plus?apm=0&aid=jgs&datum=1030, accessed August 21, 2011.

"Phonographen-Konzerte." *Phonographische Zeitschrift* 4, no. 14 (1903), 207.

"Phonographen-Streik in Frankreich." *Phonographische Zeitschrift* 6 (1905), 261.

"Phonographischer Wettstreit." *Phonographische Zeitschrift* 2, no. 1 (1901), 3.

"Photostat." *The Library Journal* 43, no. 8 (1918), 697.

"Photostat and War Collections Exhibited at Princeton." *The Library Journal* 43, no. 4 (1918), 271–273.

Plugge, Walther, and Georg Roeber. *Das musikalische Tantiemerecht in Deutschland.* Berlin: 1930.

Pollak, Hans. "Archives in Sound: An Account of the Work of the 'Phonogram-Archives' in Vienna." *The Gramophone* (April 1925), 415–418.

Power, Eugene B. *Edition of One: The Autobiography of Eugene B. Power, Founder of University Microfilms.* Ann Arbor: 1990

Prenner, Fritz. "Die Sprechmaschinenaufnahmen in ihrer Stellung zum Urheberrechte." *Phonographische Zeitschrift* 8, nos. 37, 38 (1907), 1000–1001, 1030–1032.

Price, Derek John de Solla. *Little Science, Big Science.* New York and London: 1963.

Prou, Maurice. "L'état actuel des publications de fac-similé de chartes et autres documents d'archives." In *Actes du Congrès international pour la reproduction des manuscrits, des monnaies et des sceaux: tenu à Liége, les 21, 22 et 23 août 1905*, 57–71. Brussels: 1905.

Pudor, H. "Das Phonogramm-Archiv der Wiener Akademie der Wissenschaften." *Phonographische Zeitschrift* 2, no. 6 (1901), 59–60.

Purves, Frederick. *The Grundig Book.* London: 1962.

Püttlingen, Johann Vesque von. *Das musicalische Autorrecht: Eine juristisch-musicalische Abhandlung.* Vienna: 1864.

Radio and the Composer: The Economics of Modern Music. With a Foreword by Sir Edward German. London: 1935.

Raney, M. Llewellyn. "American Trends in Textual Reproduction." In *F.I.D. Communicationes* 6 (1939), 75–79.

——. "The Decision of Paris." *The Journal of Documentary Reproduction* 1, no. 2 (1938), 151–161.

Ratisbonne, Louis, Jules Lermina, and Eugène Pouillet. *Association littéraire & artistique internationale: son histoire, ses travaux, 1878–1889.* Paris: 1889.

[Reichskartell der Musikveranstalter Deutschlands]. *Die Neugestaltung des deutschen Urheberrechts: Denkschrift der Arbeitsgemeinschaft der Verbreiter von Geisteswerken.* Berlin: [1932].

Reimer, Eduard. "Die Rechte der Autoren und Verleger bei Vervielfältigung von Zeitschriften im Wege der Mikrophotographie." In *GRUR* 50, no. 2 (1948), 98–103.

"Réunion africaine d'étude sur le droit d'auteur. Brazzaville, 5–10 août 1963. Rapport présenté par M. L'Abbée Ntahokaja (Burundi) Rapporteur général." *Le droit d'auteur* 76 (1963), 250–259.

Richter, Heinz. *Tonaufnahme für alle: Eine leichtverständliche Einführung in die Praxis der Tonaufnahme, besonders der Magnettontechnik.* Stuttgart: 1958.

Richter, Karl. *Kunst und Wissenschaft und ihre Rechte im Staate.* Berlin: 1863.

Rothgiesser, Georg. "Amerika und Deutschland als Konkurrenten auf dem Weltmarkt." *Phonographische Zeitschrift* 14, no. 29 (1913), 619–620.

Röthlisberger, Ernst. "Gesamtüberblick über die Vorgänge auf urheberrechtlichem Gebiet in den Jahren 1904, 1905 und 1906." *GRUR* 12, no. 5 (1907), 137–156.

——. "Gesamtüberblick über die Vorgänge auf urheberrechtlichem Gebiete (1902 und 1903)." *GRUR* 9, no. 1 (1904), 9–22.

——. "Urheberrecht." In *Handwörterbuch der Schweizerischen Volkswirtschaft, Sozialpolitik und Verwaltung. Vol. 3,* edited by N. Reichesberg, 1142–1148. Bern: [1903–1911].

Runge, Kurt. "Rechtsfragen um das Magnetophon." *GRUR* 53, no. 5 (1951), 234–236.

S. 2328 and H. R. 10353 Bills to Amend Section I of an Act Entitled "An Act to Amend and Consolidate the Acts Respecting Copyright," Approved March 4, 1909, As Amended by Adding Subsection F. Joint Hearings before the Committees on Patents Congress of the United States 69th Congress, First Session. April 5, 6, 7, 8, and 9, 1926. Washington, D.C.: 1926.

Sanger, George P., ed. *The Statutes at Large, Treaties and Proclamations of the United States of America from December 1863 to December 1865: Arranged in Chronological Order and carefully collated with the Originals at Washington, XIII.* Boston: 1866.

"Schellack." *Phonographische Zeitschrift* 5, no. 46 (1904).

Scherzinger, Martin Rudoy. "Music, Spirit Possession, and the Copyright Law: Cross-Cultural Comparisons and Strategic Speculations." *Yearbook of Traditional Music* 31 (1999), 102–125.

Schreiber, Heinrich. "Pflicht und Recht der Bibliotheksphotokopie." *UFITA* 7 (1934), 441–463.

——. "Photokopie und Bibliotheken: Betrachtungen zum gegenwärtigen Stand der Frage." *UFITA* 9 (1936), 41–59.

Schulze, Erich. *Das deutsche Urheberrecht an Werken der Tonkunst und die Entwicklung der mechanischen Musik.* Berlin: 1950.

——. "Geschäfte mit Musik." *GEMA-Nachrichten* 67 (1956), 5–14.

——. *Geschätzte und geschützte Noten: Zur Geschichte der Verwertungsgesellschaften.* Weinheim, Germany: 1995.

Schürmeyer, Walter. "Die Photographie im Dienste der bibliothekarischen Arbeit." *Zentralblatt für Bibliothekswesen* 50 (1933), 580–583.

Schürmeyer, Walter, and P. Th. Loosjes. "Literatur über die Anwendung von photographischen Reproduktionsverfahren in der Dokumentation." *I.I.D. Communicationes* 4, no. 2 (1937), 23–29.

Schuster, Arthur, ed. *International Research Council: Constitutive Assembly Held at Brussels, July 18th to July 28th, 1919. Reports of Proceedings.* London: 1920.

Schuster, Heinrich M. *Das Urheberrecht der Tonkunst in Österreich, Deutschland und anderen europäischen Staaten.* Munich: 1891.

——. "Die Denkschrift der deutschen Komponisten über den Urheberrechtsentwurf." *GRUR* 6, no. 1 (1901), 14–19.

Schwartzkoppen, Luise von. "Die rechtliche Zulässigkeit der Photokopie im Rechte des Auslandes und nach dem Entwurf zu einem neuen Urheberrechtsgesetz." *Zentralblatt für Bibliothekswesen* 51, no. 6 (1934), 297–311.

Seeger, Charles. "Who Owns Folklore?—A Rejoinder." *Western Folklore* 21, no. 2 (1962), 93–101.

Seeger, Pete. "The Copyright Hassle." *Sing Out!* 13, no. 5 (1963–1964), 41, 43, 45.

Seidell, Atherton. "Microfilm Copying of Scientific Literature." *Science* 89, no. 2306 (1939), 219–220.

——. "A Plan for the Dissemination of Scientific Literature by Means of Microfilms." *I.I.D. Communicationes* 4, no. 1 (1937), 24–25.

——. "The Utilization of Microfilms in Scientific Research." *Science* 89, no. 2298 (1939), 32–34.

Sevensma, T. P. "Die Bibliothek des Völkerbunds." In *Zentralblatt für Bibliothekswesen* 48 (1931), 527–529.

Shepard, Martha. "Library Service and Photocopying." *Library Resources and Technical Services* 10, no. 3 (1966), 331–335.

"Siemens Reproduktions-Automat." *I.I.D. Communicationes* 3, no. 1 (1936), insert.

Silber, Irwin. "Folk Songs and Copyrights." *Sing Out!* 9, no. 4 (1960), 31–34, 36.

Simpson, Lawrence. "The Copyright Situation as Affecting Radio Broadcasting." Reprint from *New York University Quarterly Review* IX, no. 2 (1931), 180–197.

Sinclair, Upton. *The Jungle*. London: 1906.

Smith, Adam. *Theorie der ethischen Gefühle*. Hamburg: 2004 [1759].

Smoschewer, Fritz. "Einige Gedanken über die Zusammenarbeit von Urhebern und Sendestellen." *Phonographische Zeitschrift* 7 (1927), 136–139.

——. "Zur Frage der Regelung des Rundfunks durch die Berner Konvention." *Blätter für Funkrecht: Herausgegeben im Auftrag der Reichs-Rundfunkgesellschaft m.b.H. in Berlin von Rechtsanwalt Willy Hoffmann* 1, no. 4 (1927), 41–46.

——. "Zur Frage des Urheberschutzes der wiedergebenden Künstler." *GRUR* 32, no. 1 (1927), 50–54.

Solberg, Thorvald, ed. *Copyright Enactments, 1783–1900*. Washington, D.C.: 1900.

Sousa, John Philip. "The Menace of Mechanical Music." *Appleton's Magazine* 8 (1906), 278–283.

Stevens, Rolland E. "Library Experience with the Xerox 914 Copier." *Library Resources and Technical Services* 6, no. 1 (1962), 25–29.

Stobbe, Otto. *Handbuch des deutschen Privatrechts. 2. Auflage. Band 3: Urheberrecht. Forderungsrecht*. Berlin: 1885.

Straschnov, Georges. *Le Droit d'auteur et les droits connexes en radiodiffusion, Préface de M. Julien Kuypers*. Brussels: 1948.

Striedl, Hans. *Der xerographische Rollendruck als bibliothekarisches Hilfsmittel unter Berücksichtigung von Erfahrungen an der bayerischen Staatsbibliothek*. Munich: 1959.

"Survey of Copyrighted Material Reproduction Practices in Scientific and Technical Fields." *Bulletin of the Copyright Society of the U.S.A.* 11, no. 2 (1963), 69–124.

Swingle, Walter, and Maude Swingle. "The Utilization of Photographic Methods in Library Research Work." *The Library Journal* 41, no. 11 (1916), 801–804.

Talbot, William Henry Fox. *The Pencil of Nature: New Introduction by Beaumont Newhall*. New York: 1969 [1844].

Taylor, Frederick Winslow. *The Principles of Scientific Management.* New York: 1911.

Thalheim, R. "Der erste internationale Kongress der phonographischen Industrie in Rom und die Gründung der internationalen Vereinigung der phonographischen Industrie." *UFITA* 7 (1934), 71–75.

To Amend and Consolidate the Acts Respecting Copyright. February 22, 1909. Report to accompany H. R. 28192. 60th Congress, 2nd session, House of Representatives, Report No. 2222. Washington, D.C.: 1909.

To Amend the Copyright Act. Hearings before a Subcommittee of the Committee on Patents, United States, Senate, 68th Congress, 1st Session on S. 2600, a Bill to Amend Section 1 of an Act Entitled "An Act to Amend and Consolidate the Acts Respecting Copyright," Approved March 4, 1909. April 9, 17, and 18, 1924. Washington, D.C.: 1924.

"Tradition." In *Deutsches Wörterbuch*, Vol. 21, edited by Jacob and Wilhelm Grimm, 1854–1860 [1935].

"Tradition." In *Grosses vollständiges Universal-Lexicon aller Wissenschaften und Künste*, Vol. 44, edited by Johann Heinrich Zedler, 925. Leipzig and Halle: 1745.

Traités et conventions entre la Suisse et la France: Conclus le 30 Juin 1864. Ratifiés par la France le 21 Septembre 1864, par la Suisse le 3 Octobre 1864. Convention pour la garantie réciproque de la propriété littéraire, artistique et industrielle entre la Suisse et la France, in: *Recueil officiel des lois et ordonnances.* C. Bern 1866, Vol. VIII, 305–323.

Treplin, Heinrich. "Das Bibliotheksrecht." In *Handbuch der Bibliothekswissenschaft. Zweiter Band. Bibliotheksverwaltung*, edited by Fritz Milkau, 599–634. Leipzig: 1933.

Tyerman, Barry W. "The Economic Rationale for Copyright Protection for Published Books: A Reply to Professor Breyer." *UCLA Law Review* 18, no. 6 (1971), 1100–1125.

Ulmer, Eugen. *Der Rechtsschutz der ausübenden Künstler, der Hersteller von Tonträgern und der Sendegesellschaften in internationaler und rechtsvergleichender Sicht.* Munich: 1957.

"Unberechtigtes Kopieren von Phonographen-Walzen." *Phonographische Zeitschrift* 5, no. 8 (1904), 31.

United Nations Educational, Scientific and Cultural Organization (UNESCO). *Recommendation on the Safeguarding of Traditional Culture and Folklore, Adopted by the General Conference at Its 25th Session in Paris on 15 November 1989.* Paris: 1989.

UNESCO, World Intellectual Property Organization (WIPO). *Model Provision for National Laws on the Protection of Expressions of Folklore against Illicit Exploitation and Other Prejudicial Actions.* UNESCO, OMPI: 1985.

Union internationale pour la protection des oeuvres littéraires et artistiques, *Actes de la conférence réunie à Berlin du 14 octobre au 14 novembre 1908 avec les actes de ratification.* Bern: 1910.

"Urheber." In *Grosses vollständiges Universal-Lexicon aller Wissenschaften und Künste*, Vol. 50, edited by Johann Heinrich Zedler, 1133–1134. Leipzig and Halle: 1746.

"Urheberrecht an Phonogrammen." *Phonographische Zeitschrift* 9, no. 24 (1908), 710.

Vaidhyanathan, Siva. *Copyrights and Copywrongs: The Rise of Intellectual Property and How it Threatens Creativity.* New York and London: 2001.

Van Asperen, J. P. C. "Neuzeitliche photographische Reproduktionsverfahren." *I.I.D. Communicationes* I, no. 3 (1934), 1–12 and I, no. 4 (1934), 2–24.

Vander Haeghen, G. "Le Livre de Demain." *Bulletin de l'Institut international de bibliographie* 12 (1907), 105–127.

Varmer, Borge. "Photoduplication of Copyrighted Material by Libraries." In *Copyright Law Revision. Studies prepared for the Subcommittee on Patents, Trademarks, and Copyrights of the Committee on the Judiciary United States Senate Eighty-Sixth Congress, Second Session, Pursuant to S. Res. 240, Study 15, Committee Print*, edited by Library of Congress Copyright Office, 45–76. Washington, D.C.: 1960.

Veaner, Allen B. "Developments in Copying Methods and Graphic Communication, 1965." *Library Resources and Technical Services* 10, no. 2 (1966), 199–209.

——. "Xerox Copyflo at Harvard University Library: A Study of the Costs and the Problems." *Library Resources and Technical Services* 6, no. 1 (1962), 13–24.

"Verschiedene Qualitäten für Phonographenwalzen." *Phonographische Zeitschrift* 2, no. 22 (1901), 268.

Völkerbund. *Das internationale Institut für geistige Zusammenarbeit.* Paris: 1927.

Volkmann, Ludwig. *Zur Neugestaltung des Urheberschutzes gegenüber mechanischen Musikinstrumenten: Eine Denkschrift de Lege Ferenda.* Leipzig: 1909.

Wächter, Oscar von. *Das Urheberrecht an Werken der bildenden Künste, Photographien und gewerblichen Mustern.* Stuttgart: 1877.

Warren, Samuel D., and Louis D. Brandeis. "The Right to Privacy." *Harvard Law Review* IV (1890), 193–220.

Wendland, Wend B. "Intellectual Property, Traditional Knowledge and Folklore: WIPO's Exploratory Program." *International Review of Industrial Property and Copyright Law* 33, no. 4 (2002), 485–504.

Wentzel, Fritz. "Amerikanische Vervielfältigungsgeräte auf photographischer Grundlage (Photostat, Rectigraph, Photostat-Recorder)." *Photographische Korrespondenz* 65, no. 5 (1929), 143–148.

"White-Smith Music Publishing Company v. Apollo Company." In *Cases Adjudged in the Supreme Court at the October Term, 1907*, edited by Charles Henry Butler, 1–20. New York: 1908.

Williams & Wilkins Co. v. United States. U. S. Supreme Court, Records and Briefs, 420 US 376, (1973–1974).

Wilm, Werner. "Die Neugestaltung des Urheberrechts." *Phonographische Zeitschrift* 11, no. 19 (1910), 451–452.

Wilson, Leslie. "Copyright and the Scientist." *Nature* 170, no. 4339 (1952), 1108–1109.

Winter, A. *Vorschläge für eine Vereinbarung über den redlichen Verkehr mit photomechanischen Vervielfältigungen: Vortrag gehalten auf der 8. Jahrestagung der Deutschen Gesellschaft für Dokumentation e.V. am 11.10.1956 in Bad Nauheim.* Frankfurt am Main: 1957.

WIPO. *Intellectual Property Needs and Expectations of Traditional Knowledge Holders: WIPO Report on Fact-Finding Missions on Intellectual Property and Traditional Knowledge (1998–1999).* Geneva: 2001.

——. *Records of the Diplomatic Conference for the Revision of the Berne Convention (Paris, July 5 to 24, 1971).* Geneva: 1974.

——. *Records of the Intellectual Property Conference of Stockholm, June 11 to July 14, 1967*, 1, 2. Geneva: 1971.

Zedler, Johann Heinrich. "Credit." In *Grosses vollständiges Universal-Lexicon aller Wissenschaften und Künste, Vol. 6*, 1599. Halle and Leipzig: 1733.

Zieger, Gerhard. *Vervielfältigen—aber wie? Herausgeber: Institut für Verwaltungsorganisation und Bürotechnik Leipzig.* Berlin: 1965.

4. Literature

Adrian, Johann, Wilhelm Nordemann, and Artur-Axel Wandtke, eds. *Josef Kohler und der Schutz des geistigen Eigentums in Europa.* Berlin: 1996.

Alexander, Isabella. *Copyright Law and the Public Interest in the Nineteenth Century.* Oxford: 2010.

Ashley, Tim. *Richard Strauss.* London: 1999.

Bachelard, Gaston. *Die Bildung des wissenschaftlichen Geistes: Beitrag zu einer Psychoanalyse der objektiven Erkenntnis.* Frankfurt am Main: 1987.

Baker, Nicholson. *Double Fold: Libraries and the Assault on Paper.* New York: 2001.

Bandilla, Kai. *Urheberrecht im deutschen Kaiserreich: Der Weg zum Gesetz betreffend das Urheberrecht an Werken der Literatur und Tonkunst vom 19. Juni 1901.* Bern: 2005.

Barron, Anne. "Copyright Law's Musical Work." *Social and Legal Studies* 15, no. 1 (2006), 101–127.

Belting, Hans. *Faces: Eine Geschichte des Gesichts.* Munich: 2013.

Bendix, Regina. *Amerikanische Folkloristik: Eine Einführung, bearbeitet von Nicholas H. Schaffner.* Berlin: 1995.

Benjamin, Walter. *Das Kunstwerk im Zeitalter seiner technischen Reproduzierbarkeit: Drei Studien zur Kunstsoziologie.* Frankfurt am Main: 1990 [1936].

——. "Über den Begriff der Geschichte." In *Abhandlungen. Gesammelte Schriften,* Vol. I, 2, edited by Walter Benjamin, 691–704. Frankfurt am Main: 1991 [1940/1942].

Berg, Maxine. "From Imitation to Invention: Creating Commodities in Eighteenth-Century Britain." *Economic History Review* 55, no. 1 (2002), 1–30.

Bettig, Ronald V. *Copyrighting Culture: The Political Economy of Intellectual Property.* Boulder, Col.: 1996.

Biagioli, Mario. "Aporias of Scientific Authorship." In *The Science Studies Reader,* edited by Mario Biagioli, 12–30. New York and London: 1999.

Biagioli, Mario, and Peter Galison, eds. *Scientific Authorship: Credit and Intellectual Property in Science.* New York: 2003.

Bierley, Paul Edmund. *The Incredible Band of John Philip Sousa.* Urbana, Chicago: 2006.

Biernacki, Richard. "The Social Manufacture of Private Ideas in Germany and Britain, 1750–1830." In *Wissenschaftskolleg zu Berlin, Jahrbuch 1998/99,* edited by Wolf Lepenies, 221–246. Berlin: 2000.

Bloch, Marc. *The Historian's Craft: Translated from the French by Peter Putnam with a Preface by Peter Burke.* Manchester: 1992 [1949].

Blumenberg, Hans. *Aspekte der Epochenschwelle: Cusaner und Nolaner.* Frankfurt am Main: 1976 [1966].

Bosse, Heinrich. *Autorschaft ist Werkherrschaft: Über die Entstehung des Urheberrechts aus dem Geist der Goethezeit.* Paderborn: 1981.

Bourdieu, Pierre, Luc Boltanski, Robert Castel, Jean-Claude Chamboredon, Gérard Lagneau, and Dominique Schnapper. *Eine illegitime Kunst: Die sozialen Gebrauchsweisen der Photographie.* Frankfurt am Main: 1983.

Bracha, Oren. "The Ideology of Authorship Revisited: Authors, Markets, and Liberal Values in Early American Copyright." *The Yale Law Journal* 118 (2008), 186–271.

Briggs, Asa. *The Birth of Broadcasting, Vols. I–V.* London and New York: 1961.

Bronnenmeyer, Christl. *Max Grundig.* Berlin: 1999.

Brown, Gregory S. "After the Fall: The *Chute* of a Play, *Droit d'Auteur*, and Literary Property in the Old Regime." *French Historical Studies* 22, no. 4 (1999), 465–491.

Buckland, Michael Keeble. *Emanuel Goldberg and His Knowledge Machine: Information, Invention, and Political Forces.* Westport, Conn.: 2006.

Buinicki, Martin T. *Negotiating Copyright: Authorship and the Discourse of Literary Property Rights in Nineteenth-Century America.* New York, London: 2006.

Butzmann, Frieder. "Was nicht in der Bedienungsanleitung stand: Beobachtungen bei der Entwicklung und dem Umgang mit Tonaufnahme- und Wiedergabesystemen im 20. Jahrhundert." *Technikgeschichte* 61, no. 1 (1994), 35–57.

Callon, Michel. "Die Sozio-Logik der Übersetzung: Auseinandersetzungen und Verhandlungen zur Bestimmung von Problematischem und Unproblematischem." In *ANThology: Ein einführendes Handbuch zur Akteur-Netzwerk-Theorie,* edited by Andrea Belliger and David Krieger, 51–74. Bielefeld: 2006.

Carpenter, Kenneth. "Toward a New Cultural Design: The American Council of Learned Societies, the Social Science Research Council, and the Libraries in the 1930s." In *Institutions of Reading: The Social Life of Libraries in the United States,* edited by Thomas Augst and Kenneth Carpenter, 283–309. Amherst and Boston: 2007.

Chakrabarty, Dipesh. "Europa provinzialisieren: Postkolonialität und die Kritik der Geschichte." In *Europa als Provinz: Perspektiven postkolonialer Geschichtsschreibung,* edited by Dipesh Chakrabarty, 41–65. Frankfurt am Main: 2010 [2001].

Chandler, Alfred D. *The Visible Hand: The Managerial Revolution in American Business.* Cambridge, Mass.: 1977.

Clark, John E. T. *Musical Boxes: A History and an Appreciation.* London: 1948.

Congost, Rosa. "Property Rights and Historical Analysis: What Rights? What History?" *Past & Present,* 181, no. 1 (2004), 73–106.

Coombe, Rosemary J. "Challenging Paternity: Histories of Copyright." *Yale Journal of Law and the Humanities* 6 (1994), 397–422.

——. *The Cultural Life of Intellectual Properties: Authorship, Appropriation, and the Law.* Durham, London: 1998.

Crafton, Donald. *The Talkies: American Cinema's Transition to Sound, 1926–1931.* New York: 1997.

Crisell, Andrew. *An Introductory History of British Broadcasting.* London and New York: 1997.

Cummings, Alex S. "From Monopoly to Intellectual Property: Music Piracy and the Remaking of American Copyright, 1909–1971." *The Journal of American History* 97, no. 3 (2010), 659–681.

Dahl, Peter. *Radio: Sozialgeschichte des Rundfunks für Sender und Empfänger.* Reinbek bei Hamburg: 1983.

Daston, Lorraine, and Peter Galison. "The Image of Objectivity." *Representations* 40 (1992), 81–128.

Decherney, Peter. "Copyright Dupes: Piracy and New Media in Edison v. Lubin (1903)." *Film History* 19 (2007), 109–124.

Dölemeyer, Barbara. "Wege der Rechtsvereinheitlichung. Zur Auswirkung internationaler Verträge auf europäische Patent- und Urheberrechtsgesetze des

19. Jahrhunderts." In *Aspekte europäischer Rechtsgeschichte. Festgabe für Helmut Coing*, edited by Christoph Bergfeld et al., 65–85. Frankfurt am Main: 2002.

Dommann, Monika. "08/15, QWERTY, PAL-SECAM, Paletten und MP3: Standards als kulturelle Artefakte." In *Geltung und Faktizität von Standards*, edited by Thomas M. J. Möllers, 253–260. Baden-Baden: 2009.

——. "Dokumentieren: Die Arbeit am institutionellen Gedächtnis in Wissenschaft, Wirtschaft und Verwaltung (1895–1945)." *Jahrbuch für europäische Verwaltungsgeschichte* 20 (2008), 277–299.

——. "Mobile Medien, reguliertes Eigentum." In *Bildregime des Rechts*, edited by Jean B. Joly, Cornelia Vismann, and Thomas Weitin, 249–267. Stuttgart: 2007.

——. "Papierstau und Informationsfluss: Die Normierung der Bibliothekskopie." *Historische Anthropologie* 16, no. 1 (2008), 31–54.

——. "Rechtsinstrumente: Die Übersetzung von Technik in Recht." *Schweizerische Zeitschrift für Geschichte* 55, no. 1 (2005), 17–33.

——. "Recording Prints, Reading Films: Mikrofilme, amerikanische Kosmopoliten und die Entdeckung des Copyrightproblems in den 1930er Jahren." *Zeitschrift für Medienwissenschaft* 2, no. 2 (2010), 73–83.

——. "Schutz vor Kodak! Die Schaffung einer Privatsphäre für Porträts um 1900." In *Fotografien im 20. Jahrhundert. Verbreitung und Vermittlung*, edited by Annelie Ramsbrock, Annette Vowinckel, Malte Zierenberg, 235–252. Göttingen: 2013.

Downey, Gregory John. "Constructing 'Computer-Compatible' Stenographers: The Transition to Real-Time Transcription in Courtroom Reporting." *Technology and Culture* 47, no. 1 (2006), 1–26.

Dussel, Konrad. *Deutsche Rundfunkgeschichte*. Constance: 2010 [1999].

Eco, Umberto. *Apokalyptiker und Integrierte: Zur kritischen Kritik der Massenkultur*. Frankfurt am Main: 1984 [1964].

Edgerton, David. *Warfare State: Britain, 1920–1970*. Cambridge: 2006.

Ehrlich, Cyril. *Harmonious Alliance: A History of the Performing Right Society*. Oxford and New York: 1989.

——. *The Piano: A History*. London: 1976.

Erler, Adalbert. "Josef Kohler." In *Handwörterbuch zur deutschen Rechtsgeschichte*, Vol. II, edited by Adalbert Erler, 925–927. Berlin: 1978.

Estivals, Robert. *Le dépôt légal sous l'ancien régime de 1537 à 1791*. Paris: 1961.

Fessmann, Ingo. *Rundfunk und Rundfunkrecht in der Weimarer Republik*. Frankfurt am Main: 1973.

Fickers, Andreas. *Der "Transistor" als technisches und kulturelles Phänomen. Die Transistorisierung der Radio- und Fernsehempfänger in der deutschen Rundfunkindustrie 1955 bis 1965*. Bassum, Germany: 1998.

Fisher, William W. "Geistiges Eigentum—ein ausufernder Rechtsbereich: Die Geschichte des Ideenschutzes in den Vereinigten Staaten." In *Eigentum im internationalen Vergleich (18.—20. Jahrhundert)*, edited by Hannes Siegrist and David Sugermann, 265–291. Göttingen: 1999.

Fleischer, Arndt. *Patentgesetzgebung und chemisch-pharmazeutische Industrie im deutschen Kaiserreich (1871–1918)*. Stuttgart: 1984.

Fleischhauer, Wolfgang. "Eigentümlichkeit: Ein Beitrag zur Wortgeschichte." In *Herkommen und Erneuerung: Essays für Oskar Seidlin*, edited by Gerald Gillespie and Edgar Lohner, 56–63. Tübingen: 1976.

Fögen, Marie Theres. "Die ungeliebten Kinder der Rechtswissenschaft." In *opuscula*, edited by Andrea Büchler, 88–96. Zurich, St. Gallen: 2009.

Foucault, Michel. "Die Wahrheit und die juristischen Formen." In *Schriften in vier Bänden: Dits et Ecrits. Herausgegeben von Daniel Defert und François Ewald unter Mitarbeit von Jacques Lagrange, Vol. 2*, edited by Michel Foucault, 669–792. Frankfurt am Main: 2002 [1994].

Fuchs, Eckhardt. "Der Völkerbund und die Institutionalisierung transnationaler Beziehungen." *Zeitschrift für Geschichtswissenschaft* 54, no. 10 (2006), 888–899.

Gaiba, Francesca. *The Origins of Simultaneous Interpretation: The Nuremberg Trial.* Ottawa: 1998.

Gaines, Jane M. "Early Cinema's Heyday of Copying: The Too Many Copies of L'Arroseur arrosé (The Waterer Watered)." *Cultural Studies* 20, no. 2–3 (2006), 227–244.

Gauss, Stefan. *Nadel, Rille, Trichter: Kulturgeschichte des Phonographen und des Grammophons in Deutschland (1900–1940).* Cologne: 2009.

Geimer, Peter. *Theorien der Fotografie zur Einführung.* Hamburg: 2009.

Gelatt, Roland. *The Fabulous Phonograph, 1877–1977.* London: 1977 [1954].

Gillespie, Tarleton. *Wired Shut: Copyright and the Shape of Digital Culture.* Cambridge, Mass.: 2007.

Goehr, Lydia. *The Imaginary Museum of Musical Works: An Essay in the Philosophy of Music.* Oxford: 1992.

Goldstein, Paul, *Copyright's Highway: From Gutenberg to the Celestial Jukebox.* Stanford: 2003 [1994].

Grimm, Dieter. "Die Bedeutung des Rechts in der Gesellschaftsgeschichte: Eine Anfrage." In *Perspektiven der Gesellschaftsgeschichte*, edited by Paul Nolte, Manfred Hettling, Frank-Michael Kuhlemann, and Hans-Walter Schmuhl, 47–57. Munich: 2000.

———. *Recht und Staat der bürgerlichen Gesellschaft.* Frankfurt am Main: 1987.

Gumbrecht, Hans Ulrich. "Modern, Modernität, Moderne." In *Geschichtliche Grundbegriffe. Historisches Wörterbuch zur politisch-sozialen Sprache, Vol. 4*, edited by Otto Brunner, Werner Conze, and Reinhart Koselleck, 93–131. Stuttgart: 1978.

Gumbrecht, Hans Ulrich, and Karl Ludwig Pfeiffer, eds. *Materialität der Kommunikation.* Frankfurt am Main: 1995.

Gundlach, Robert W. "Retrospective on Xerography and Chester F. Carlson." In *Technology of Our Times: People and Innovation in Optics and Optoelectronics*, edited by Frederick Su, 56–62. Washington, D.C.: Society of Photo-Optical Instrumentation Engineers, 1990.

Habermas, Rebekka. *Diebe vor Gericht: Die Entstehung der modernen Rechtsordnung im 19. Jahrhundert.* Frankfurt am Main, New York: 2008.

———. "Eigentum vor Gericht: Die Entstehung des modernen Rechtsstaates aus dem Diebstahl?" *Werkstatt Geschichte* 42 (2006), 25–43.

———. "Von Anselm von Feuerbach zu Jack the Ripper: Recht und Kriminalität im 19. Jahrhundert." *Rechtsgeschichte* 3 (2003), 128–163.

Hagen, Wolfgang. *Das Radio: Zur Geschichte und Theorie des Hörfunks—Deutschland/USA.* Munich: 2005.

Hansen, Mathias. *Richard Strauss: Die Sinfonischen Dichtungen.* Kassel, Germany: 2003.

Hartmann, Frank, ed. *Vom Buch zur Datenbank: Paul Otlets Utopie der Wissensvisualisierung.* Berlin: Avinus, 2012.

Heesen, Anke te. *Der Zeitungsausschnitt: Ein Papierobjekt der Moderne.* Frankfurt am Main: 2006.

Hefti, Ernst. "Das Urheberrecht im Nationalsozialismus." In *Woher kommt das Urheberrecht und wohin geht es? Wurzeln, geschichtlicher Ursprung, geistesgeschichtlicher Hintergrund und Zukunft des Urheberrechts,* edited by Robert Dittrich, 165–180. Vienna: 1988.

Heide, Lars. *Punched-Card Systems and the Early Information Explosion 1880–1945.* Baltimore: 2009.

Herren, Madeleine. *Hintertüren zur Macht: Internationalismus und modernisierungsorientierte Außenpolitik in Belgien, der Schweiz und den USA 1865–1914.* Munich: 2000.

Hesse, Carla. "Enlightenment Epistemology and the Laws of Authorship in Revolutionary France, 1777–1793." *Representations* 30 (1990), 109–137.

Hilderbrand, Lucas. *Inherent Vice: Bootleg Histories of Videotape and Copyright.* Durham, N.C.: 2009.

Hirschman, Albert O. *Shifting Involvements: Private Interest and Public Action.* Princeton: 1982.

Hoffmann, Christoph. "Vor dem Apparat: Das Wiener Phonogramm-Archiv." In *Bürokratische Leidenschaften: Kultur- und Mediengeschichte im Archiv,* edited by Sven Spieker, 281–294. Berlin: 2004.

Hughes, Steve, and Nigel Haworth. *The International Labour Organization (ILO): Coming in from the Cold.* London and New York: 2011.

Hutter, Michael. *Neue Medienökonomik.* Munich: 2006.

——. "On the Construction of Property Rights in Aesthetic Ideas." *Journal of Cultural Economics* 19 (1995), 177–185.

Jasanoff, Sheila. *Science at the Bar: Law, Science, and Technology in America.* Cambridge, Mass. etc.: 1995.

Jaszi, Peter. "On the Author Effect: Contemporary Copyright and Collective Creativity." In *The Construction of Authorship: Textual Appropriation in Law and Literature,* edited by Martha Woodmansee and Peter Jaszi, 29–56. Durham, N.C., and London: 1994.

——. "Toward a Theory of Copyright: The Metamorphosis of 'Authorship.'" *Duke Law Journal* 2 (1991), 455–502.

Jauss, Hans Robert. "Literarische Tradition und gegenwärtiges Bewusstsein der Modernität." In *Literaturgeschichte als Provokation,* edited by Hans Robert Jauss, 11–66. Frankfurt am Main: 1970.

Johns, Adrian. "Intellectual Property and the Nature of Science." *Cultural Studies* 20, no. 2 (2006), 145–164.

——. *Piracy: The Intellectual Property Wars from Gutenberg to Gates.* Chicago and London: 2009.

——. "Pop Music Pirate Hunters." *Daedalus* (Spring 2002), 67–77.

Johnston, William Dawson. *History of the Library of Congress, Vol. I, 1800–1864.* Washington, D.C.: 1904.

Jones, Steve. "Music and Copyright in the USA." In *Music and Copyright,* edited by Simon Frith, 67–85. Edinburgh: 1993.

Kenney, William Howland. *Recorded Music in American Life: The Phonograph and Popular Memory, 1890–1945*. New York, Oxford: 1999.

Kevles, Daniel J. "Patents, Protections, and Privileges." *Isis* 98 (2007), 223–331.

Khan, B. Zorina. *The Democratization of Invention: Patents and Copyrights in American Economic Development, 1790–1920*. New York: 2005.

Kittler, Friedrich A. *Aufschreibesysteme 1800/1900*. Munich: 1995.

———. *Austreibung des Geistes aus den Geisteswissenschaften: Programme des Poststrukturalismus*. Paderborn: 1980.

———. *Grammophon, Film, Typewriter*. Berlin: 1986.

Klingenberg, Eberhard. "Vom persönlichen Recht zum Persönlichkeitsrecht: Zur Entwicklung der Urheberrechtstheorie im 19. Jahrhundert." *Zeitschrift der Savigny-Stiftung für Rechtsgeschichte: Germanistische Abteilung* 96 (1979), 183–208.

"Koch-Hesse, Robert." *Munzinger Online/Personen—Internationales Biographisches Archiv.* Available at http://www.munzinger.de/document/00000005560, accessed August 23, 2011.

Koskenniemi, Martti. *The Gentle Civilizer of Nations: The Rise and Fall of International Law, 1870–1960*. Cambridge, U.K. and New York: 2002.

Kraft, James P. "Musicians in Hollywood: Work and Technological Change in Entertainment, 1926–1940." *Technology and Culture* 35 (1994), 289–314.

Krige, John. *American Hegemony and the Postwar Reconstruction of Science in Europe*. Cambridge, Mass., and London: 2006.

Ladas, Stephen Pericles. *The International Protection of Literary and Artistic Property, Vols. 1 & 2*. New York: 1938.

Laing, Dave. "Copyright and the International Music Industry." In *Music and Copyright*, edited by Simon Frith, 22–39. Edinburgh: 1993.

Lange, Britta. "Archiv und Zukunft: Zwei historische Tonsammlungen Berlins für das Humboldt-Forum." *Trajekte* 10, no. 20 (2010), 4–6.

Latour, Bruno. *La fabrique du droit: Une ethnographie du Conseil d'Etat*. Paris: 2002.

———. *Science in Action: How to Follow Scientists and Engineers Through Society*. Cambridge, Mass.: 1987.

Lefebvre, Thierry. "Dr. Eugène-Louis Doyen und die Anfänge des Chirurgie-Films." *montage/av: Zeitschrift für Theorie & Geschichte audiovisueller Kommunikation* 14, no. 2 (2005), 69–77.

Levie, Françoise. *L'homme qui voulait classer le monde: Paul Otlet et le Mundaneum*. Brussels: 2006.

Litman, Jessica. "Copyright Legislation and Technological Change." *Oregon Law Review* 68, no. 2 (1989), 275–361.

Loewenstein, Joseph. *The Author's Due: Printing and the Prehistory of Copyright*. Chicago: 2002.

———. "The Script in the Marketplace." *Representations* 12 (1985), 101–114.

Löhr, Isabella. "Der Völkerbund und die Entwicklung des internationalen Schutzes geistigen Eigentums in der Zwischenkriegszeit." *Zeitschrift für Geschichtswissenschaft* 54, no. 10 (2006), 890–910.

———. *Die Globalisierung geistiger Eigentumsrechte: Neue Strukturen internationaler Zusammenarbeit 1886–1952*. Göttingen: 2010.

Long, Pamela O. "Invention, Authorship, 'Intellectual Property,' and the Origin of Patents: Notes toward a Conceptual History." *Technology and Culture* 32, no. 4 (1991), 846–884.

——. *Openness, Secrecy, Authorship: Technical Arts and the Culture of Knowledge from Antiquity to the Renaissance*. Baltimore: 2001.

Luhmann, Niklas. *Das Recht der Gesellschaft*. Frankfurt am Main: 1995.

——. *Die Realität der Massenmedien*. Wiesbaden: 2004 [1995].

——. *Gesellschaftsstruktur und Semantik: Studien zur Wissenssoziologie der modernen Gesellschaft*. Frankfurt am Main: 1993.

Machlup, Fritz, and Edith Penrose. "The Patent Controversy in the Nineteenth Century." *The Journal of Economic History* 10, no. 1 (1950), 1–29.

Maisonneuve, Sophie. *L'invention du disque 1877–1949: Genèse de l'usage des médias musicaux contemporains*. Paris: 2009.

Maracke, Catharina. *Die Entstehung des Urheberrechtsgesetzes von 1965*. Berlin: 2003.

May, Christopher. *The World Intellectual Property Organization: Resurgence and the Development Agenda*. London, 2007.

Mayer, Alexander. *Grundig und das Wirtschaftswunder*. Erfurt, Germany: 2008.

McSherry, Corynne. *Who Owns Academic Work? Battling for Control of Intellectual Property*. Cambridge, Mass.: 2001.

Melis, Guido. "Giannini, Amedeo." *Dizionario Biografico degli Italiani* 54 (2000). Available at http://www.treccani.it/enciclopedia/amedeo-giannini/, accessed September 2, 2011.

Mischler, Ernst. "Richter, Karl Thomas." *Allgemeine Deutsche Biographie* 28 (1889), 489–491. Available at http://www.deutsche-biographie.de/sfz68893.html, accessed August 5, 2013.

Mort, Joseph. *The Anatomy of Xerography: Its Invention and Evolution*. Jefferson, N.C.; London: 1989.

——. "Xerography: A Study in Innovation and Economic Competitiveness." *Physics Today* 47 (April 1994), 32–38.

Nanz, Tobias, and Bernhard Siegert, eds. *ex machina: Beiträge zur Geschichte der Kulturtechniken*. Weimar: 2006.

North, Douglass C. *Institutionen, institutioneller Wandel und Wirtschaftsleistung*. Tübingen, Germany: 1992 [1990].

Oberholzer-Gee, Felix, and Koleman Strumpf. "The Effect of File Sharing on Record Sales: An Empirical Analysis." *Journal of Political Economy* 115, no. 1 (2007), 1–42.

Ord-Hume, Arthur W. J. G. *Clockwork Music: An Illustrated History of Mechanical Musical Instruments from the Musical Box to the Pianola, from Automaton Lady Virginal Players to Orchestrion*. London: 1973.

Osterhammel, Jürgen. "Anthropologisches zum Freihandel." In *Menschen und Märkte: Studien zur historischen Wirtschaftsanthropologie*, edited by Wolfgang Reinhard and Justin Stagl, 353–369. Vienna: 2007.

——. *Die Verwandlung der Welt: Eine Geschichte des 19. Jahrhunderts*. Munich: 2009.

——. *Geschichtswissenschaft jenseits des Nationalstaats: Studien zu Beziehungsgeschichte und Zivilisationsvergleich*. Göttingen: 2001.

Owen, David. *Copies in Seconds: How a Lone Inventor and an Unknown Company Created the Biggest Communication Breakthrough Since Gutenberg—Chester Carlson and the Birth of the Xerox Machine*. New York and London: 2004.

Parin, Paul. *Die Leidenschaft des Jägers: Erzählungen*. Hamburg: 2003.

Pasler, Jann. *Composing the Citizen. Music as Public Utility in Third Republic France*. Berkeley, Calif.: 2009.

Pathé. *Premier Empire du Cinéma*. Paris: 1994.

Patterson, L. Ray. *Copyright in Historical Perspective*. Nashville: 1968.

Peters, John Durham. "Helmholtz und Edison: Zur Endlichkeit der Stimme." In *Zwischen Rauschen und Offenbarung: Zur Kultur- und Mediengeschichte der Stimme*, edited by Friedrich Kittler, Thomas Macho, and Sigrid Weigel, 291–312. Berlin: 2002.

——. "The Uncanniness of Mass Communication in Interwar Social Thought." *Journal of Communication* 46, no. 3 (1996), 108–123.

Petersson, Niels P. *Anarchie und Weltrecht: Das Deutsche Reich und die Institutionen der Weltwirtschaft 1890–1930*. Göttingen: 2009.

Pfaller, Robert. *Die Illusionen der anderen: Über das Lustprinzip in der Kultur*. Frankfurt am Main: 2002.

Piguet, Jean-Claude. *Les faiseurs de musiques: Histoire de la boîte à musique à Sainte-Croix. Les fabricants de musiques*. Sainte-Croix, Switzerland: 1996.

Plumpe, Gerhard. *Der tote Blick: Zum Diskurs der Photographie in der Zeit des Realismus*. Munich: 1990.

——. "Eigentum—Eigentümlichkeit: Über den Zusammenhang ästhetischer und juristischer Begriffe im 18. Jahrhundert." *Archiv für Begriffsgeschichte* 23 (1979), 175–196.

Pollard, Sidney. "Free Trade, Protectionism, and the World Economy." In *The Mechanics of Internationalism*, edited by Martin H. Geyer and Johannes Paulmann, 27–53. Oxford: 2001.

Read, Oliver, and Walter L. Welch. *From Tin Foil to Stereo: Evolution of the Phonograph*. Indianapolis: 1976 [1959].

Ricketson, Sam. *The Berne Convention for the Protection of Literary and Artistic Works: 1886–1986*. London: 1987.

Rose, Mark. *Authors and Owners: The Invention of Copyright*. Cambridge, Mass.: 1993.

Ryan, John. *The Production of Culture in the Music Industry: The ASCAP-BMI Controversy*, Lanham, Md.: 1985.

Saint-Amour, Paul K., ed. *Modernism and Copyright*. New York: 2011.

Saxer, Daniela. *Die Schärfung des Quellenblicks: Forschungspraktiken in der Geschichtswissenschaft 1840–1914*. Munich: 2013.

Schmidt, Manuela Maria. *Die Anfänge der musikalischen Tantiemenbewegung in Deutschland: Eine Studie über den langen Weg bis zur Errichtung der Genossenschaft Deutscher Tonsetzer (GDT) im Jahre 1903 und zum Wirken des Komponisten Richard Strauss (1864–1949) für Verbesserungen des Urheberrechts*. Berlin: 2005.

Schmoeckel, Mathias, and Matthias Maetschke. *Rechtsgeschichte der Wirtschaft: Seit dem 19. Jahrhundert*. Tübingen: 2008.

Schrage, Dominik. *Psychotechnik und Radiophonie: Subjektkonstruktionen in artifiziellen Wirklichkeiten 1918–1932*. Munich: 2001.

Schulze, Erich. *Hundert Jahre Berner Konvention*. Frankfurt am Main: 1987.

Schwartz, Hillel. *The Culture of the Copy: Striking Likenesses, Unreasonable Facsimiles*. New York: 1996.

Scott, Katie. "Authorship, the Académie, and the Market in Early Modern France." *Oxford Art Journal* 21, no. 1 (1998), 27–41.

Seckelmann, Margrit. *Industrialisierung, Internationalisierung und Patentrecht im Deutschen Reich 1871–1914*. Frankfurt am Main: 2006.

Seville, Catherine. *The Internationalisation of Copyright Law: Books, Buccaneers, and the Black Flag in the Nineteenth Century*. Cambridge etc.: 2009.

Shera, Jesse H. "Herman Howe Fussler." *Library Quarterly 53*, no. 3 (1983), 215–253.

Sherman, Brad, and Lionel Bently. *The Making of Modern Intellectual Property Law: The British Experience, 1760–1911*. Cambridge: 1999.

Sherman, Brad, and Alain Strowel, eds. *Of Authors and Origins: Essays on Copyright Law*. Oxford: 1994.

Siefert, Marsha. "Aesthetics, Technology, and the Capitalization of Culture: How the Talking Machine Became a Musical Instrument." *Science in Context 8*, no. 2 (1995), 417–449.

Siegfried, Detlef. *Time Is on My Side: Konsum und Politik in der westdeutschen Jugendkultur der 60er Jahre*. Göttingen: 2006.

Siegrist, Hannes. *Advokat, Bürger und Staat: Sozialgeschichte der Rechtsanwälte in Deutschland, Italien und der Schweiz (18.—20. Jahrhundert)*, Vols. 1 & 2. Frankfurt am Main: 1996.

——. "Die Propertisierung von Gesellschaft und Kultur: Konstruktion und Institutionalisierung des Eigentums in der Moderne." In *Entgrenzung des Eigentums in modernen Gesellschaften und Rechtskulturen*, edited by Hannes Siegrist, 1–52. Leipzig: 2007.

——. "Geistiges Eigentum im Spannungsfeld von Individualisierung, Nationalisierung und Internationalisierung: Der Weg zur Berner Übereinkunft von 1886." In *Europa und die Europäer: Quellen und Essays zur modernen europäischen Geschichte*, edited by Rüdiger Hohls, Iris Schröder, and Hannes Siegrist, 52–61. Stuttgart: 2005.

——. "Geschichte und aktuelle Probleme des geistigen Eigentums (1600–2000)." In *E-Merging Media: Kommunikation und Medienwirtschaft der Zukunft*, edited by Axel Zerdick et al., 313–332. Berlin: 2004.

Siegrist, Hannes, and David Sugarman, eds. *Eigentum im internationalen Vergleich (18.–20. Jahrhundert)*. Göttingen: 1999.

Solberg, Thorvald. *Copyright Legislation: A Retrospective Summary*. [Washington, D.C.: 1929].

Southern, Eileen. *The Music of Black Americans: A History*. New York and London: 1983.

Steinmetz, Willibald. *Begegnungen vor Gericht: Eine Sozial- und Kulturgeschichte des englischen Arbeitsrechts (1850–1925)*. Munich: 2002.

Sterling, Christopher Hastings, and John Michael Kittross. *Stay Tuned: A Concise History of American Broadcasting*, Belmont, Calif.: 1990.

Sterne, Jonathan. *The Audible Past: Cultural Origins of Sound Reproduction*. Durham: 2003.

——. "The Mp3 as Cultural Artifact." *new media & society 8*, no. 5 (2006), 825–842.

Stiglitz, Joseph E. "Knowledge as a Global Public Good." In *Global Public Goods: International Cooperation in the 21st Century*, edited by Inge Kaul, Isabelle Grunberg, and Marc A. Stern, 308–325. New York: 1999.

Stokes, Simon. *Art and Copyright*. Oxford: 2001.

Strathern, Marilyn. "Potential Property: Intellectual Rights and Property in Persons." *Social Anthropology IV*, no. 1 (1996), 17–32.

——. *Property, Substance, and Effect: Anthropological Essays on Persons and Things.* London and New Brunswick, N.J.: 1999.

Streeter, Thomas. "Broadcast Copyright and the Bureaucratization of Property." In *The Construction of Authorship: Textual Appropriation in Law and Literature,* edited by Martha Woodmansee and Peter Jaszi, 303–326. Durham, N.C. and London: 1994.

Stumpf, Carl. "Das Berliner Phonogrammarchiv." *Internationale Wochenschrift für Wissenschaft, Kunst und Technik* 2 (1908), 226–246.

Tanner, Jakob. "Property rights, Innovationsdynamik und Marktmacht: Zur Bedeutung des schweizerischen Patent- und Markenschutzes für die Entwicklung der chemisch-pharmazeutischen Industrie." In *Die neue Schweiz: Eine Gesellschaft zwischen Integration und Polarisierung (1910–1930),* edited by Andreas Ernst and Erich Wigger, 273–303. Zurich: 1996.

Teubner, Gunther. "Global Bukowina: Legal Pluralism in the World Society." In *Global Law Without a State,* edited by Gunther Teubner, 3–28. Aldershot, U.K.: 1997.

Thompson, Emily. "Machines, Music, and the Quest for Fidelity: Marketing the Edison Phonograph in America, 1877–1925." *The Musical Quarterly* 79, no. 1 (1995), 131–171.

——. *The Soundscape of Modernity: Architectural Acoustics and the Culture of Listening in America, 1900–1933.* Cambridge, Mass.: 2002.

Trentmann, Frank. *Free Trade Nation Commerce, Consumption, and Civil Society in Modern Britain.* Oxford: 2008.

Vec, Miloš. "Aushöhlung des Staates? Selbst-Normierung im Staat der Industriegesellschaft als historisches Problem." *Rechtshistorisches Journal* 19 (2000), 517–532.

——. "Kurze Geschichte des Technikrechts: Von den Anfängen bis zum Ersten Weltkrieg." In *Handbuch des Technikrechts,* edited by Martin Schulte, 3–60. Berlin: 2003.

——. *Recht und Normierung in der Industriellen Revolution: Neue Strukturen in der Normsetzung in Völkerrecht, staatlicher Gesetzgebung und gesellschaftlicher Selbstnormierung.* Frankfurt am Main: 2006.

——. "Verspäteter Gesetzgeber: Der Regelungsbedarf für technische Entwicklungen." *Frankfurter Allgemeine Zeitung,* February 13, 2002, N4.

——. "Weltverträge für Weltliteratur: Das Geistige Eigentum im System der rechtsetzenden Konventionen des 19. Jahrhunderts." In *Grundlagen und Grundfragen des Geistigen Eigentums,* edited by Louis Pahlow and Jens Eisfeld, 107–130. Tübingen: 2008.

Vismann, Cornelia. "Action Writing: Zur Mündlichkeit im Recht." In *Zwischen Rauschen und Offenbarung: Zur Kultur- und Mediengeschichte der Stimme,* edited by Friedrich Kittler, Thomas Macho, and Sigrid Weigel, 133–151. Berlin: 2002.

——. *Akten: Medientechnik und Recht.* Frankfurt am Main: 2001.

——. *Medien der Rechtsprechung, herausgegeben von Alexandra Kemmerer und Markus Krajewski.* Frankfurt am Main: 2011.

——. "Tele-Tribunals: Anatomy of a Medium." *Grey Room* 10 (Winter 2003), 5–21.

Vogel, Martin. "Deutsche Urheber- und Verlagsrechtsgeschichte zwischen 1450 und 1850. Sozial- und methodengeschichtliche Entwicklungsstufen der Rechte von Schriftstellern und Verlegern." *Archiv für Geschichte des Buchwesens* XIX (1978), 2–190.

Vogt, Ralf M. *Die urheberrechtlichen Reformdiskussionen in Deutschland während der Zeit der Weimarer Republik und des Nationalsozialismus.* Frankfurt am Main: 2004.

Vortmann, Jürgen. "Nieberding, Arnold." *Neue Deutsche Biographie* 19 (1998), 214. Available at http://www.deutsche-biographie.de/sfz71805.html, accessed August 5, 2013.

Wadle, Elmar. "Der Bundesbeschluss vom 9. November 1837 gegen den Nachdruck." *Geistiges Eigentum: Bausteine zur Rechtsgeschichte, Vols. 1 & 2.* Munich: 2003 [1996], 1:222–265.

——. "Die Entfaltung des Urheberrechts als Antwort auf technische Neuerungen." *Technikgeschichte 52*, no. 3 (1985), 233–243.

——. "Entwicklungsschritte des Geistigen Eigentums in Frankreich und Deutschland." In *Eigentum im internationalen Vergleich (18.–20. Jahrhundert),* edited by Hannes Siegrist and David Sugermann, 245–263. Göttingen: 1999.

Wallis, Roger, Charles Baden-Fuller, Martin Kretschmer, and George Michael Klimis. "Contested Collective Administration of Intellectual Property Rights in Music: The Challenge to the Principles of Reciprocity and Solidarity." *European Journal of Communication* 14 (1999), 5–32.

Warfield, Patrick. "John Philip Sousa and 'The Menace of Mechanical Music.'" *Journal of the Society for American Music 3*, no. 4 (2009), 431–463.

Weber, Max. *Wirtschaft und Gesellschaft: Grundriss der verstehenden Soziologie.* Tübingen: 1980 [1922].

Wehler, Hans-Ulrich. *Deutsche Gesellschaftsgeschichte, Vol. 1–5.* Munich: 1987–2008.

Weibel, Peter. "Die Frage der Fotografie im Wiener Aktionismus als die Frage nach Autor und Autonomie in der Fotografie." In *Die Zukunft der Bilder: Medienentwicklung und Recht—25 Jahre VG BILDKUNST,* edited by Gerhard Pfenning, VG BILD-KUNST, and Michael Schwarz, 108–137. Göttingen: 1993.

Westermann, Andrea. *Plastik und politische Kultur in Westdeutschland.* Zurich: 2007.

Wiessner, Matthias. "Die DDR und das internationale Urheberrechtsregime." In *Entgrenzung des Eigentums in modernen Gesellschaften und Rechtskulturen,* edited by Hannes Siegrist, 249–267. Leipzig: 2007.

Winthrop-Young, Geoffrey. *Friedrich Kittler zur Einführung.* Hamburg: 2005.

Wolf, Reinhard. "Mussolini und die Filesharing-Jäger." *Die Tageszeitung,* April 15, 2008. Available at http://www.taz.de/!15890/, accessed September 2, 2011.

Woller, Hans. *Gesellschaft und Politik in der amerikanischen Besatzungszone: Die Region Ansbach und Fürth.* Munich: 1986.

Woodmansee, Martha. "The Genius and the Copyright: Economic and Legal Conditions of the Emergence of the 'Author.'" *Eighteenth-Century Studies* 17, no. 4 (1984), 425–448.

Woodmansee, Martha, and Peter Jaszi, eds. *The Construction of Authorship: Textual Appropriation in Law and Literature.* Durham, N.C., and London: 1994.

Zannos, Susan. *Chester Carlson and the Development of Xerography.* Bear, Del.: 2002.

Zeitschrift für Medien- und Kulturforschung 1 (2010): Schwerpunkt "Kulturtechnik," 101–219.

Ziegler, Susanne. "Erich M. von Hornbostel und das Berliner Phonogramm-Archiv." In *Vom tönenden Wirbel menschlichen Tuns: Erich M. von Hornbostel als Gestaltpsychologe, Archivar und Musikwissenschaftler. Studien und Dokumente,* edited by Sebastian Klotz, 146–168. Berlin: 1998.

Index